The Racist Fantasy

Psychoanalytic Horizons

Psychoanalysis is unique in being at once a theory and a therapy, a method of critical thinking and a form of clinical practice. Now in its second century, this fusion of science and humanism derived from Freud has outlived all predictions of its demise. **Psychoanalytic Horizons** evokes the idea of a convergence between realms as well as the outer limits of a vision. Books in the series test disciplinary boundaries and will appeal to scholars and therapists who are passionate not only about the theory of literature, culture, media, and philosophy but also, above all, about the real life of ideas in the world.

Series Editors

Esther Rashkin, Mari Ruti, and Peter L. Rudnytsky

Advisory Board

Salman Akhtar, Doris Brothers, Aleksandar Dimitrijevic, Lewis Kirshner, Humphrey Morris, Hilary Neroni, Dany Nobus, Lois Oppenheim, Donna Orange, Peter Redman, Laura Salisbury, Alenka Zupančič

Volumes in the Series:

Mourning Freud by Madelon Sprengnether
Does the Internet Have an Unconscious?: Slavoj Žižek and Digital Culture by Clint Burnham
In the Event of Laughter: Psychoanalysis, Literature and Comedy by Alfie Bown
On Dangerous Ground: Freud's Visual Cultures of the Unconscious by Diane O'Donoghue
For Want of Ambiguity: Order and Chaos in Art, Psychoanalysis, and Neuroscience by Ludovica Lumer and Lois Oppenheim

The Racist Fantasy

Unconscious Roots of Hatred

Todd McGowan

BLOOMSBURY ACADEMIC
NEW YORK • LONDON • OXFORD • NEW DELHI • SYDNEY

BLOOMSBURY ACADEMIC
Bloomsbury Publishing Inc
1385 Broadway, New York, NY 10018, USA
50 Bedford Square, London, WC1B 3DP, UK
29 Earlsfort Terrace, Dublin 2, Ireland

BLOOMSBURY, BLOOMSBURY ACADEMIC and the Diana logo
are trademarks of Bloomsbury Publishing Plc

First published in the United States of America 2022

Cover design by Eleanor Rose
Cover image © Getty Images

Library of Congress Cataloging-in-Publication Data

Names: McGowan, Todd, author.
Title: The racist fantasy : unconscious roots of hatred / Todd McGowan.
Description: New York : Bloomsbury Academic, 2022. | Series: Psychoanalytic
horizons | Includes bibliographical references and index. |
Summary: "The Racist Fantasy lays out the fundamental fantasy structure that
underlies a racist psyche as it develops in capitalist modernity"–Provided by publisher.
Identifiers: LCCN 2022009689 (print) | LCCN 2022009690 (ebook) |
ISBN 9781501392818 (hardback) | ISBN 9781501392801 (paperback) |
ISBN 9781501392825 (epub) | ISBN 9781501392832 (pdf) |
ISBN 9781501392849
Subjects: LCSH: Prejudices–Psychological aspects. | Racism–Psychological
aspects. | Subconsciousness. | Capitalism.
Classification: LCC BF575.P9 M35 2022 (print) | LCC BF575.P9 (ebook) |
DDC 155.8/2–dc23/eng/20220708
LC record available at https://lccn.loc.gov/2022009689
LC ebook record available at https://lccn.loc.gov/2022009690

ISBN: HB: 978-1-5013-9281-8
          PB: 978-1-5013-9280-1
          ePDF: 978-1-5013-9283-2
          eBook: 978-1-5013-9282-5

Series: Psychoanalytic Horizons

Typeset by Integra Software Services Pvt. Ltd.

To find out more about our authors and books visit www.bloomsbury.com
and sign up for our newsletters.

For Ryan Engley
Who came from the same place

Contents

Acknowledgments

Thanks to Routledge for permission to publish a revised version of "The Bedlam of the Lynch Mob: Racism and Enjoying through the Other," in Sheldon George and Derek Hook, eds., *Lacan and Race: Racism, Identity, and Psychoanalytic Theory* (New York: Routledge, 2021), 19–34. If it still existed, I'm sure that *Culture Critique* would have given me permission to publish a much-revised version of "Fantasies of the Unsexualized Other, Or, The Naïveté of the Arab Mind." *Culture Critique* 1.2 (2009). I'll thank them in absentia. Furthermore, James Godley gave me a chance to work out some of these ideas in a talk at Dartmouth College, and Allan Pero did the same at the University of Western Ontario.

Haaris Naqvi at Bloomsbury has been incredibly supportive of this project from the moment I brought it to the press. I would also like to thank the Psychoanalytic Horizons series editors at Bloomsbury—Mari Ruti, Esther Rashkin, and Peter Rudnytsky—for their enthusiastic embrace of the book, when a thoroughgoing rejection led me to believe that no one would find anything in it worth considering.

Thanks to my football teammates at Earlham College, who showed me how integrated intimacy might be tried. It was an interesting failure, because the interracial bond depended, unfortunately, on a shared and militant homophobia.

My mother, Sandi McGowan, taught me the importance of taking a stand against racism no matter what the personal cost. She endured mockery, ridicule, ostracism, and finally banishment from her in-laws thanks to her refusal to countenance their open displays of racism, but at no point did she relent in her critique of them, which had a decisive influence on me as a child. Whenever we left them, I would receive a lesson from her on the evil of their racism and its malignant effect on the world. For her trouble, my dying grandfather threw her out of his hospital room with the declaration, "Sandi, this is for family only." He was a bigot right up to the end. She, on the other hand, chose universal nonbelonging over racist belonging. I suppose I should thank my father's family as well, for giving me a firsthand look at how the racist fantasy delivered enjoyment to its adherents. Their obscene enjoyment was always instructive. My brother Wyk McGowan also took up the politics of antiracism since I can remember, undoubtedly due to our mother's influence.

My own in-laws, Jane Neroni and Del Neroni, have always been politically committed to fighting for equality, which is a not unpleasant surprise, given the usual contingencies that come with being related by marriage.

My twin sons, Dashiell and Theo Neroni, patiently guided me into the world of hip hop, but their guidance must have been tendentious because I somehow found myself at a heavy metal concert with one of them.

Certain people have made the University of Vermont a relatively hospitable place to write a book: Sarah Alexander, Andrew Barnaby, Emily Bernard, Bill Falls, John Waldron, and Hyon Joo Yoo. They are individually and collectively cogent arguments against relocation.

Bea Bookchin has been a role model for me on integrating theoretical speculation with practical politics. I was always almost convinced by her rejection of the state, but then … something happened.

Thanks to LACK, which offers a non-place where theory counts more than status, where everyone is no one. Anna Kornbluh and Russell Sbriglia have been especially crucial in offering me thoughts that might derail this project in ways that it needed to be derailed. Our occasional online chats have thankfully replaced actual interpersonal interactions for me.

I appreciate the support of Clint Burnham, Joan Copjec, Matthew Flisfeder, Scott Krzych, Don Kunze, Juan Pablo Lucchelli, Hugh Manon, Quentin Martin, Jonathan Mulrooney, Carol Owens, Kenneth Reinhard, Frances Restuccia, Molly Rothenberg, Stephanie Swales, Louis-Paul Willis, Jean Wyatt, and Cindy Zeiher. They have helped to create a universe where theoretical speculation matters more than the banality of real life.

Thanks to Sheila Kunkle for batting around ideas with me about how to theorize the racist fantasy. She is one of those within the world of psychoanalytic thought committed on the ground to this fight, which she approaches like one of Alain Badiou's militants. Of course, she pays the price as a result.

I worked out many of the ideas in this book with my podcast partner, Ryan Engley. I appreciate him for knowing when to cut me off on the show. Unfortunately, that skill could not be employed with this book, which is why it has a certain endless quality to it.

Thanks to Slavoj Žižek for bringing the importance of enjoyment in racism to the fore and opening the door for so many of us. If I've stolen some of his ideas here, it's only fair.

As he is wont, Walter Davis read the entire book and had many corrections. If the book is now too correct, it's his doing.

Jennifer Friedlander provided an invaluable reading that clarified the direction that I was taking to me, even when I didn't want to be taking it. Thanks to her and fellow comrade Henry Krips.

Thanks to Richard Boothby for his constant encouragement. Even when Rick knows I've written something disastrous, he manages to find one little point worth lauding. I hope someday to merit what he has said about me, but time is running out.

I owe an immense debt of gratitude to Daniel Cho, who read an early draft of the book with immense care and offered numerous possible paths for improvement. I didn't take him up on any because I wanted to keep the book just the right amount of shitty.

Sheldon George read an early version of the book and offered crucial directions for revision and development. I wish that his encyclopedic knowledge of *Star Trek* could have been useful for this project, but unfortunately "Let That Be Your Last Battlefield" cannot function as the last word on racism.

Mari Ruti's reading of the manuscript reorganized my line of thinking. She is thus completely to blame for all the organizational problems that resulted. But her faith in what is said here was so complete that it almost caused me to believe as well. Thankfully, I retained my skepticism.

Hilary Neroni made the most important additions and excisions. Without her, I have written nothing at all.

Finally, thanks to Walter Davis, Paul Eisenstein, and Hilary Neroni, who showed me that we could be together apart and that being apart is the best way of being together.

Introduction: Hiding the Unconscious

Racism persists even when people know better. It manifests itself not only among the uneducated but also among the highly educated, even among those educated in the problem of racism. While education plays an integral role in the fight against racist structures and attitudes, education alone lacks the power to dislodge the psychic resonance that racism has. This is because, in addition to being a social structure, racism also speaks to the psyche. Its recalcitrance as a social structure stems in part from the role that it plays within the psyche.

This book aims to explore the psychic resonance that racism has. To do so, it will consider the role that the unconscious plays in racism. What is unconscious about racism is not its destructiveness or its unjustness but the way that it produces enjoyment for the racist. At first blush, the notion that racism produces enjoyment seems difficult to reconcile with the vileness and hatred that come to mind with the image of racism. Enjoyment does not rush to the fore of people's minds when they think of racism. But the connection between racism and enjoyment makes more sense if one thinks of enjoyment as what goes beyond mere pleasure, as an experience of excess that transcends the realm of pleasure and pain. It seems clear that the racist partakes in something excessive, that racism itself is excessive. This excess takes the racist beyond morality, rationality, and self-interest. Even in its structural form, racism's excessiveness provides a site for the enjoyment of those invested in the structure.[1]

This enjoyment is most evident in conspicuous displays of racism. On the night of November 9, 1938, the Nazi *Sturmabteilung* (SA) killed approximately a hundred Jews, damaged thousands of Jewish businesses, and destroyed hundreds of synagogues all over Germany. *Kristallnacht* or the Night of Broken Glass was a frenzy of racist destruction. But it was also a way for Nazis to enjoy themselves at the expense of the Jews they beat and killed. Nazi racism licensed the rampant destruction of property and killing of people that otherwise would have been impermissible within German society. The law and social convention prohibited this type of excess, but racism permitted the SA to go beyond the limits that would otherwise have constrained their attitudes and behavior. They could run amok. Racism allows for an enjoyment of transcending limits, as the violence of *Kristallnacht* shows.

The psychic appeal of racism always involves some excess and thus involves enjoyment, which is pleasure taken to the extreme point at which it ceases to be simply pleasurable. Most racist enjoyment does not take the form of Nazi violence. The extremity of *Kristallnacht*, however, reveals what's at stake in the less conspicuous forms of racism. Although other forms of racism don't go as far as that of Nazi violence, they partake in the same enjoyment. Let's look, for instance, at the racism lurking in Hollywood's midcentury attempt to be antiracist— the musical *South Pacific* (Joshua Logan, 1958). The film (based on a successful Broadway play) recounts the Second World War romance between Nellie Forbush (Mitzi Gaynor) and Emile de Becque (Rossano Brazzi). As the romance develops, Nellie finds out that Emile had children with his first wife, who was Polynesian. For Nellie, this rules out Emile as a potential marriage partner. Racism drives Nellie to drop the romance rather than become stepmother to children she views as racially other.

The film is critical of this racism. It even includes a song, "You've Got to Be Carefully Taught," that specifically denounces racism as the inculcation of hatred in children, and it openly champions interracial marriage, even as it shows the resistance that interracial marriage raises.[2] But this antiracism occurs alongside a racist depiction of the South Pacific islands as a site of unrestrained enjoyment. The film centers this enjoyment on the island of Bali Ha'i, the home of purported exotic rituals and alluring women, which attracts the desire of the American soldiers stationed nearby, specifically Luther Billis (Ray Walston) and Joe Cable (John Kerr). Racism constructs Bali Ha'i as a place where one can go to experience an excess that is available nowhere else, an excess that will bring forth an unrivaled enjoyment. Racism aligns this excess with the figure of the racial other, in this case, the inhabitants of Bali Ha'i.

In the early part of the film, we see Bali Ha'i only from a distance with soft clouds around its mountain peaks and a green aura surrounding its base. An instrumental version of the romantic song "Bali Ha'i" plays softly in the background during the long shots of the exotic island. This adds to the association of the island with excessiveness. The figure of Bloody Mary (Juanita Hall) builds up the image of the island as a place to enjoy, as she tells Joe that the island itself is calling out to him and inviting him to find an unsurpassable enjoyment there. Once on the island, as Mary brings Joe to her daughter Liat (France Nuyen), we see them walk through an Edenic pathway replete with lush vegetation, flowing waterfalls, and streams of sunlight coming down through the trees. At the end of the path lies Mary's very young daughter Liat, who runs to kiss Joe after they exchange just a few words in French. By placing her in a beautiful setting and shooting her in soft focus, *South Pacific* depicts Liat, who is Vietnamese, as a figure of unbridled enjoyment.[3] The film highlights her racial otherness as the source of this enjoyment that immediately seduces Joe, as he wants to partake in it. Even though he later gives in to his own racism and rejects Liat, he does subsequently change his mind and try to return to her. His death in battle prevents this reunion and thus prevents a depiction of interracial marriage.[4]

While *South Pacific* doesn't endorse any overt racist violence like that which occurs during *Kristallnacht*, it nonetheless enacts the psychic appeal that underlies this violence. Despite the differences between them, both the film and *Kristallnacht* reveal that racism occurs through a fantasy structure that delivers enjoyment to the racist. This enjoyment can take the form of extreme violence or extreme eroticism, but in both cases, it appears as excessive in relation to the restrictions of everyday life. The racist fantasy plays a central role in the perpetuation of racism because this fantasy provides a matrix through which racism becomes enjoyable for its perpetuators.

But fantasy is not the only form that racism takes. First and foremost, racism is an ideology, an ideology that proclaims racial difference and a racial hierarchy. This ideology provides a necessary support and sustenance for capitalist society. Capitalism cannot function without racism, which is why a racist ideology must arise and continue to predominate within the capitalist universe. Historians and theorists have pointed out the mutual imbrication of capitalism and racism. From W. E. B. Du Bois and Eric Williams to Cedric Robinson and Charisse Burden-Stelly, thinkers have shown capitalism's structural dependence on racism.[5] In *Black Marxism*, Robinson clarifies how this relationship works. He notes that capitalism creates "delimited material well-being and a racial consciousness that at one and the same time removed an entire section of the working classes, the Blacks, from the possibility of access to that well-being while also supplying a fictive measure of status to non-Black workers."[6] Racist ideology enables certain members of the working class to feel as if they belong to the capitalist society that otherwise exploits them while relegating others to a state of even greater exploitation. A racial hierarchy greases the wheels of capitalist production. Racism permits capitalist society to cut off the dissatisfaction that would otherwise call it into question. But this ideology does not explain everything.

While racist ideology can give those invested in it a certain symbolic status and a sense of superiority associated with that, it does not provide enjoyment. Racist ideology gives those invested in it a sense of identity, a sense of belonging that the racial other doesn't have, but identity alone is not enough to ensure capitulation. This is why a racist fantasy is necessary to supplement it. Fantasy supplies the enjoyment that ideology leaves to the side. It explains racism's psychic resonance in a way that racist ideology alone cannot.

Racist ideology begins by presupposing race as a biological fact: it links various characteristics to each race—intelligence as Asian, connection with the earth as Native American, and so on, in the traditional Western version of this ideology. This distribution of characteristics justifies the racial hierarchy that is the ideology's end point. Modern slavery would be unthinkable without racist ideology providing the support for it. As a result of this ideological support, white Europeans could believe in their own existential superiority and in their ultimate biological right to enslave Africans, an act that plays a foundational role in the development of the capitalist system. Racist ideology creates an existential divide between races, so that those who believe themselves to be members of the white race do not consider their slaves to be equal fellow humans. The US Constitution could tally slaves as three-fifths of a citizen precisely because racist ideology creates an existential difference in the first place. This ideology is more or less conscious among those invested in it, while the racist fantasy is not. Its power stems from the fact that it is primarily unconscious.

The unconscious investment is the central pillar of racism's intransigence. Unless one takes the unconscious as the starting point for making sense of racism's appeal, the mystery of the enduring power of racism is impossible to decipher. As Achille Mbembe puts it, "Racism is practiced without one's being conscious of it. Then one expresses one's amazement when someone else draws attention to it or takes one to task. It feeds our hunger for entertainment and allows us to escape the ambient boredom and monotony."[7] Understanding the origins and historical wrongs of racism, while wholly necessary in the fight against it, does not extirpate its influence. In addition to historical and political education, the struggle against racism requires an engagement with the unconscious.

Because the racist fantasy operates primarily in the unconscious, it is more widespread than racist ideology. There are people with no conscious commitment to the racist ideology who nonetheless subscribe unconsciously to the racist fantasy. This fantasy can affect even those who know better, even those who consciously believe themselves to be antiracist. This can go from anticipating a certain behavior because of race to allowing race to determine who belongs to one's inner circle of friends. It might involve living in a gated community justified by the fear of crime. It can even include something relatively innocuous like befriending someone because one wants to have a Black or an Asian or a white friend. It can manifest itself in the act of seeing race as a defining characteristic when one first looks at a person. Or it can appear as refusing to consider racism as a systemic feature of capitalism and insisting that class exploitation is always more important than racism. The effect of racism in contemporary society is striking and impossible to miss—the vast structural inequality alone is impossible to miss—but the investment in racism is primarily subtle and disguised. The latter helps to sustain the former, which is why the latter demands our attention.

While there are societal and historical factors that produce racism, the continued existence of racism depends in part on psychic causes. To explain racism as the effect of solely historical factors is to leave unanswered the question of why racism develops in the first place and why people accept the racist ideas that history passes down to them. Just as one can find a historical cause for racism, one could equally find a cause for antiracism. This is what Jean-Paul Sartre is getting at in *Being and Nothingness* when he notes, "the cause, far from determining the action, appears only in and through the project of an action."[8] The historical cause of racism has an effect only insofar as people take it up in what they do. And in order to take it up, they must find something appealing about the racist mindset.

To return to the famous antiracist song from *South Pacific*, being carefully taught is not enough to produce a racist or a racist society. If racism didn't deliver some psychic benefit or satisfaction, no one would be a racist, no matter what their history or material situation. This has to be a factor in thinking about why racism endures. While those embracing racist ideas may not be consciously aware of this satisfaction, it must nonetheless be at work. The satisfaction that racism provides functions not just for people who openly embrace racist ideas like Nazis or Klan members but for many who don't, which is why it is so difficult to eradicate racism. This satisfaction occurs through the racist fantasy, which does its work unconsciously.

The inability to abandon racist ideas and behaviors in spite of knowledge about their fallaciousness further lets us know that racism is not the result of a conscious choice but has its grounding in the unconscious. There must be something about racism that compels people to indulge in it despite knowing better. They must find in racist ideas and actions an unconscious benefit that they would never consciously avow. Although many, perhaps most, people today consciously will themselves not to be racists, they nonetheless find themselves drawn unconsciously to the enjoyment that racism delivers, an enjoyment that resists their will.

When we look at the terminology deployed in the contemporary combat against racism, one might mistakenly assume that the combatants have already taken the unconscious into account. The predominance of the term *unconscious bias* specifically names this aspect of the psyche. But this apparent nod to the unconscious is ultimately misleading. Although the term *unconscious bias* has become a regular part of the antiracist lexicon, the analysis of the unconscious has not. In fact, the proponents of the term often take pains to distinguish their thought from Sigmund Freud's.

In *Blindspot*, their leading work on unconscious bias, Mahzarin Banaji and Anthony Greenwald make this distinction clear. They assure readers that "an understanding of the unconscious workings of the mind has changed greatly in the century since Freud's pathbreaking observations."[9] According to Banaji and Greenwald, Freud's unscientific conception of the unconscious has given way to a scientifically verifiable one. Thank God, we have now collectively moved beyond Freud's failure to be scientific enough.[10] But in the process of this shift, what has been lost is Freud's insistence on the radical otherness of the unconscious in relation to consciousness.[11] By moving beyond Freud, we conveniently moved beyond the unconscious itself.

The problem manifests itself in the second part of the term *unconscious bias*. *Bias* suggests a distortion of knowing and highlights that the problem is confined to how people know. This term indicates the belief that racism represents a failure to know accurately. According to this line of thought, racists have deviated from straightforward perception and thereby fallen into bias. But once one begins with the premise that the problem of racism is a problem of knowing, one necessarily misses the radicality of the problem. Armed with this understanding, one might imagine that in order to correct unconscious bias, a racist society just needs some education that teaches people that their biases are unfounded. All we need to do, in short, is to fill in the gaps of knowledge.

According to this position, the racist doesn't know enough or hasn't had enough experiences. The assumption here is that racism stems from not being acquainted with otherness or simply not knowing enough people who are racially different. When we start with this position, the path to ending racism focuses on awareness. It attempts to raise the consciousness of those who hold racist attitudes or who act in racist ways. If racism stems from ignorance, we fight it with knowledge, including knowledge about how we know and how prejudices make their way into the process of knowing. This is the type of antiracism—the primary manifestation of which is diversity training—associated with the term *unconscious bias*. Even for those who don't employ the term, it marks the predominant form of antiracism in contemporary society.

But if racism is unconscious, this means that the problem is not simply a deficit of knowledge but a surfeit of enjoyment. People enjoy at odds with how they know. That is to say, they enjoy not in spite of knowing better but because they know better. Their unconscious investment in racism delivers an enjoyment that comes at the expense of what they know. No matter how much they know better, this enjoyment will find a way to manifest itself. The member of the SA that burns down a Jewish business or kills a Jew on *Kristallnacht* knows that this destruction violates the law or social mores, but the knowledge of violating social norms is the key to the enjoyment that these activities produce. This is why instruction alone cannot alter how people enjoy. It can actually have the perverse effect of augmenting their racist enjoyment rather than eliminating it.

The interchangeability of the term *unconscious bias* with *implicit bias* makes the problem with this line of action clear. The reference to the unconscious is really just a reference to what is not currently being thought. It does not have anything to do with the unconscious that psychoanalysis theorizes—and thus cannot touch on the role that an unconscious racist fantasy plays in racist society. The type of theorizing about racism that sees it in terms of *unconscious bias* implicitly categorizes racism as an epistemological problem.

Unconscious bias denotes racism that persons have without knowledge, not the part of racism that resists knowledge, which is the effect of the unconscious. The unconscious isn't simply a lack of knowledge. It is what one does without being able to know it consciously. The unconscious acts ahead of our knowledge and becomes visible through its acts, which is why other people can see our unconscious more clearly than we can. It is not our hidden thoughts but is expressed in what we do. We act out the unconscious that we cannot avow to ourselves.

It falls to psychoanalytic interpretation to address the unconscious as it appears in people's actions. But there has been only a limited amount of interpretations of racism along psychoanalytic lines. The primary blame for this lies with psychoanalytic theorists, who have too often left the terrain of antiracist critique to those without any investment in the psychoanalytic conception of the unconscious. This failure to think about the psychic effects of racism begins with Sigmund Freud and continues through the major second and third generation psychoanalytic theorists.[12] For its part, psychoanalytic practice has largely dropped the ball by not recognizing racism as a psychic pathology. As David Eng and Shinhee Han put it, "to the extent that a patient or clinician almost never initiates therapy to examine his or her racism, racism is not seen as a psychopathology but is rather normalized as an everyday practice."[13] Rather than being part of the solution to racism, psychoanalysis has been part of the problem.

Although Frantz Fanon begins the psychoanalytic interpretation of racism in 1952 with the publication of *Black Skin, White Masks* in French, his turn to psychoanalysis for critiquing racism has had only a few to take it up.[14] Fanon himself devoted the rest of his brief life to the anticolonial struggle, which caused his analysis of racism to take a back seat. Following (and critical of) Fanon, Hortense Spillers works to inject psychoanalytic thinking into the social field where racism is operative.[15] For his part, David Marriott insists on the necessity of considering the role that the unconscious plays both in racism and in the response to it. We must account for, according to Marriott, "the place of the black imago in the white unconscious—a place marked by murderous aggression and a phobic transferal of feelings of loss onto the black other."[16] Marriott recognizes that without attention to the unconscious, an important part of racism will remain unconsidered. In addition to Marriott, other important inheritors of Fanon's legacy include Anne Anlin Cheng, Kalpana Seshadri, David Eng, Sheldon George, and Antonio Viego.[17]

In *Trauma and Race: A Lacanian Study of African American Racial Identity*, George depicts the role that enjoyment plays in racism, which is why this is such a groundbreaking work. As George sees it, repressed trauma for Black subjects occurs at the same location as white enjoyment. He writes, "the white subject's *jouissance* becomes the instrument of African Americans' confrontation with trauma."[18] In racist violence, this becomes evident. The white subject represses the source of its enjoyment, while the Black subject represses the trauma. In this way, racism becomes, for George, an affair of the unconscious. George not only advocates on behalf of Fanon's concern for the role of the unconscious in racism but extends this interpretation to the terrain of enjoyment, which George sees at work most prominently in the violence of slavery. Slavery is not just a symbolic structure built on domination. It is also, for George, an apparatus that allows whites to enjoy through the suffering of Black slaves. They enjoy the violent dominance, the sexual exploitation, and the total humiliation of the racial other.[19] Although the racism of this structure is evident, the way that it produces enjoyment is unconscious, which is why George stresses it.

Since the unconscious manifests itself in people's actions, it is, much more than their sense of identity, the basis of who they are. Although the unconscious status of racism renders it difficult to extirpate, the unconscious is also the source of the desire to rid oneself of racism. In this sense, the political valence of the unconscious is radically open: it obfuscates how people enjoy their racism while at the same time generating the desire that goes beyond this racism and the enjoyment that corresponds to it. The unconscious is at once a prison and the key to the prison's door. The escape requires rearranging how people relate to their enjoyment, but this necessitates taking stock of how unconscious racism functions.

The fundamental unconscious manifestation of racism appears in the racist fantasy. The terrain of the racist fantasy is, somewhat surprisingly, a region that psychoanalytic theorists have not fully explored.[20] The racist fantasy organizes the subject's enjoyment through a scenario that relates this subject to a racial other, who acts as the source of this enjoyment, as is clear in the figure of Liat in *South Pacific*. As a young Vietnamese woman, Liat embodies the racial other in the fantasy structure that *South Pacific* creates both for the American solider Joe Cable and for the spectator. The position of the racial other in the fantasy gives the fantasy its racist hue.

This fantasy sustains its power despite the status of the overt racist ideology. When people claim that there has been tangible progress concerning racism, they focus on the lessened acceptance of racist ideology with its clear racial hierarchy. This ideology that foregrounds biological races and their inequality no longer has widespread social acceptance. But critics of this progressive narrative rightly point out the persistence of racism in the wake of this ideology. This persistence takes place in large part through the racist fantasy.[21]

Taking an understanding of the unconscious as our point of departure, we should reverse the relationship between racism and knowledge. People have a bias in their knowing because of racism;

racism is not a result of a bias in their knowing. To find the root of racism we must look not at mistakes in knowing but at successes in enjoying, at moments like *Kristallnacht* and the long shot of Bali Ha'i toward the beginning of *South Pacific*. These successes occur through fantasy. An analysis of racism that focuses on the unconscious must take fantasy as its starting point because fantasy is the way that subjects unconsciously organize their enjoyment. Although the content of the racist fantasy is different in different times and places, the form remains the same. The racist fantasy is the basis for the enjoyment of racism. The racism that proliferates in individuals and institutions gains such traction because of its psychic resonance. Racism remains intractable as long as it remains enjoyable.

The Racist Fantasy

Imagine There's an Other

Fantasy delivers enjoyment. The appeal of fantasy lies in its ability to provide a largely unconscious structure that organizes the enjoyment of those fantasizing. Fantasy provides a scenario through which subjects relate to an object that they desire. Through this scenario, one has a path laid out to the desired object, a path whose difficulty feeds the enjoyment that fantasy produces. If fantasy simply presented direct access to the desired object, it would fail to facilitate enjoyment and be ineffectual as a fantasy.

This is why, when I'm in high school, I fantasize about going to Harvard rather than about going to the local community college. The difficulty of getting into Harvard—or even the impossibility, given my academic acumen—plays the key role in the enjoyment that the fantasy provides. If everyone easily got into Harvard, I would not waste my time fantasizing about it. For this reason, teens don't fantasize about getting into the local community college. Harvard's admission standards function as the implicit obstacle in the fantasy that provides the source of the enjoyment that the fantasy offers. Even a simple fantasy like this one shows that fantasy depends on the obstacle that lies on the path to the fantasy object. Although the fantasy seems to involve nothing but a pleasant object—being enrolled at Harvard—it necessitates an obstacle to that pleasant object in order to produce enjoyment.

The fantasy narrative allows the subject to experience its lack and then overcome that lack by moving past an obstacle in order to obtain its object of desire, such as admission to Harvard or, perhaps more typically, the affection of a new romantic partner. This is the basic narrative that fantasy lays out. Through this imaginary scenario, fantasy enables one to enjoy in a way that would be impossible without it. The enjoyment does not stem from obtaining the object but from the erection of an obstacle that renders the object desirable—the difficulty of getting into Harvard or the impossibility of the would-be romantic partner accepting my overtures. There is no object simply desirable in itself outside of any fantasy structure. The fantasy creates desirability through the erection of the obstacle. This is why fantasy focuses on the obstacle rather than the successful obtaining of the object, which always appears like an afterthought.[1]

It is because fantasy works by thwarting desire rather than immediately quenching it that fantasy works so well as a vehicle for racism. Racism penetrates into a variety of fantasies, often doing so even when those fantasizing consciously believe themselves to be free of any racist thoughts. But my claim is that there is one fundamental racist fantasy that provides the structure for how racism produces enjoyment. By examining various manifestations of racism throughout modern history, we can see how widespread this fantasy is. While there are obviously variations on the basic structure, it nonetheless provides the paradigm that informs all of these variations. It is what I will refer to as the racist fantasy.

The racist fantasy, like all fantasies, has three primary figures—the subject, the object desired, and the obstacle to that object. Even though the object appears as what the subject desires to obtain, the object is actually unimportant in the fantasy. The only significance that the object of the racist fantasy has is that it is unattainable. It might be unlimited wealth, the most attractive person, or world renown. Any of these could play the part of the object of desire within the racist fantasy. What's notable is that none of these objects necessarily point to any racism. They could be the object of desire in any sort of fantasy, not exclusively a racist one. As long as it is unattainable, the object in the racist fantasy can be any object. Unattainability is initially what kickstarts the subject's desire for it. But what characterizes the racist fantasy and differentiates it from other forms of fantasy is that the obstacle to the object—what bars the subject's access to unrestrained enjoyment—is the racial other.[2]

Every fantasy has an obstacle, but fantasy becomes racist when it places the racial other in the position of the obstacle. This is what differentiates the racist fantasy from, say, the capitalist fantasy: the obstacle is the racial other in the racist fantasy, not other capitalists. The racial other's difference from the subject of the fantasy is crucial because it is this difference that enables the racial other to act as a barrier to the subject's desire.

The fantasy's key player is the racial other. Functioning as an obstacle, this figure gives the desired object a sublime value that it otherwise wouldn't have and thus provides the subject with access to an unrestrained enjoyment that it otherwise wouldn't have. Admission to Harvard is worthless if everyone gets in. Even the fantasy of dating the most attractive guy imaginable would not supply any enjoyment were this guy readily available. Availability suffocates desire, which feeds on absence. The obstacle introduces scarcity into the fantasy, and scarcity produces value.[3]

As the fantasized obstacle to complete enjoyment, the racial other is responsible for all the subject's—and the society's—failures. This presence of this figure in the fantasy is what gives the racist fantasy its racist hue. The fantasy defines the subject through the racial other that threatens it, which gives both the subject and the object of desire a wholly secondary and insignificant status within the structure. All the fantasy's attention rests on the figure of the racial other who acts as the vehicle for the enjoyment that the racist fantasy produces. The racial other functions as the fantasized obstacle that makes the object of desire—incredible wealth, social status, a sexual partner—into what the racist cannot have.

The Obstacle Course

The structure of fantasy necessarily focuses on the obstacle. In this sense, the racist fantasy, with its emphasis on the racial other as the obstacle barring access to the desired object, is not an exceptional fantasy structure. Although other fantasies might not partake in the racism of the racist fantasy, they share the preoccupation with the obstacle. The obstacle is not just an obstacle but also a site of access to enjoyment that would be impossible without it. The point of fantasy is not, as one might expect, to carve out an imaginary path to the desired object but to create an obstacle that produces enjoyment for the subject by forcing it into an indirect pursuit of this object. In the fantasy, we enjoy not having the object because this inflates the object's value. Enjoyment is always tied to an absence, not a presence. One enjoys the nation not when it seems secure but at the moment it becomes threatened. Flags fly when war breaks out, not during long periods of peace. What one doesn't have can transcend the realm of what merely is, which is why it opens up the possibility of enjoyment beyond the limit of what is.

The crucial thinker in uncovering the importance of the obstacle for our constitution of both ourselves and the world is Johann Gottlieb Fichte. Fichte follows closely on the heels of Immanuel Kant and attempts to solve certain problems that Kant's system leaves open. But in doing so, he discovers the significance of the obstacle in the path of desire. Although Fichte never theorizes fantasy, his thought has clear implications for how we conceive of the role of the obstacle in fantasy. This becomes apparent in his chief philosophical work, the *Wissenschaftslehre* (poorly translated as the *Science of Knowledge*).

In this work, Fichte argues that we create ourselves and the world through an act of self-positing or self-determination, but this positing always encounters an obstacle that both limits it and drives it onward.[4] The obstacle is also an impetus. Without the obstacle, our self-positing would lack any incentive to develop itself and keep going, which is why the obstacle is also an impetus. The name that Fichte uses to describe this obstacle is the *Anstoss*, which means, conveniently, both obstacle and impetus at the same time. The ambivalence of this German word serves Fichte's purposes perfectly, as it enables him to register the fecundity of the obstacle.[5]

The term *Anstoss* has crucial implications for the understanding of fantasy. The *Anstoss* or obstacle marks the point at which fantasy blocks the path to the object and, simultaneously, the point at which it provides access to enjoyment. The obstacle in a fantasy is precisely what provides arousal for the subject fantasizing. The obstacle is at once an impetus. When looking at fantasy, one should always regard the obstacle in the fantasy through the lens of Fichte's term *Anstoss*. The *Anstoss* prohibits the subject from attaining the desired object, but it also entices the subject by opening up an enjoyment that would be impossible without the *Anstoss*.[6]

Hollywood cinema, which is the great fantasy factory of the capitalist universe, spends most of its time creating obstacles to objects of desire rather than focusing on the objects of desire themselves. We should pause to take stock of the strangeness of this phenomenon, which is immensely instructive for gaining insight into how fantasy works. In Hollywood cinema, the attainment of the object of desire is confined to a brief coda at the end of the film, no matter what the genre. The lion's share of every Hollywood film's running time is devoted to the obstacle that prevents access to this object. This is especially apparent in romantic comedies and action thrillers. But nowhere is it better illustrated than in Frank Capra's *It's a Wonderful Life* (1946), which dwells for over two hours on the defeats and struggles of George Bailey (James Stewart) and devotes a scant five minutes to the moment he obtains his object of desire—evidence of everyone's love for him. Although it is an uplifting Christmas film, it is also primarily a film about the series of seemingly intractable obstacles that George Bailey encounters. The enjoyment of the film resides in these obstacles (including George's own nonexistence in the scenario created by his guardian angel), not in the final triumph. One enjoys the fantasy of *It's a Wonderful Life*, if one does, because one enjoys the obstacles that block the path to the desired object. The pleasure of attaining the desired object at the end is fleeting and forgettable. It contrasts with the sustained enjoyment that the obstacles to this object provide in the film. Obstacles preoccupy fantasy's narrative because they are the source of the enjoyment it produces, though one's conscious focus may remain on the desired object that they obstruct.

The fantasy object might be a particular commodity, a lifestyle, or even a type of social status. But whatever it is, it promises unrestrained enjoyment for the subject. Every fantasy aims at an object that holds within it the secret of enjoyment for the one caught up in the fantasy. The fantasy narrates the passage that the subject takes to arrive at the object of desire. For one caught up in a fantasy, the object appears to have the utmost importance. It seems as if it is the nodal point of the fantasy. But despite this belief, the actual object of desire has no importance whatsoever.

We invest ourselves in the value of our fantasy objects and believe them to have an intrinsic worth. This is why, it seems, that we fantasize about them. But the fantasy object has its worth in regard to the position that it occupies within the fantasy, not intrinsically. The causal relationship between the fantasy and the object is the opposite of what we imagine: we don't fantasize about the object because of its importance; it has this importance because we fantasize about it.[7]

If we return to the example of *It's a Wonderful Life*, this becomes evident. Before he sees the town of Bedford Falls turn into Pottersville as a result of his own fantasmatic disappearance, George Bailey regards the town as worthless, and we as spectators share in this evaluation. He laments wasting his life in this small town that served only to destroy his great dreams, and we share in his frustration. After he loses Bedford Falls when it becomes Pottersville in the filmic fantasy, George changes his tune and expresses his love for the town. All its defects cease to be reasons for hating it and become reasons for appreciating it, both for George and for the spectator. But Bedford Falls has this new status solely because the fantasy of the film narrates its transition into the horrible Pottersville and thereby places an obstacle in the way of George enjoying it. The town doesn't change at all. George's evaluation of it changes due to an angel repositioning it in his fantasy structure and in the fantasy structure of the spectator watching the film. When watching *It's a Wonderful Life* and investing oneself in its fantasy, one enjoys Pottersville, the horrible obstacle to the object, not Bedford Falls, which is the object itself. But the source of this enjoyment remains unconscious. Consciously, Pottersville functions purely as an obstacle in the way of getting back to Bedford Falls. By interpreting the fantasy structure, however, we can see where the enjoyment lies.

Fantasy renders ordinary objects into objects of desire by making them unattainable. This is its magic act, which it performs through the obstacle. The obstacle transforms the ordinary object into a site of unrestrained enjoyment by getting in the way of access to it. Thanks to the effect of the obstacle, the object of desire ceases to be ordinary. The object becomes just out of reach, thereby making an unrestrained enjoyment seem possible at the same time that the fantasizing subject doesn't have it.[8] Even if the fantasy shows the subject deprived of the object, it nonetheless depicts the object as possible. The fantasized obstacle allows one to fantasize an enjoyment that cannot exist. Outside the fantasy structure, the subject simply confronts the traumatic impossibility of its desire.

Impossibilities Are Possible

Fantasy doesn't just make the impossible possible. It does so, ironically, by placing a barrier between the subject and its object. Fantasy necessarily involves a barrier that bars access to the object. By prohibiting access to the impossible object, fantasy creates the illusion that the object is attainable but for the prohibition or obstacle that stands in the way. This barrier enables the subject to avoid encountering the disappointment of actually obtaining the object—and recognizing that the object doesn't contain the hidden enjoyment that the subject attributed to it. As the fantasy stages it, if the subject were to obtain this object, it would achieve an enjoyment without any restriction, that is, an enjoyment that cannot possibly exist, since we enjoy through limits, not beyond them. As a result, the fantasy must place an obstacle in front of the object so that this lie doesn't get exposed.

The obstacle creates the illusion of a possible satisfaction that would exist with the realization of desire, which is why the obstacle is also an impetus. The basic deception of fantasy is that our desire can be realized. Outside of fantasy, the realization of desire is its dissipation. Desire aims at an object but satisfies itself by missing the object and not realizing itself. The failure of desire to find the perfect object is its mode of satisfaction. The structure of desire distinguishes between sustaining satisfaction through relating to the object from a distance and its impossible realization in which desire would obtain the object, an act that would reveal the inherent failure of the object to provide the promised satisfaction. Obtaining the desired object has the effect of deflating the object and subtracting its value from it. In this sense, outside the fantasy, one cannot obtain the desired object without eliminating what makes it desirable. Fantasy rectifies this impossibility of desire through the obstacle that enables desire's realization to seem possible. The obstacle possibilizes the impossibility of desire.

In this sense, the fundamental task of fantasy is to transform an impossible satisfaction that no one could attain into a prohibited satisfaction that becomes unattainable due to the fantasized obstacle that prevents the subject from having its object. Fantasy plays the central role in the psyche because it performs this operation. Even though fantasy is primarily unconscious, it enables people to believe consciously in the possibility of a satisfaction that they cannot have. It allows them to come into touch with a transcendent impossibility that makes everyday life bearable. Through fantasy, one can imagine an enjoyment without lack, but this is possible only via the creation of an obstacle that bears responsibility for the failure to attain this enjoyment. This process enables one to enjoy the obstacle while believing oneself to be enjoying the prospect of having the desired object itself.

Let's look at another simple fantasy. I fantasize that I'm playing football for Cincinnati Bengals, an American professional football team. The fantasy produces enjoyment for me not through the object—being a member of the professional football team—but through the obstacle that bars access to this object—the difficulty of achieving this object. In contrast to the racist fantasy, here the obstacle and the object seem closely aligned, perhaps even the same thing. After all, being a member of a professional football team is almost impossible, given the paucity of positions available and the number of athletes who would like to play. But this is precisely the point. The obstacle to joining the team makes being a member of the team enjoyable. I'm actually enjoying this obstacle when I imagine myself running on the field among the other professional players. Without this obstacle, there is no difference between playing for the Bengals and playing in the sandlot with my friends, which I never fantasize about. The former is more enjoyable than the latter in the fantasy because of the obstacle to the former. The obstacle is an impetus to enjoy that allows me to access an enjoyment that would otherwise be off-limits.

But no one recognizes that the obstacle is the source of enjoyment while caught up in a fantasy. One always experiences it as a barrier that thwarts access to the perfect enjoyment that one strives to attain. What is unconscious about the fantasy is not the enjoyment that it provides but the location of this enjoyment. One consciously identifies one's enjoyment with the object while the knowledge of the true site of enjoyment, the obstacle, is unconscious. The connection between the obstacle and enjoyment is what necessarily remains unconscious for the subject. One cannot consciously experience what blocks one's pleasure—the obstacle—as the source of enjoyment. Consciousness misses the path through which the fantasy delivers enjoyment. While enjoyment itself is not unconscious, the connection to what produces it is.

The Selflessness of the Racist

The fantasy structure itself minimizes the part that the racist plays in it. Thus, the enjoyment that racism produces seems to come from others, not from the subject itself, even though it is the product of the subject's own act of fantasizing. In this way, the racist fantasy works to hide racism from the racist. The fantasy not only makes the victim of racism guilty for blocking the racist's enjoyment. It also exculpates the racist from any involvement in the proceedings. Through the fantasy, racists see the activity of the racial other but not their own. The subject of the racist fantasy believes itself to be a victim.

The evanescence of the subject is a conspicuous feature of all fantasizing. When he discusses the logic of fantasy in an eponymous seminar devoted to this subject, Jacques Lacan points out that fantasy produces enjoyment for the subject by eliding the subject's activity. He states, "the I as such is precisely excluded in the fantasy."[9] Rather than narrating the subject actively attaining the object of desire, fantasy reduces the subject to a passive position. It is the obstacle, not the subject, that is the star of the fantasy.[10] As a result, the racial other is a more compelling figure in the fantasy than the racist subject.

Looking at the canonical works of American literature, the priority of the racial other becomes evident. In the racist fantasy structure of this literature, the subject is white, and the racial other is Black. In her commentary on racism in American literature, Toni Morrison notices that writers tend to depict Black characters with a complexity that white characters lack. She claims, "If we follow through on the self-reflexive nature of these encounters with Africanism, it falls clear: images of blackness can be evil *and* protective, rebellious *and* forgiving, fearful *and* desirable—all of the self-contradictory features of the self. Whiteness, alone, is mute, meaningless, unfathomable, pointless, frozen, veiled, curtained, dreaded, senseless, implacable. Or so our writers seem to say."[11] The bland quality of whiteness in the American imagination that Morrison identifies testifies to the impact of the racist fantasy. This fantasy sees the racial other as a barrier to access to the object, but at the same time, it characterizes this figure as the site of an endlessly appealing enjoyment in contrast with the white subject. The racial other has a vitality that the white subject lacks, and racists imagine that this vitality is actually the source of their continued lack. The subject of the fantasy, whether this subject is white or not, is a blank screen. It gains its coloring from the racial other.[12]

The appeal of the racial other in the fantasy is inextricable from the threat that it poses. It is as an obstacle that race operates for the subject, but this obstacle is at once an impetus that triggers enjoyment.

The racial other bars the subject from enjoying the desired object by monopolizing the object for itself and in this way offers the subject access to an enjoyment that it otherwise wouldn't have. The illegitimate enjoyment of the racial other occurs at the expense of the fantasy's subject, but the subject enjoys through this other and finds the key to its own enjoyment in that imputed to the racial other.[13]

In *Mein Kampf,* Hitler provides a paradigmatic version of the racist fantasy, one that exposes the role that the racial other has in monopolizing the object for itself. Describing a Jewish youth seducing a German girl, he writes, "With satanic joy in his face, the black-haired Jewish youth lurks in faith for the unsuspecting girl whom he defiles with his blood. With every means he tries to destroy the racial foundations of the people he has set out to subjugate."[14] In his fantasy, Hitler figures the Jew as one who accesses the privileged object—the German female—and thereby bars German men from this object. The racial other is able to experience what Hitler calls "satanic joy," a joy off-limits to Germans. The Jew provides access for Hitler to an illicit enjoyment.

As a result of this fantasy, the Jew provides the paradigm for Hitler's own enjoyment, figuring a way for Hitler to enjoy through this obstacle to enjoyment. Via the fantasy, he and his followers can experience the satanic joy monopolized by the Jews. By appealing to this fantasy, Hitler is able to attract the German nation to his project. The fantasy and the possibility for unrestrained enjoyment that it promises have an incredible mobilizing power, a power that completely outstrips the self-interest of those caught up in it. The racist fantasy has been successful because it offers people a clear reason for why they aren't enjoying in the way that they imagine they could—it explains the tedium of people's lives—and a path through which to accede to unrestrained enjoyment through the racial other.[15]

Although Hitler clearly states the fantasy and seems to be conscious of it, what is unconscious is the relationship to enjoyment that the fantasy maps out. Hitler does not know—and cannot know, so long as he remains Hitler the anti-Semite—how he enjoys through the satanic joy of the Jew. Hitler believes that his enjoyment lies in the figure of the unsuspecting German girl whom the Jewish man seduces, but this is where the fantasy misleads the racist. The racist fantasy elevates the object of desire—the unsuspecting German girl, to use Hitler's terms—into the apparent source of enjoyment, obscuring that it is really the obstacle, the Jew, who provides enjoyment for the racist. Hitler is an anti-Semite insofar as he refuses to take responsibility for his own enjoyment, insofar as he locates this enjoyment in the figure of the Jew. We see here how parasitic the racist's enjoyment is: Hitler enjoys through the satanic joy of the Jew that he despises. The step out of the racist fantasy occurs when one sees the enjoyment that one experiences as one's own and ceases associating it with the racial other.

Field Work

We know that a fantasy is racist not because of the status of the subject in the fantasy but because of the central role that the racial other plays in it. We shouldn't look at the subject but at the erection of the racial other. This other enjoys in the subject's stead and thus triggers resentment. The racist fantasy produces a different and privileged relationship to enjoyment in the racial other that provides the basis for what we see as racial difference. Racial difference exists through the way that the racist fantasy deploys enjoyment according to race. It is not that racial difference first exists and then brings with it different relationships to enjoyment.

Racism produces racial difference. This is a point hammered home convincingly by Karen and Barbara Fields in their masterpiece *Racecraft*. They write, "Disguised as race, racism becomes something Afro-Americans are, rather than something racists do. Racists and apologists for racism have long availed themselves of the deception."[16] Anytime that we hear someone talking about the problems created by racial difference, we should, according to the Fields sisters, translate this talk immediately into the terms of racism. Talk about race instead of racism is always ideological and has the effect of ensconcing us in the trap of attempting to tolerate difference instead of focusing on eradicating racism.[17]

In order to see how racism produces race in the way the Fields sisters suggest, we should return to the thought of Sheldon George, who focuses on the factor of enjoyment in the analysis of racism. For George, enjoyment is always present when racism is at work. Racism produces race through its distribution of the relationships to enjoyment.[18] Racial difference has a thoroughly fantasmatic origin. It emerges out of the racist fantasy and the way that this fantasy organizes enjoyment. The great accomplishment of Sheldon George's *Trauma and Race* is that it establishes the primacy that enjoyment (or jouissance) has in constituting racial difference. This imaginary difference comes into being as a way of distributing enjoyment in the social order. George claims, "it is ultimately *jouissance* that grounds difference, establishing this difference through its circumscription of the fantasy object."[19] The fantasy always depicts the racial other's enjoyment as illegitimate, as a violation of the law, of morality, or of social mores. The racial other becomes enshrined as racial as a result of the position as the obstacle that this figure has in the racist fantasy.

There are multiple versions of the racist fantasy in which different identities figure in the positions of the fantasy. One version could have a Chinese subject and a Korean racial other, another could have a German subject and a Jewish racial other, while another could have a Hutu subject and a Tutsi racial other. In one traditional American version of the racist fantasy, the racial other can be a Black man who enjoys white women at the expense of white men. This version of the fantasy has played an important role throughout American history and continues to be a factor in the distribution of enjoyment in contemporary American society. This version of the racist fantasy does not, however, have a monopoly in the United States. There are versions of the racist fantasy that place Black women, Asians, Native Americans, Arabs, Mexican immigrants, and others in the position of the racial other.

According to the version of the fantasy where the Black man is the obstacle, this figure's superior sexual prowess renders him more able to please white women. The fantasy produces the sexual vitality of Black masculinity. Against such a fantasmatic challenger, the white man has no chance to measure up. In this sense, the racist fantasy does not clearly and simply establish the white man's superiority in all domains, as we might expect a racist fantasy to do. As a sexual being, the Black man, the racial other, thoroughly dominates the white man in the fantasy, which is why he is an unsurmountable obstacle to the complete enjoyment of white women. He is able to enjoy in a way that white men cannot, so he not only explains their failures but provides them a form of enjoyment with which to identify.[20] They access enjoyment through the obstacle of the racial other. The obstacle is at once an obstacle and a portal of access.

The fantasy is racist insofar as it grants the Black man an inherent sexual superiority that leads to the victory over white men with white women. In *Black Skin, White Masks*, Frantz Fanon offers a compelling account of this phenomenon. He writes, "For the majority of Whites the black man represents the (uneducated) sexual instinct. He embodies genital power out of reach of morals and taboos. As for white women, reasoning by induction, they invariably see the black man at the intangible gate leading to the realm of mystic rites and orgies, bacchanals and hallucinating sexual sensations."[21] Just as Hitler fantasizes about the Jew's satanic joy when seducing a white German woman, Fanon recognizes that whites imagine an excess of Black enjoyment when fantasizing about Black men seducing white women. Fanon points out that this scenario serves as a justification for white aggression, an aggression that has no motivation in actual events.

Fanon also points out how this same collective fantasy structure operates for white women. They too partake in the enjoyment of the obstacle. The obstacle to white society's enjoyment serves for white women invested in the racist fantasy as an "intangible gate" that opens to an enjoyment unimaginable without this figure. If we think of the white woman's fantasy as simply an individual fantasy, the Black man is not an obstacle to any object. But in the collective fantasy, he plays the role of an obstacle, which is precisely what makes him a site of unrestrained enjoyment for the white women that Fanon discusses. Were the Black man not functioning as an obstacle within the collective racist fantasy, he would not appear as a figure of excess to the racist white woman.

The prevailing white racist relation to the fantasy of Black enjoyment is envy. The racist fantasy produces an envious form of enjoyment. One can even see the envy of the racial other's sexual enjoyment in critiques of this figure's sexism. According to Achille Mbembe, it is often difficult to separate the critique from the racist fantasy. In *Necropolitics*, he states, "Just as in the colonial era, the disparaging interpretation of how Negroes and Muslim Arabs treat their women engages in a mix of voyeurism and envy—envy of the harem."[22] The interpretation that Mbembe discusses stems from a fantasized assessment of the racial other's sexual superiority to the racist subject. This superiority gives this figure an advantage when it comes to enjoying the desired object. It also gives the racist subject a site for its own enjoyment through fantasy.

The racial other always has an enjoyment advantage deriving from its fantasized racial inheritance. In the fantasy, it is a genetic gift, like athletic ability or intelligence. But what makes possible its victory over the subject in the fantasy is not just this inheritance but also the other's willingness to bypass the symbolic restrictions that the subject observes. In other words, on the terrain of sex, the racial other cheats. In the racist fantasy, the figure does not obey the constraints of civilized society that the subject abides by. The fantasized racial other uses seduction and ultimately has recourse to violence in order to enjoy the object in a way that the subject cannot.

This is what we see operative in the case of Hitler's anti-Semitic rant against the seductive power of the Jew in *Mein Kampf*. The violence that Hitler unleashes against the Jews originates in this fantasized vision of their advantages when it comes to sexual relations. The racial other's sexual enjoyment is what gives racist violence its ferocity. It is a ferocity driven by the libido. From the perspective of the fantasy, extreme violence is necessary to combat the excesses of the racial other's enjoyment advantage. But this extreme violence doesn't just combat an excess; it reproduces it in the guise of eliminating it. The racist subject feeds off the enjoyment that it imputes to the racial other in the fantasy, especially when the racist is destroying this other. The victim of racism suffers for the crime of serving as the site of enjoyment for the racist in the racist's own fantasy.

The aim of the fantasy is the production of enjoyment, which it accomplishes through its vision of the racial other. The racist fantasy locates enjoyment in the figure of the racial other that both accesses the fantasy object and blocks the subject's path to this object. Thus, despite reviling this racial other, the racist subject must unconsciously identify with this figure in order to access the enjoyment that it hoards for itself. The racial other is the only one enjoying in the fantasy. The racist enjoys through the target of the racism, an action that is only possible through the mechanism of fantasy.

Fantasy helps to explain the contradictory attitude displayed toward slaves during the epoch of American slavery. Saidiya Hartman perfectly describes this phenomenon in her account of the creation of the suffering of the slave as a spectacle. In *Scenes of Subjection*, she writes, "The constitution of blackness as an abject and degraded condition and the fascination with the other's enjoyment went hand in hand. Moreover, blacks were envisioned fundamentally as vehicles for white enjoyment."[23] The image of Black enjoyment didn't serve the economic rationale of slavery, but it did add to its psychic reward for the enslavers. This was an enjoyment that the whites could partake in without recognizing themselves as complicit in it.

In the racist fantasy, the subject does not recognize itself as the one enjoying. The racist fantasy is structured around the idea that the racial other monopolizes enjoyment for itself. Through the structure of the fantasy, the subject experiences this enjoyment of the other as enjoyment that it should properly have. But the fantasy doesn't go on to depict the subject regaining the enjoyment that the racial other has taken from it. In the fantasy, the subject is only a victim deprived of enjoyment.[24] The racist subject enjoys through the racial other, even if racism involves putting this other to death. The subject's enjoyment attained through the fantasy depends on the figure that the subject hates.

The privileged role that the racial other's enjoyment plays in the racist's fantasy life becomes clear when we look at illicit sexual practices. In *The Autobiography of Malcolm X*, Malcolm X describes his days as a pimp in New York City, where he would constantly see the dynamics of the racist fantasy in action across gender differences in his white clientele. He writes, "In all of my time in Harlem, I never saw a white prostitute touched by a white man." Instead, white prostitutes played the part of the desired object in the racist fantasy. On their own, they embodied no enjoyment. In order to do so, they required an obstacle. Malcolm X continues, "They would participate in customers' most frequent exhibition requests—a sleek, black Negro male having a white woman."[25] By watching the Black man enjoying the white woman, the white man partakes in the Black man's enjoyment of the object, which is the only enjoyment that he can access. The white man imputes an excess to the Black man that enables the white man to be excessive through watching the other. The racial other is a fantasized obstacle directly interceding between the subject and the object of desire. It is this obstacle that provides the fantasized enjoyment. The ostracized position that the Black man occupies enables him to be the site of enjoyment in the fantasy.

Malcolm X provides a perfect description of the contours of the racist fantasy. White customers pay to watch a Black man having sex with a white woman because they fantasize that the Black man's enjoyment outstrips anything they would be capable of themselves. The white woman genuinely becomes desirable only when the Black man is having sex with her. Outside of this fantasized relationship, she is just an ordinary object. Fantasized Black enjoyment elevates her out of her ordinariness.

This dynamic is not confined to white male customers of white female prostitutes. Malcolm X goes on to recount the activity of a pimp who sends Black male prostitutes to white female customers. He learns from the woman in charge of this enterprise that her clients demand absolute blackness in their sexual servants. According to Malcolm X, "She told me that nearly every white woman in her clientele would specify 'a black one'; sometimes they would say 'a *real* one', meaning black, no brown Negroes, no red Negroes."[26] Just as much as the white men watching Black men and white women, these white women ensconce themselves in the racist fantasy. They attribute an unrestrained enjoyment to the Black man and attempt to access this through the sex act. Unlike the white men, they locate themselves as the desired object in the fantasy, not the subject, so that they interact directly with the racial other rather than watching this other in action. But this works only insofar as they invest themselves in the same collective racist fantasy as the white men watching the Black men with white women. The fantasy is the same, but their way of identifying themselves within it is different. It enables them to do what the white men can only watch.

After chronicling these iterations of the racist fantasy enacted by whites, Malcolm X chalks them up to white perversion. He doesn't recognize the enormity of the insight that this behavior points toward. It is not simply one group's unique perversion but a basic structure of racism as such. His experience exposes the matrix of the racist fantasy, a fantasy that envelopes not just perverse white New Yorkers but everyone living in a racist world. When one looks at sexual practices, one sees how fantasies play themselves out. Sexual practices bespeak the underlying fantasy structure. What Malcolm X sees seems far removed from events such as racist massacres or the Holocaust, but the same racist fantasy that produces the scenarios that Malcolm X describes is also the one that leads to atrocity after atrocity.

The behavior of the white men visiting prostitutes in New York stems from the same position as Hitler's horror at the satanic joy of the Jew seducing German women. Even though Hitler annihilates Jews rather than paying to watch them actually have sex with German women, the fantasy structures underlying these two activities cannot be distinguished. The point for both is to discover an unrestrained enjoyment that they cannot have without the racial other. They look to this other for what they believe they cannot have themselves.

Enjoying the Radio

Spike Lee's *Do the Right Thing* (1989) explores the damage that the fantasy figure of the racial other does to those who occupy this position.[27] The racist fantasy drives the hostility present in the film and ultimately plays the central role in the explosion of violence that culminates the film. Throughout the film's running time, Lee depicts tensions on a sweltering summer day in Brooklyn that swirl around the racist fantasy. *Do the Right Thing* focuses on the protest of Buggin' Out (Giancarlo Esposito), who leads a campaign for Sal (Danny Aiello), owner of Sal's Pizzeria, to include photos of some Black people on the pizzeria's Wall of Fame. Sal restricts the photos to Italian luminaries such as Joe DiMaggio, Frank Sinatra, and Al Pacino, despite the fact that a largely Black clientele keeps him in business. Buggin' Out's response to the lack of Black figures that he sees at Sal's remains within the logic of representation. He simply wants to see Black faces on the wall and threatens a boycott until Sal complies. Despite leading the protest against Sal, Buggin' Out is not the primary racialized fantasy figure in *Do the Right Thing*. He ends up being a minor figure within the film's politics.

The film remains neutral to the protest and to Buggin' Out's liberal politics of representation. There are indications that Lee finds this protest beside the point, as Mookie (Spike Lee) and his sister Jade (Joie Lee) and most of the other Black characters show no interest in participating. In addition, when we see Buggin' Out in search of allies in the local community, he receives mockery rather than support. In one case, he approaches a group of three older men on the street who all reject his entreaties. The last, Sweet Dick Willie (Robin Harris), is the most derisive. He tells Buggin' Out, "Hell no, goddammit. Sal ain't never done nothing to you before man, and me neither. Hear me? What you ought to do is boycott that goddamn barber that fucked up your head." The comedy of this insult, which comes at the expense of Buggin' Out's vision of politics and his unique haircut, suggests that boycotting to change the representation on the wall will be inefficacious.[28]

But the protest against Sal's Wall of Fame does ultimately expose the racist fantasy underlying American society, which is the film's central concern. Although Buggin' Out is not himself a figure of fantasized racial enjoyment, his protest nonetheless provides the occasion that brings this figure out. The protest comes to a head when Buggin' Out and Radio Raheem (Bill Nunn) confront Sal in the Pizzeria while Radio Raheem's boombox blasts loud rap music. Lee shoots the confrontation in a rapid series of close-ups with Public Enemy's "Fight the Power" (the song that Radio Raheem is playing) drowning out everyone's screams. As the tension escalates in the scene, it is clear that the loud music overwhelms Sal psychically because it serves as the vehicle for Black enjoyment within his fantasy frame. He experiences the music as the imposition of a foreign enjoyment on him, an imposition that leaves him unable to think clearly, let alone enjoy himself. Lee shoots the scene in a way that overwhelms the spectator with music, rapidly changing images, and jarring angles.

When Sal explodes in anger, he destroys the boombox with his baseball bat and repeatedly screams a racist epithet at Buggin' Out and Radio Raheem. Even though Buggin' Out is the voice of the protest and Sal's principal antagonist in the scene, it is the figure of Radio Raheem who occupies the position of the racial other who has monopolized enjoyment in Sal's version of the racist fantasy. It is Radio Raheem's music that overwhelms everyone in the scene and that Sal violently acts against with his baseball bat. The primary violence that ensues occurs between Sal and Radio Raheem, as the latter lashes out against Sal for destroying his radio. Ultimately, the police arrive and place Radio Raheem in a chokehold that kills him.

It is important that the violence surrounds Radio Raheem rather than Buggin' Out. This violence is not a response to Black protest but to Black enjoyment. One of the great achievements of Lee's film is to show the political function of enjoyment. It does not involve Buggin' Out because Buggin' Out is not a figure of enjoyment. Despite his sincere politics, almost no one in the film can take him seriously. His political action doesn't trigger Sal's racist outburst. Radio Raheem, with his imposing size and loud music, does.

By portraying Radio Raheem as the figure of Black enjoyment, Lee makes clear the fantasy status of this figure. His excessiveness is clearly just a fantasy that has no basis in the filmic reality. Sal experiences Radio Raheem as the site of unrestrained enjoyment (which becomes evident through low angles and the music in the scene). The presence of him and his music poses no physical danger to Sal. But it does pose a fantasized danger on the level of enjoyment. Lee's film demands that the spectator recognize what the recoil from this enjoyment costs—namely, the life of Radio Raheem.

Although Sal experiences Radio Raheem as a figure of excess, he isn't one. Throughout the film, Radio Raheem engages in no excessive acts of enjoyment. Spike Lee makes sure to show him as calm and unobtrusive throughout the film before the conflict at Sal's. He never enjoys without restraint. We never see him taking drugs, participating in an orgy (or even having sex), wielding a gun, or hanging out with a gang. His soft-spoken demeanor completely belies the unrestrained enjoyment that Sal attributes to him. While he does carry a boombox around with him at all times, he does not wield his music in a hostile manner. The structure of the film shows that Radio Raheem and his loud music represent threatening enjoyment only in the racist fantasy, not in the film's social reality.

The fate of Radio Raheem in the film also reveals that once one enters into the fantasmatic position of the racial other, there is really nothing that one can do personally to escape. Radio Raheem never acts as a threatening figure. He doesn't fit into the traditional stereotypical behaviors of the racial other, and yet the white characters in the film, beginning with Sal and followed by the police, treat him as a threat nonetheless. The threat that these characters recognize in him is a threat that they fantasize into existence. It appears once they see him in the position of the racial other. It is not part of the social reality.

This distinction is crucial to the political charge of *Do the Right Thing*. Doing the right thing, in the film's idiom, signifies rejecting the racist fantasy that relies on an image of the racial other's threatening enjoyment.[29] Only by rejecting this fantasy does one accede to an antiracist subjectivity. But the fantasy has such power over the white characters in the film that it seems almost impossible to avoid. The fantasy is not simply an option for most people. It is part of the world they are born into.

A Formal Question

The racist fantasy is a form that can accommodate different contents. This is why its target can be so variable. Take, for instance, contemporary anti-immigrant attitudes in Europe and the United States. Many immigrants are poor women with young children alongside them. As such, they do not seem to pose an obstacle to anyone's sexual enjoyment, much less that of the stereotypical strong white male. But if we look closer at the opposition to undocumented immigration, the same logic of the racist fantasy becomes apparent.

The mother and child who come to a developed country as undocumented immigrants do so in order to escape a desperate situation. They are not fleeing wealth and abundance. Otherwise, they would not uproot their lives and make the dangerous trip to a place that broadcasts high and low that it doesn't want them. Many liberals see this as a sign of the inherent virtue of immigrants: they are willing to make great sacrifices to ensure a better life for themselves and their children. But this willingness to do whatever it takes is precisely what worries those opposed to immigration and what places the immigrant in the position of the obstacle to enjoyment in the racist fantasy.

Just as within a certain version of the racist fantasy the Black man transgresses every barrier to decorum that white men respect in order to enjoy white women, another version posits the immigrant as willing to do what ordinary citizens will not. This willingness is not even hidden in the fantasy but is part of public discourse about immigration, even among its champions. Those who defend immigration proclaim that immigrants are willing to do the unpleasant work for a pittance that no one else is willing to do. Although it is not strictly sexual enjoyment, this willingness to work jobs that the subject will not work for less than the subject will take represents a way of figuring the immigrant as an obstacle to the citizen's enjoyment. The immigrants' very willingness to do what citizens won't testifies to their ability to enjoy in a way that citizens cannot and at the expense of citizens' own enjoyment.

Not only does the immigrant perform work that citizens will not perform for a wage that they will not accept, according to the racist fantasy, the immigrant does so without acceding to the rules that govern the social order. The immigrant as an immigrant has the status of one who doesn't belong to the social order. The social restrictions that apply to citizens don't apply to immigrants, who have no clear place within the social order. Although being undocumented seems to carry nothing but disadvantages, from the perspective of the racist fantasy, it signifies the clear advantage of benefiting from the social order without being subjected to its laws. Undocumented immigrants have a much greater fantasmatic power due to their lack of documentation, which indicates how the law fails to sink its teeth into them.

The immigrant provides enjoyment for the racist subject by functioning as a barrier to the object of desire and by modeling the enjoyment with which the subject can identify. The more that immigrants become marginalized and fall outside the social order— the more they exist in an oppressed situation—the more they appear to partake in the enjoyment that the racist fantasy attributes to them. Far from eliminating their access to enjoyment, their oppressed status signifies their access to it in the racist fantasy.

The racist fantasy can even imagine an entire part of the world as a site of illicit enjoyment that occurs in the stead of the subject's homeland. This is what occurs in the phenomenon that Edward Said diagnoses as *Orientalism*. The Orientalist looks to the East for a sexual thrill that the repressiveness of Western morality precludes. As Said puts it in his celebrated account, "the Orient was a place where one could look for sexual experience unobtainable in Europe."[30] This sexualization of an entire region of the world can only take place as a result of the ubiquity of the racist fantasy. The region becomes dangerously sexual through the role that the racial other plays in blocking the racist subject's enjoyment. But by traveling to the East or even reading about it, one could enter into the enjoyment that this obstacle obtains for itself. One could traverse the barrier that separates the subject from the racial other's enjoyment.

The sexual fascination with the East that Said describes is inseparable from the violence of colonization and empire. This sexuality is not just a lure for the Western subject. It is also a threat that must be domesticated. In this sense, the East both entices and repels due to the position that it occupies within the racist fantasy. Much like the fantasized version of the Black man that Malcolm X discusses, it arouses the white man sexually and aggressively.

There is no psyche that doesn't rely on fantasy. Fantasy creates the pathways for our desire and enables us to relate to objects through a shared social reality. Racism takes advantage of our reliance on fantasy and inserts itself into this primary psychic operation. The point is not ridding ourselves of fantasy—this is impossible—but recognizing that the obstacle is the source of enjoyment rather than a hindrance to it. On the basis of this revelation, one can abandon one's racism. Taking responsibility for one's own enjoyment is the essential step toward an antiracist subjectivity. Once one does this, the racial other ceases to be a fantasized obstacle to one's enjoyment because one sees the obstacle as one's own. The struggle against racism involves education and experience, but it must touch the level of fantasy in order to eradicate the psychic investment in racism.

Once one grasps the obstacle in the fantasy as a formal structure that provides enjoyment, the racist content of this form ceases to be necessary. The formal interpretation of the fantasy frees the subject from its reliance on racism. Pointing out that racism functions as a form rather than only as a content is precisely what the best antiracist jokes make evident. One of these begins with the question: What do you call a Black man walking on the moon? The answer: An astronaut. Another begins: Bicyclists and Jews are responsible for our economic problems. The response: Why Jews? The response to the response: Why bicyclists?

In both cases, the joke relies on the respondent's racist assumption, which it subsequently explodes.

Each joke reveals that the racial other is a formal position that functions regardless of its content. One expects to see difference, due to the effect of racism, and one sees sameness. One sees an astronaut rather than a racist stereotype. The jokes illustrate that racism has nothing to do with race, that the racist fantasy that identifies a racial other could target any group—bicyclists instead of Jews. The racist fantasy posits the racial other as this formal obstacle that the racist does not recognize as formal. Racists are blinded to form by the light of content. The antiracist joke attempts to dim this content in order to expose the form.

Let's examine a third joke along these lines. A Jewish guy walks into a bar, sees the bartender, and exclaims, "Thanks for Pearl Harbor!" The bartender responds, "I'm Chinese, not Japanese." The Jewish guy says, "Chinese, Japanese, what's the difference?" The next day, he comes back to the bar. The bartender says to him, "Thanks for the Titanic." The Jewish guy is perplexed. The bartender explains, "Iceberg, Goldberg, what's the difference?" The significance of this joke lies in its ability to focus on the form that produces racism no matter what its content. Here, we see how supposed racial difference can be equated to words rhyming. It is nothing more substantial than that. By shifting people's focus from content to form, the antiracist joke works psychically against the power of the racist fantasy, which relies on people not recognizing form.

The turn to form entails a recognition of the impossibility of the desired object, which makes clear the insignificance of the obstacle. The object itself contains its own obstacle that derives from its own inherent impossibility. One can experience the object as constitutively lost, as containing its own inaccessibility, and then the racial other ceases to be necessary within the fantasy. When one sees the racist fantasy as a form, one can strip the racism away from it and enjoy without relying on the racial other as an obstacle. This is the path to antiracist fantasizing.

Enjoyment Über Alles

The racist fantasy endures as a result of the enjoyment it produces, but enjoyment itself is not a straightforward phenomenon. It is not simply pleasure. Instead, enjoyment is a pleasure that goes too far and thereby produces suffering. The suffering is not incidental to the enjoyment but essential to it. When we enjoy, we inevitably suffer our enjoyment. This is because enjoyment is always tied to sacrifice. Sacrifice produces an absence, a lack that gives us something to enjoy insofar as it isn't there. Unlike present objects, absent objects give us access to something transcendent, something that goes beyond the confines of the social order. Sacrifice is the way that we produce these absent objects. Absence corresponds to a sublime excess, and it is this excess that we enjoy when we enjoy what we have sacrificed.

While the social order demands productivity aimed at the social good, enjoyment works through the destruction of all goods. We enjoy insofar as we are what Sigmund Freud calls discontents (*Unbehagen*) in our culture.[31] Enjoyment is thus a counterforce to society, a force that constantly threatens to blow society apart, despite the fact that the social order relies on enjoyment to fuel its productivity. Enjoyment appeals to us—we will sacrifice anything, even our lives, in order to enjoy—but the nature of its dramatic appeal also triggers fear. As Jacques Lacan points out, we constantly retreat from our own enjoyment. In his *Seminar XIII*, he states, "if there is a fear, it is the fear of enjoying. Enjoyment being properly speaking an opening for which no limit is seen."[32] Enjoyment goes too far and undermines our prospects for the good life, which is why we often recoil from it. I enjoy through destroying my own good or the good of others, not by simply making things better for myself. Society and everyone within it function by employing this destructiveness for productive ends, using the destruction of the good as an indirect means of fomenting the social good.

Enjoyment is always disturbing because it challenges the confines of the social order. We cannot just integrate enjoyment smoothly into this order. While every social order needs some enjoyment to energize it, enjoyment threatens society, as well as those who partake in it. I recoil from my own enjoyment because I see in it the destruction of my own symbolic identity and social status, which I sacrifice in order to enjoy. The excess of enjoyment acts as a permanent threat to what I am in society. In light of the threat that it poses, we constantly hide our enjoyment from others or try to displace it. Everyone must wrestle with the excess of enjoyment, but by imputing enjoyment to the racial other in the racist fantasy, one avoids confronting oneself as an enjoying subject.[33] One avoids confronting one's own excessiveness. The primary function of the racist fantasy lies in attributing one's enjoyment to the racial other and to excuse the subject from responsibility for its own enjoyment.

The excess of enjoyment seems clearest in the extreme actions that separate speaking beings from the rest of the world—wild orgies, drug addiction, serial killing, overeating, parachuting, fast driving, or sports fandom. In each of these domains, people go beyond what society sanctions in order to do damage (or potential damage) to themselves. Even if society allows overeating or parachuting, it lets us know that these are dangerous activities that put our lives in jeopardy. The societal warning that accompanies both activities indicates the enjoyment that they supply and adds to this enjoyment. Enjoyment involves sacrificing oneself. This is why there is a thrill of enjoyment attached to shooting up heroin or eating Twinkies. In both cases, we know that we are sacrificing ourselves. The nutrition information—or information about the lack of nutrition—on the Twinkies package serves the same role as an anti-drug public service announcement: both establish the product as a site of illicit enjoyment. They let us know that by indulging we are sacrificing our health.

The enjoyment of extreme activities stands out as a conspicuous form of enjoyment. Drinking too much, engaging in risky sexual acts, gambling away one's savings—these extreme activities provide enjoyment by going beyond established norms. But the transgression alone is not enjoyable. It becomes enjoyable because the act involves the sacrifice of the good. The harm that one does to oneself or to others creates a sublimity beyond the everyday that one is able to enjoy. The extreme act enables one to transcend the confines of a restrictive social reality as the sacrifice propels one beyond it.

But these extreme acts are also misleading because enjoyment most often manifests itself much more subtly. Just as much as a drunken binge, gossip about a coworker or singular devotion to one's work can function as sites of excess that produce enjoyment. In these cases, one enjoys within social regulations. I may even find enjoyment through excessive capitulation—always coming to class on time and always raising my hand whenever the teacher asks a question. This excessive obedience produces the enjoyment of showing up one's classmates. If everyone did it, no one would do it. One enjoys when one does too much, even if this *too much* is obedience. The point is the disjunction between one's subjectivity and the symbolic identity that one occupies, between who one is and what one is. One gossips more than one should (or more viciously), or one works twice as hard as required. Enjoyment does not even require doing too much but simply feeling too much in a situation.

Enjoyment often comes in groups. When we cheer on the national football team in the World Cup, we enjoy our nation. At this moment, we are not simply loyal citizens but gain a surplus enjoyment from our sense of belonging to the nation that is superior to others (if it's winning the match). The shiver that runs down the German's spine when Germany wins the World Cup is the indication of enjoyment that derives from everything that one is not. Religious ceremonies also partake in this enjoyment of belonging that works only insofar if it also excludes. I can enjoy being a Christian only insofar as I know that Jews and Muslims aren't. In this way, I'm enjoying the sacrifice of the outsiders that constitutes me as a member of the group. As a believer, I enjoy my own salvation through the eternal damnation of the nonbeliever. Without this sacrifice of the other, it is impossible to enjoy one's religious faith.

Perhaps the greatest account of the enjoyment attached to extreme acts occurs in David Cronenberg's *Crash* (1996), in which numerous characters gain erotic stimulation from participating in reenactments of famous car crashes. Although it seems strange to enjoy crashing a car, the film makes it clear that the enjoyment derives directly from the self-destruction of the car crash. The threat that these crashes pose to the lives of those involved is precisely the point. The closer that they come to death, the more enjoyment they find. In the film, Cronenberg will show a close-up of a scar created by a car crash, and it is difficult to distinguish the scar from a sexual organ. The car crash has an erotic value in the film. The extreme event brings enjoyment because it enacts a destruction of one's own good and enables one to experience a transcendent moment beyond all social restrictions.

The importance of the film *Crash* for understanding the concept of enjoyment lies in the link that it forges between suffering and enjoyment. Enjoyment is not just extreme pleasure but a pleasure that one suffers when pleasure goes too far. Driving a little fast might be pleasurable, but it is the crash that brings enjoyment. There is always a danger attached to enjoyment, either physical or just psychic. In this sense, it both draws us in—we will do anything in order to enjoy—and at the same time repulses us. We spend much of our time retreating from our enjoyment because of the suffering that it entails. This is the appeal of enjoying vicariously through the other. We try to create a situation where someone else does the suffering while we do the enjoying. We strive for a situation akin to the joke in Ernst Lubitsch's classic *To Be or Not to Be* (1942), where Nazi Colonel Ehrhardt (Sig Ruman) explains that in Polish concentration camps the Nazis do the concentrating while the Poles do the camping. Like the Nazis in Lubitsch's film, we want to enjoy while others suffer, but this never works out. In order to enjoy, we always have to pay the price in suffering. The racist fantasy has such a lasting appeal because it promises enjoyment without suffering.[34] But suffering is integral to any enjoyment, even that produced by the racist fantasy. Racism is clearly horrific for the victim of racism, but it's even a bad deal for racists themselves because it never delivers on this promise of a suffering-free enjoyment.

The racist fantasy offers a way to both experience the excessiveness of enjoyment and retreat from it. This is why it draws in so many people. One sees oneself as free of the stain of enjoyment while enjoying through the fantasized excesses of the racial other. So far, so good. Fantasy delivers enjoyment while insulating the enjoying subject from the suffering that it entails. But the problem is that in order to provide this enjoyment, the fantasy must abase the subject fantasizing. To fantasize is to accede to self-abasement, a logic present in the racist fantasy as much as in any other. One envisions the other enjoying in one's fantasy—the racial other who hoards the desired object—and thus enjoy vicariously, but this enjoyment always occurs at one's own expense. In addition to primarily damaging the victim of racism, racism also harms the racist. The subject of the fantasy is the dupe of the enjoying other. People submit to the racist fantasy for the promise of free enjoyment, but they always come away having suffered, having paid for their enjoyment. Of course, the victims of racism suffer far more directly, but from the perspective of the racist invested in the fantasy, this suffering always looks like enjoyment. This is why it is so hard for members of the oppressing group to acknowledge the oppression that the racial other endures.

Bikini Atoll

A remarkable instance of the racist fantasy being realized occurred in France in 2016. French authorities passed a law banning the burkini, a form of beachwear for women that covers the entire body and the head. The burkini, so the authorities argued, violated French laicity, the restriction on public displays of religious clothing and symbols. Keeping the burkini off French beaches was a way of keeping religion out of French public life. When police accosted a woman wearing a burkini on a Nice beach in 2016 and forced her to partially remove it, this event made headlines across the world. Whereas decades ago authorities would force women to cover themselves on beaches, now they demanded that they take clothes off. Unlike the bikini, the burkini offended the police because it entered into their fantasmatic scenario. They could walk past thousands of women in bikinis without becoming aroused, but one burkini triggered the racist fantasy. The law enabled the police to tell themselves that they were just doing their duty, but the fact that it took four officers to prompt the middle-aged woman to remove part of the burkini indicates the degree of psychic disturbance that it caused. They saw the excess of enjoyment in the woman's excessive clothing.

The burkini bespoke the excess of enjoyment in the way that it covered the body too much. It aroused the ire of French authorities because it indicated the refusal of certain Muslim women—most often immigrants—to curtail their excessive self-sacrifice. The fact that French society viewed the burkini as evidence of the Muslim woman's capitulation to patriarchy contributed to the enjoyment that the authorities saw in this outfit. The woman clearly suffered their adherence to her religion's dress code, a suffering that equaled enjoyment in the minds of the French onlookers. French society located enjoyment in the immigrant wearing the burkini. This was the point at which the society capitulated to the racist fantasy. By outlawing this type of clothing, French authorities attacked their own fantasy. But this attack through the law didn't eliminate the fantasy but nourished it, persuading people that immigrant women were the embodiments of obscenity, an obscenity that manifested itself in displays of excessive modesty.[35]

It is not just the Islamic woman in a Burkini who posed a threat to French enjoyment. It is Islam as such. Even though French hostility to Islam targets a religion rather than a race, this hostility operates just like racism. The vast majority of Muslims in France are Arab or African, and French Islamophobia treats these Muslims as racial others, not as figures of religious difference. Religious difference alone does not represent a danger.

As a racial other imagined within the racist fantasy, however, the Muslim menaces the French way of life. This figure represents an obstacle to French access to the object of desire. In *Republic of Islamophobia*, James Wolfreys explains how French society inserts Muslims in the racist fantasy, even though he doesn't use these terms. As he puts it, "A lurid and sensationalised vision of Islam was routinely depicted in the media, persistently linking Muslims to fanaticism, creating and reinforcing the notion that Islam posed an intransigent threat to Western values."[36] This omnipresent threat to French society and its form of enjoyment explodes through events like the Burkini affair in Nice. As long as Muslims fit within the racist fantasy propagated in France, they will represent unrestrained enjoyment no matter what they do and no matter how they are attired.

The French example shows that enjoyment can appear anywhere, as much in the covering of the body as in the overt display of the body. It can appear in how one restricts sexuality, not just in how one expresses sexuality (because the restriction of sexuality is its expression). What characterizes all instances of enjoyment is that they involve an excessive relationship to the order of signification. Enjoyment always violates the norm, even if it violates the norm by adhering to it too enthusiastically. The suffering that it produces stems from going too far.

The racist fantasy arises on the basis of an attempt to enjoy without suffering. But fantasy never delivers enjoyment without also delivering the suffering that makes it possible. No suffering, no enjoyment. Recognizing this, recognizing the necessary connection between our enjoyment and suffering, is a key to breaking the racist form of the fantasy and its hold over people. People indulge in this fantasy because it promises that one can access enjoyment on the cheap. But enjoyment is only worthwhile when we pay for it with the suffering that it entails. We cannot have a society without enjoyment, but one can take responsibility for one's own enjoyment. This means accepting the suffering that enjoyment demands, which is the antiracist gesture. Antiracism requires giving up the fantasy of an enjoyment without suffering and recognizing one's enjoyment as one's own, not that of the other.

Pan Racism

The racist fantasy is a structure that operates regardless of the actual identity of those occupying the various positions within the fantasy. This fantasy infects white Americans, the French authorities, and even the Haitians who turned against the darker skinned slaves during the Haitian Revolution.[37] It operates in vastly different societies and in varied historical epochs, even those that may lack institutional forms of racism. It persists because it is the site at which racism produces enjoyment. Racism appeals to people as a result of the enjoyment that it provides, which is why the racist fantasy plays such a crucial role in the perpetuation of racism. Unlike racism, the racist fantasy does not discriminate. Anyone can become invested in this fantasy, and it can place anyone in the position of the racial other.

Being a victim of the racist fantasy in one of its versions does not immunize one from partaking in another version of it. For instance, it is possible for a Black subject to subscribe to a racist fantasy that places Jews or Arabs—or just darker skinned people—in the position of the racial other.[38] Just because one belongs to a group that typically occupies the position of the racial other in the fantasy does not preclude anyone from taking up the position of the racist subject. One can always find someone to fantasize as a racial other.

In different parts of the world, the racist fantasy operates differently. In France, it targets immigrants. In Japan, it targets the Chinese. In Rwanda during the 1990s, it targeted Tutsis. In each case, the racist fantasy generates the enjoyment that feeds racist social structures and mindsets. While the subject of this fantasy is often white, there is no essential link between whiteness and this position. Any identity can occupy the position of the subject of the racist fantasy and view any other identity as the racial other. No one is immune from the reach of the racist fantasy due to a specific racial identity, even though its benefits more clearly redound to some than to others.

The racist fantasy is a shared social structure rather than the product of the derangement of certain individuals. To think of racism—and the attempt to solve racism—in terms of the individual is to succumb to liberal mythology and fail to see its structural status. No one individual invented it, and no one individual is responsible for its perpetuation. No individual is guilty for the emergence of the racist fantasy, but all individuals who invest themselves in it are guilty for keeping it alive.

Although individuals are necessary to sustain the fantasy, it is a part of the basic social structure that forms individual existence within the society. It is on the social level where the fantasy dominates that the real battle against racism takes place.

To say that a society is racist is to say that a racist fantasy underlies its social order. Although racist social structures and institutions are vital for the perpetuation of racist society, the racist fantasy is what makes this racism enjoyable for those who indulge in it. That's why it is so important to understand. Fantasy is essential to the maintenance of the social order. It offers people a way to imagine overcoming their dissatisfaction through accessing what the social order constitutively denies them. The racist fantasy promises people what they can't get elsewhere.

The Fantasy's Breadth

There Are Only Two Races

It always seems like a progressive gesture when we acknowledge that social problems such as racism are more complex than commonly thought. By introducing additional variables, we point the way beyond binary thinking. Binary thinking seems too simple, too reductive, so it must indicate progress when we surpass it. My contention, however, is that understanding how the racist fantasy operates requires thinking in terms of two basic positions. There is the racist subject and the racial other. These structural positions function regardless of the racial identity of those occupying them. Thinking about a multiplicity of racial identities makes it difficult to recognize how the racist fantasy produces enjoyment for the racist because it obscures the relationship between the racist subject and the racial other. This relationship that occurs in the racist fantasy occurs in a variety of manifestations in the modern universe. It is not just confined to one group or one region.

In today's theoretical world, binary thinking stands in great disrepute, thanks largely to the past efforts of deconstructive and assemblage theorists, who in different ways have shown a way beyond the binary. They reveal that binaries are unstable and ultimately unsustainable. Led in radically different ways by Jacques Derrida and Gilles Deleuze, such thinkers make it their project to conceptualize alternatives to binarism.

Deconstruction is dead and buried. But perhaps the principal legacy that lives on—as a specter of Derrida—is the effort to undermine binary thinking.[1] Deconstruction undermines binary thinking by destabilizing it. In an interview in the collection *Positions*, Derrida makes his clearest statement on deconstruction's relation to binarism. He states, "In a classical philosophical opposition we are not dealing with the peaceful coexistence of a *vis-à-vis*, but rather with a violent hierarchy. One of the two terms governs the other (axiologically, logically, etc.), or has the upper hand. To deconstruct the opposition, first of all, is to overturn the hierarchy at a given moment."[2] The first gesture of deconstruction is smashing the hierarchies involved in binary oppositions. The second gesture is eliminating such oppositions altogether, thereby enabling us to work toward a world without hierarchies.

As Derrida sees it, binarism is the basis for hierarchy. Doing away with the binary is thus a crucial step in doing away with the hierarchy.[3] There certainly is something to this, if for no other reason than it is difficult to conceive of any binary oppositions that do not involve a clear hierarchy: man and woman, white and Black, or even tall and short. If everyone began to think of race in terms of a panoply of races, it would become much more difficult to sustain racist beliefs. The elimination of the binary should lead eventually to a cosmopolitan view of the world—or so the thinking goes.[4]

Gilles Deleuze and Félix Guattari have a similar goal, though their path toward it is substantively different. Deleuze and Guattari view binary thinking as rooted in the logic of identity, which they undermine by thinking in terms of rhizomes and assemblages. Instead of binary oppositions, they see flows. Hence, they are much more concerned with the multiplicities generated through racial intermixture than they are in the binary structure that the racist attempts to enforce. Until we embrace the move from binarism to rhizomatic thinking, they suggest, we will remain stuck with the oppressive hierarchies that sustain our society's racism.

Deleuze and Guattari's theoretical emphasis on the minority and its proliferation leads them to view the racial minority as inherently multiple. In an instructive passage from *A Thousand Plateaus*, they write, "there is no race but inferior, minoritarian; there is no dominant race; a race is defined not by its purity but rather by the impurity conferred on it by a system of domination."[5] To be racialized, for

Deleuze and Guattari, implies that one has become impure and thus part of a multiplicity, no longer confined to a position within a binary opposition. What's appealing about Deleuze and Guattari's position is that it presents the target of racism as the privileged ontological position. But what's missing in this schema is an explanation for why racism appeals to the racist. An understanding of the appeal of racism is also missing in the attempt to deconstruct the binary opposition between races. Attention to the source of this appeal is the advantage that theorizing racism in terms of the racist fantasy—and the relation between the racist subject and the racial other—provides.

When it comes to racism, those who reject the binary opposition point out that the issue doesn't come down just to Black and white but necessarily involves a multiplicity of races. According to this line of thinking, the analysis of racism must consider how Asians and Native Americans, for instance, mitigate the opposition between European and African (or white and Black). By expanding the problem in this way, I break out of the rigid binary thinking that is itself inextricable from racism. Breaking out of a racial binary appears ipso facto to challenge the racism that requires binary thinking. But thinking about racism in terms of a multiplicity of races actually proves a barrier to grasping how the racist fantasy works to distribute enjoyment.

While every racial identity seems distinct, this distinctiveness disappears in the context of how the social order produces and distributes enjoyment. It does so according to the logic of fantasy, and this logic does not respect particular distinctions. While it may be true in the social reality that we experience a panoply of racial distinctions, fantasy does not operate with such fine tuning. It works on the basis of the racist subject indulging in it and the racial other that it uses as a figure of illicit enjoyment blocking the subject's own access to enjoyment.

When we think in terms of the racist fantasy and its distribution of enjoyment, racism concerns only two races, that of the racist subject and the racial other. Even though those occupying each position can change radically, the structure remains the same. While different racial groups can take up the position of the subject or the racial other—a Korean subject and a Chinese other, a white subject and a Native American other, or a light-skinned Black subject and a dark-skinned Black other—racism is fundamentally a black and white issue, even when it doesn't involve Black and white. To move beyond this binary is to miss the role that racist enjoyment plays in defining social existence. When we think in terms of the complexities of racial difference, we miss the simplicity of the racist fantasy and its distribution of enjoyment.[6]

Since race has no biological status, thinking in terms of race is necessary only insofar as we need to assess the impact of racism on society. Racism forces the issue of race on everyone, but outside of the structures of racism, race does not exist. For any other purpose, race is simply an inadequate and tendentious mode of division that will have the effect of hardening patterns of racialist thinking that contribute to racism. This is why Paul Gilroy insists that "'race' should be approached as an afterimage—a lingering effect of looking too casually into the damaging glare emanating from colonial conflicts at home and abroad."[7] This is why insisting on the reality of multiple races mistakes an ideological structure for a real distribution of identities.

To invoke multiple races is to court the risk of accepting the existence of race as a fact, of the belief that it is something real. In this sense, there is a danger in tallying up the differences between the races or attributing specific qualities to them. Such a procedure risks promoting the view that race is the cause of racism rather than its result. In order to understand how racism works and continues to affect contemporary society, we must always look at race in terms of the structure of racism.

Karen and Barbara Fields make clear exactly why we should not try to think in terms of multiple races. They see that thinking in terms of races obfuscates racism under the patina of race. Making this move naturalizes race and turns it into the reason for racism rather than the result. In their *Racecraft*, the Fields sisters point out that "*Race appears to be a neutral description of reality because of the race-racism evasion, through which immoral acts of discrimination disappear, and then reappear camouflaged as the victim's alleged difference.*"[8] Once we accept that multiple races actually exist, we contribute to making racism invisible beneath the blinding visibility of race. The fundamental lure of racist society is race. One creates racists by convincing people that there is such a thing as race. Once one accepts this starting point, one has already succumbed to racist thinking. Instead, one must see race as the product of racism. The radical and difficult lesson of *Racecraft* is that whenever we see race we must recognize the racist act that produces race as a visible category. The racist gesture makes the racial other that it targets.[9]

What the movement to get beyond binarism misses is the power of the binary to reveal an underlying fantasmatic structure. The structure of the fantasy is a binary one, which is why we should continue to think of racism in terms of the binary opposition that it produces. Fighting against racism requires understanding the effects of racism, not obscuring these effects beneath the chimera of multiplicity. Until we stop fantasizing, we will be inextricably bound up with binary logic. That is to say, we will always be bound up with binary logic, no matter how much it seems to be retrograde.

The Creation of Racial Difference

Racism as it is activated in the racist fantasy involves an opposition between two distinct positions, not relations between a multitude of different races. What identity inhabits each of these two positions is utterly contingent and unimportant for the analysis of how racism functions. It doesn't matter if the racist is white and the victim of racism is Black or if the racist is Japanese and the victim is Korean. The structure prevails over whoever occupies the positions within it. The opposition between the racist subject and the racial other expresses the basic structure of racism.

This is why one can see the dynamic of the racist fantasy at work even where there seems to be no racial difference at all—in events such as the 1994 Rwandan genocide. The Rwandan genocide was an outburst of racist violence rooted in the racist fantasy. The majority group in

Rwanda, the Hutus, perpetuated this violence against the minority Tutsis. During this period of terror, over half a million Rwandan Tutsis died, and some 250,000 were raped at the hands of the Hutu majority. Those murdered were almost all brutally hacked to death with machetes.

The conflict that led directly to the genocide was a civil war between Tutsis and Hutus. In 1990, a group of Tutsi refugees invaded Hutu-ruled Rwanda from a position in Uganda. This struggle endured for four years and culminated in the assassination of the Hutu President of Rwanda, Juvénal Habyarimana, when his plane was shot down on April 6, 1994. This attack ended a peace agreement and restarted the civil war. The very next day the response to the attack came in the form of a genocidal assault on the Tutsis.[10]

Despite appearances, it was not Black on Black violence but an instance of the racist subject lashing out against the racial other, responding to the logic of the fantasy. The Hutus saw the Tutsis as a racial other. The violence occurred with Hutus in the position of the racist subject and Tutsis in that of the racial other. It provides a revelatory moment of the potential for horrible brutality lying ready to be activated within the racist fantasy. The Tutsis found themselves caught up in the Hutu racist fantasy, and many of them paid the ultimate price for it.

Hutu media outlets helped to develop the racist fantasy that had already been propagated throughout the social order. Such a media effort occurs in almost every region where we see the racist fantasy at work. It provides emotional support for the fantasy. What these media outlets said about the Tutsis indicates the prominence of the racist fantasy in Rwandan society during the 1990s. One particularly nefarious newspaper, *Kangura*, characterized the Tutsis as a clear threat to Hutu enjoyment. Among its infamous "Hutu Ten Commandments," the paper proclaimed, "Every Hutu male must know that all Tutsis are dishonest in their business dealings. They are only seeking ethnic supremacy."[11] By characterizing the Tutsis in this way, *Kangura* assisted in cementing the logic of the racist fantasy among the Hutus. The commandments reveal the Tutsis in the position of the racial other, operating as an obstacle to Hutu enjoyment.[12]

The Hutus committing the murders often knew the Tutsis whom they killed. They slaughtered from half a million to a million Tutsis, while also raping many Tutsi women. The sexual violence highlights the disturbing enjoyment at work in the genocide. The perpetuators were responding to the racist fantasy and attempting to eliminate the obstacle that they saw in the Tutsis, which is why they turned to sexual violence.

One of the basic ways for making sense of the Rwandan genocide is to consider it as the expression of ancient tribal hatreds. We should do whatever we can to avoid this completely ideological way of looking at Rwanda. Despite the fact that this approach appears to respect the particular history of the situation, it is actually the typical racist approach, one that strips the contemporary political struggle out of mass violence and attempts to distance the events from those analyzing them. Western commentators often use this strategy when talking about the conflict in the Mideast, which conveniently forgets that this conflict originates with the establishment of current political conditions. In the case of Rwanda, this type of analysis must impose the notion of tribal difference on the Hutus and Tutsis, groups that actually bled into each other in precolonial Rwanda. Although Hutu and Tutsi became distinct ethnicities under colonialism, they did not have that status in precolonial times. They did not have an ancient ethnic opposition informing their relations.[13]

Taking colonial history into account, it is tempting, in the opposite direction, to understand the Rwandan genocide through the decades leading up to it, in which European colonial powers favored the group that eventually became the victim of a genocide. Rather than being the result of ancient hatreds, the genocide would be the fruit of European colonialism. It is true that German and Belgian colonial regimes enforced the division between Tutsi and Hutu, giving Tutsi priority in the government and the economy. As Scott Straus points out in his important book *The Order of Genocide*, "Under Belgian colonialism, Belgian anthropologists even 'scientifically' measured the differences between the Hutus and the Tutsis. And, critically, in the 1930s Belgian colonial officers issued identity cards that labeled Rwandans according to their ethnicity. European race thinking also became the basis for allocating power in the colonial system."[14] The Belgian preference for the Tutsis produced resentment among the Hutus, who suffered greater oppression under colonialism.

This history seems to lead to a clear interpretation that views the genocide as revenge for the privilege that the Tutsis had under colonial rule. The problem with this interpretation is that the Hutus had power in Rwanda since 1962 and even gained recognition from Belgian authorities, a fact that reveals the inadequacy of this historicist explanation of the genocide. The colonial past functioned as a justification for the genocide but was important primarily for the Tutsi position in the fantasy that it reinforced.

In the Hutu version of the racist fantasy, the Tutsis, blessed with the endorsement of the colonial powers, hoarded the enjoyment that properly belonged to the Hutus. The colonial past gave the Hutu leaders an image of Tutsi privilege that framed the Tutsis as the obstacle to Hutu enjoyment. Although it seems strange to talk about genocide in terms of enjoyment, this is actually the only way to make sense of its otherwise illogical process. The genocide was an attempt—just like the lynchings in America or the extermination in Nazi Germany—to recuperate this enjoyment, fantasized as stolen by the Tutsis, for the Hutus themselves.

Even though there was a third identity in Rwanda, the Twa, the primary opposition was between the Hutus and the Tutsis. The Hutu majority focused their racist animus on Tutsis and disregarded other groups. The insignificance of the Twa during the genocide lends support to the contention that racism is fundamentally an affair of two parties—the racist subject and the racial other. The Hutu concern was not purifying the land (which is why they ignored the Twa) but recuperating the enjoyment that the racial other, the Tutsis, had illegitimately appropriated for themselves. This opposition between the Hutus and the Tutsis as symbolic identities derives from fantasy, not from actual historical conditions. This is why it is important to clarify, as Mahmood Mamdani does in an account of the genocide, that "Hutu and Tutsi are political, not cultural, identities."[15] Political identities form through fantasy structures, and it is the racist fantasy that undergirds this opposition and ultimately drives the genocide.

The genocide is significant for understanding the racist fantasy because it reveals that the fantasy can operate regardless of the actual race identity of those involved. It can become activated when the people involved have more or less the same skin color, as long as those involved commit themselves to the idea of the existence of a racial other. The racist fantasy is not the exclusive possession of Southerners in the United States or French colonialists in Africa. Unfortunately, neither the United States nor Europe has a monopoly on this kind of fantasizing and the violence that results from it, even though these regions have taken it up more than others. There is no barrier to where it might manifest itself. The fantasy proliferates everywhere and incorporates all sorts of identities within it. No one is immune to it simply on the basis of a racial identity. This is because the racist fantasy can transform any racial identity into the figure of the racial other monopolizing enjoyment. A key component in the fight against racism is countering this fantasy and figuring out its structure.

An Unnatural Disaster

The historical situation in early twentieth-century Japan is far removed culturally and politically from that of the United States in the twenty-first century or Rwanda in the 1990s. And yet, within this radically different historical constellation, one can see the same racist fantasy form. Despite variations in who occupies the position of the racist subject and the racial other, it is clear, when one looks closely, that the same fantasy is operative. By looking at a specific outbreak of racist violence in Japan, we can take stock of how the racist fantasy functions in a different cultural situation with a different history and with different social rules. Examining the form that racism takes in Japan reveals that the racist fantasy can become installed wherever an idea of racial hierarchy exists.

On September 1, 1923, a violent earthquake struck Japan. The Great Kanto Earthquake wrought unprecedented destruction and completely upended Japanese society.[16] Its violence was unprecedented in modern Japanese history. But the natural disaster did not necessarily immediately imply a political disaster. Natural disasters are always incipient political events, even though no one knows right away how they will turn out politically. They create an opportunity—opening the possibility for a recognition of the universal connection between everyone in a society insofar as everyone is thrust into the same position because of the disaster. The natural disaster exposes the universality in lack. No one appears to have it all when disaster strikes—it hits rich and poor alike—and this is what makes the social bond become apparent.

In this sense, natural disasters play a potentially emancipatory role in society. They allow people to see that they form a collectivity in the face of the natural destruction. Bare survival depends on people coming together to take collective political action. This is precisely why right wing leaders and their followers, when confronted with a natural disaster, sense the political danger. Their reaction is almost always to translate the disaster into the terms of warfare. If the disaster becomes a war, any idea of universality evaporates within the opposition between the friend and enemy that a war provides. Rightist leaders characterize the disaster as an enemy that the nation can fight in order to unify the nation and thereby eliminate the possible recognition of universality that does not respect national borders that the disaster creates.

But the reaction to a disaster can go even further. Instead of characterizing the disaster itself as an enemy, one can identify an enemy as responsible for the disaster.[17] By doing so, one turns the politics of the disaster on its head—transforming a potential moment of emancipatory universality into a struggle between friend and enemy. This is what happens in the Kanto region of Japan on September 2, 1923. The destructiveness of the earthquake was massive. It not only razed countless buildings in the area and killed 100,000 people, but it also led to multiple fires that unleashed even more destruction. These fires blazed throughout the next couple of days and facilitated a reactionary political response.

No one thought to blame anyone else for the earthquake itself. But the fires provided an occasion for the racist fantasy to become active. The fires led to the slaughter of thousands of Koreans living in the area. Although there were only 20,000 Koreans living in the Kanto region at the time of the earthquake (just a fraction of the overall population), they became the target for racist violence because of the position that they occupied in the racist fantasy. According to the fantasy, they were starting blazes that destroyed Japanese life and Japanese enjoyment. Thanks to this explanatory logic, the Japanese in the devastated area had a culprit for their devastation, someone to blame for their inability to enjoy other than the earth itself. By managing to produce the Koreans as the enemy responsible for the damage of the Kanto Earthquake, the Japanese populace changed the political valence of the earthquake.

Despite the relatively low Korean population in the Kanto region, the Japanese citizens largely viewed the Koreans as intruders who were illicitly taking jobs, wealth, and even women. Because of their lowly status in Japanese society, the Korean workers, as figures of nonbelonging, were figures of enjoyment. The fact that Korean workers did not belong to Japan society—they were not citizens—gave them, according to the logic of the fantasy, an enjoyment advantage. They were getting away with something without paying the price that Japanese citizens did. As a result, through their enjoyment, these workers appeared as the fantasmatic obstacle to Japanese enjoyment. They enjoyed in the stead of the Japanese in the fantasy structure. This meant disaster for the Koreans because a significant number of Japanese citizens saw them through the structure of the racist fantasy.

The fantasy of the Korean workers as an obstacle to Japanese enjoyment becomes clear if one looks at the type of rumors that swirled about the Koreans in the earthquake's aftermath. Rumors reveal fantasies rather than facts. The rumors that gain social currency are the ones that resonate with the ruling fantasy space. If they didn't, no one would believe them, and they would quickly die out. This is why we should pay strict attention to what rumors are popular: they provide an opening into the prevailing fantasy structure that we otherwise wouldn't have. Unfortunately for the Koreans living in Japan in 1923, rumors about them all resonated with the racist fantasy.

For the Japanese subjects who participated in the massacre of the Koreans, the Koreans fit into the position of the obstacle in the racist fantasy. According to the ruling racist fantasy at the time, they committed precisely the sort of acts that obtruded on Japanese access to objects of desire and thus blocked Japanese enjoyment with their own. The rumors almost exclusively focused on enjoyment. According to J. Michael Allen's account of the situation, the rumors included the following: "widespread arson by Koreans," "murders committed by Koreans," "Koreans poisoning wells," and "Koreans organizing into large groups to prepare for attacks on Japanese residents."[18] These rumors did not just justify after the fact the massacre of Koreans that took place. They were the driving force behind it, and they emerged directly out of a racist fantasy that identified Koreans as the racial other obstructing Japanese enjoyment and enjoying in the stead of the Japanese. Without this fantasy in place, the massacre simply would not have been possible.

The Koreans could play this role in the fantasy because of their position in Japanese society. They were there as an excess labor force. They did not belong to Japanese society, and their nonbelonging placed them in a position to block Japanese access to a desired object. In this case, the desired object was life prior to the onset of the destructive earthquake, a normal life that the earthquake had eviscerated, the enjoyment of everyday life, a life envisioned as irretrievably lost. After the earthquake, that object became completely unattainable, which transformed it into fantasmatic material. Everyday life only becomes enjoyable once one can figure it as irretrievably lost, not when one has constant access to it. After a world-altering earthquake, everyday life could become an impossible desired object. Within the racist fantasy structure, the Koreans living in the Kanto region provided a visible barrier to this lost possibility.

But Korean positioning within the racist fantasy went even further. According to the fantasy that was in force at the time, they didn't just cause destruction in the aftermath of the earthquake, they were also raping Japanese women. This is where one can see the clear outlines of the racist fantasy, every bit as much as in the most outrageous Ku Klux Klan or Nazi violence. As Byung Wook Jung notes (referring to research done by Kim Puja), "in 1923, a false rumor that Korean males had attempted to rape Japanese women was gradually established as a 'rapist myth.' This became one of the major motivations that brought about the massacre of Koreans, which was provoked by the national and patriarchal consciousness of Japanese males collectively."[19] The rapist myth develops in order to ensconce the Korean workers in the fantasy position of the racial other: they enjoy Japanese women in a way that blocks the ability of Japanese men to do so. This positioning is what occasions the brutal violence of the massacre that follows the earthquake.

The rapist myth plays a crucial role in understanding the massacre insofar as it underlines the sexual nature of the racist violence. The Japanese citizens involved in the massacre had to view the Koreans as sexual competitors who were illicitly gaining an advantage over them in order to perpetuate the killings. This illicit Korean enjoyment posed a threat to Japanese enjoyment. But it also gave the Japanese an opportunity to enjoy themselves through their fantasies: the Japanese enjoyed through the Korean obstacle to their enjoyment, not in spite of this obstacle. This is the key point in understanding how the racist fantasy delivers enjoyment. When the Japanese eliminated the Koreans, they attempted to annihilate the racial other's enjoyment. In doing so, they simultaneously struck at their own enjoyment, which is why such massacres can only provide hollow victories, regardless of the participants' lack of moral qualms. Although the violence itself provides a compensatory enjoyment, it is fleeting relative to the enjoyment that the fantasy produces.

Not only did Japanese civilians, military personnel, and police officers kill Koreans in the period of time after the Great Kanto

Earthquake, but they killed them with extreme brutality. This brutality lets us know that we are dealing with enjoyment. Excessive violence arises only when enjoyment is in play. In "The Great Kanto Earthquake and the Massacre of Koreans," Sonia Ryang describes the horror of these killings. She writes, "the killings were judicious: dismembering of body parts while alive or dead, disfiguring, death by torture—in other words, none too efficiently, many were put to slow painful death, the process of which took hours or days."[20] The excessive violence of the massacre was a response to the excesses of enjoyment that the Japanese assailants attributed to their Korean victims. The excess in the violence attempts to uncover the sexual excess attributed to the victims.

When one looks at the accounts of the violence in the Kanto Earthquake Massacre, it becomes difficult to distinguish between the assault on Koreans and a lynching in the American South or the description of a Hutu militia eliminating Tutsis. The violence echoes across social and cultural barriers because the racist fantasy gains a foothold in the psyche across these barriers. Its power stems from its double function: it both enables the racist to access an impossible enjoyment in the other while allowing this same racist to eliminate the other attached to that enjoyment, apparently leaving just the enjoyment for the subject. But this denouement is always a disappointing one for the racist, which is why one racist act is never enough. Racism demands to be continually fed in order to produce the enjoyment that the racist always finds fading away with the elimination of the racial other.

Lightening Up in Bollywood

The role that the racist fantasy has played in Hollywood is well known. From the depiction of the menace that Black enjoyment poses to white society in D. W. Griffith's *The Birth of a Nation* (1915) to the Black buffoonery shown in *A Day at the Races* (Sam Wood, 1937) to the use of blackface to signify whites accessing enjoyment in *Holiday Inn* (Mark Sandrich, 1942), the emphasis on Black enjoyment runs throughout the history of Hollywood. Despite the massive cultural and formal differences that separate Bollywood cinema from this history, it too partakes of the same racist fantasy. Even though India does not share the legacy of slavery with the United States and became a nation through breaking from a colonial power, it nonetheless deploys some of the same racist tropes that one finds in Hollywood. Perhaps the most important of these tropes are blackface and brownface.[21]

Blackface and brownface are used to signify excess. Light-skinned actors put on blackface or brownface in order to indicate that they are accessing the enjoyment associated with blackness in the racist fantasy.[22] The use of blackface and brownface doesn't just occur on the margins of Bollywood. It intrudes in perhaps the most famous Bollywood product—*Mother India* (Mehboob Khan, 1957). This film is one of the greatest box office successes in the history of Indian cinema and was the first Bollywood film nominated for an Academy Award. It tells the story of Radha (Nargis), who is the eponymous mother of a village. She recounts her traumatic past, which includes her husband abandoning her, a flood destroying her land, and her infant child dying. Most important, it includes her finally killing one of her sons who developed into an unruly bandit. It is here that the racist fantasy intervenes.

This son, Birju (Sunil Dutt), becomes a figure of wanton enjoyment, partially in response to the suffering he and his family endured at the hands of a brutal moneylender, Sukhilala (Kanhaiya Lal). But from the time he is a very young boy (played by Sajid Khan), Birju behaves aggressively toward everyone with whom he interacts, including his grandmother, which indicates his proclivity for enjoying at the expense of others. In one of the first scenes when Birju appears as an adult, we see him lying on a pile of grain with a sickle next to him. He uses the sickle to threaten Sukhilala, when he comes for his share of the crops. Here, Birju is a threatening presence, even though Sukhilala is the film's villain.

The film contrasts Birju with his lighter skinned older brother, Ramu (Rajendra Kumar), who is the obedient son. The two fight on several occasions in the film. Each time Ramu defends civility against the excesses perpetuated by Birju. The association of Birju with enjoyment receives an extra emphasis through his darkened skin, which results from the use of brownface. The filmmaker has Sunil Dutt appear in brownface to indicate the path of criminality that he takes. In the second half of the film, when the spectator sees him as an adult, he quickly becomes a sexual predator and ultimately adopts the life of a bandit as the village exiles him. The village ostracizes him due to his constant assaults on the young women of the village and his refusal to give up harassing them. At one point, the entire village pursues Birju with torches and tries to smoke him out of his hiding spot, much like the Klan's pursuit of Gus (Walter Long), a white actor in blackface, in *Birth of a Nation*. After this occurs, he occupies the exact position of the racial other, which is undoubtedly why he needed to appear in brownface. But the film does not allow him to remain a threat at large. He returns to the village, kills the moneylender Sukhilala, and kidnaps Sukhilala's daughter (whom he has sexually threatened earlier in the film). As Birju rides off with Sukhilala's daughter to rape her, Birju's mother Radha must eliminate his excessiveness herself. The final event of the flashback is her shooting her own son in the back as he rides off.

Although *Mother India* does not exhibit the degree of racism that we see in *The Birth of a Nation*, it plays an almost parallel role in Bollywood to the one that Griffith's film plays in Hollywood. That is, it inaugurates Bollywood as a producer of major movie events. *Mother India* is an epochal film. But as with *The Birth of a Nation*, one cannot subtract the film's investment in the racist fantasy from its success. Although the brownface of Birju pales in comparison with Griffith's apology for the Ku Klux Klan when it comes to their degree of racism, the investment in an underlying racist fantasy is similar. Although Bollywood films employed brownface prior to *Mother India*, its success helped to ensconce the racist fantasy within the cinematic apparatus. The use of brownface became standard fare.

Unlike in Hollywood, the use of skin darkening has not disappeared from Bollywood. As recently as 2019, a hit Bollywood film, *Bala* (Amar Kaushik, 2019), resorted to skin darkening for its star. Bhumi Pednekar plays Latika Trivedi, who is a studious girl constantly suffering setbacks due to her dark skin, which the film uses brownface to indicate. *Bala* clearly tries to use skin darkening to critique racism rather than to exhibit it. The problem is that the film actually shows the darkened Latika as an obstacle to the enjoyment of her friend Bala (Ayushmann Khurrna).

As Bala prepares to marry, Latika interrupts the ceremony and exposes Bala's castration—that is, she reveals to his would-be bride that Bala is actually bald. This puts an end to the wedding and ruins Bala's relationship. At the end of the film, Bala ceases to be ashamed at his baldness and returns to Latika. He asks Latika to marry him, but she is preparing to marry someone else and rejects him.

Even though Latika leads Bala to accept himself as he is and ends up as his friend, she acts in the film as a barrier to his enjoyment. She both blocks his marriage to someone else and then refuses his offer of marriage. In this sense, her dark skin reveals the position that she occupies within the racist fantasy. She enjoys her darkness, and this enjoyment functions as an obstacle for Bala's own enjoyment. Despite the clear antiracist intentions of the filmmaker, *Bala*, like the earlier brownface film *Mother India*, succumbs to the racist fantasy.

The continued prevalence of this fantasy in Bollywood shows just how widespread the racist fantasy is. One could examine the history of Bollywood and find the same fantasy structure that haunts the history of Hollywood. Just as the greatest directors in Hollywood succumbed to the racist fantasy on occasion, we can see the same tendency among Bollywood's most decorated figures.[23]

The Sexualized Sheik

Most fantasies of the racial other sustain a remarkable consistency. Some, like that of the avaricious Jew, have endured in relatively the same form for an incredibly long time. Until very recently, the role of the Arab in the racist fantasy partook of the same consistency. The Arab man was the embodiment of extreme sexual enjoyment: he lived an exotic life in the desert; he had access to the mystical secrets of the East; and, most importantly, he was a great lover. Often, the Arab man's amorous power required a harem of women to satisfy. With his voracious sexual appetite, the Arab man had a central position in the racist fantasy, where his libido could block that of the fantasy's subjects. Although the Arab man was not as threatening a figure as the Black man, he nonetheless fit within the racist fantasy through his fantasized hypersexualization.

This fantasy image of the Arab man found its most iconic representation in the figure of Rudolf Valentino as he appeared in *The Sheik* (George Melford, 1921) and the more acclaimed sequel *Son of the Sheik* (George Fitzmaurice, 1926).[24] With his mysterious sexuality, the Sheik, like Valentino himself, has a magnetic effect on women and arouses extreme jealousy in other men. As the Sheik, Valentino stands in for an eroticism that spans the entire Arab world. One sees in him a form of sexual enjoyment that transcends anything accessible in Europe or America.

Valentino's films provide a textbook instance of Orientalism, as described by Edward Said. In *Orientalism*, Said points out that Europe uses the figure of the Orient as a site of sexual exploration of what one couldn't do at home. He claims that "the association is clearly made between the Orient and the freedom of licentious sex."[25] *The Sheik* and *Son of the Sheik* are in no way idiosyncratic. In all forms of Western art—films, novels, poetry, paintings, and music—an association with the Arab world was an association with unrestrained sexual enjoyment. Orientalism is itself a version of the racist fantasy. It places the Arab in the position of the one who monopolizes the object in the place of the fantasy's subject.

This image of Arab sexuality, despite its long dominance in the Western fantasy structure, has largely disappeared.[26] While it might seem at first thought that its abeyance is an event to celebrate—an indication that we are moving beyond certain forms of racism—the actuality of depictions of Arab men dump cold water on such hopes.

As the image of the hypersexualized Arab man has waned, a new image has taken its place, one that remains fully within the structure of the racist fantasy.

A complete reversal has occurred that nonetheless sustains the fantasy structure. The Arab man no longer has an uncontrollable libido. Instead, he has become a figure of near-total repression. Far from monopolizing the object for himself, he refuses it and demands that the object completely recede from his view. This change is part of a new fantasy image involving the Arab man.

Fantasies of the Unsexualized Other

The fantasy figure of the Arab man (and the related fantasy of the Arab woman) that has emerged in recent years emphasizes his lack of sexual enjoyment rather than his sexual prowess. This figure is sexually inexperienced and naïve, unable and unwilling to involve himself erotically with women. In this current racist fantasy, the Arab man avoids women rather than surrounding himself with a harem of them. His sexual innocence distinguishes him from the sexually enlightened subject of the fantasy.

The fantasmatic Arab man is ruthlessly violent, but he is not sexual. With the emergence of fear about Arab terrorism and the increase in concern about Islamic fundamentalism, the fantasy of the Arab, as it has undergone this dramatic and unprecedented transformation, has also become the predominant fantasy of the racial and ethnic other in the West, displacing other fantasies that had been far more significant. As this fantasy has changed, it has at precisely the same time become central.

The shift in the form of the fantasy of the Arab should be shocking to us because it appears to run completely counter to the fundamental ideological task of the fantasy of the racial other. The fantasy of the racial other involves associating this figure with extreme enjoyment, the enjoyment that can enter into the social order only in a disavowed form. The enjoyment attributed to the racial other drives the subjects within the social order, but it does so indirectly. The fantasy of the enjoying racial other allows subjects to enjoy themselves through the racial other while believing themselves to be free of the obscenity that they locate in this figure.

Given the traditional function that the fantasy of the racial other plays in a subject's psychic life, the emergence of the Arab bereft of sexual enjoyment and naïve concerning matters of sexuality seems inexplicable. Of course, fantasies portraying the racial other as naïve or unintelligent have a long history. But what is different about these fantasies is that they also associated rampant sexuality with the absence of intelligence.

The prevailing fantasy reveals not that the Arab man is a sexual threat to the Western woman but that her sexuality actually threatens him. Within the fantasy structure, the Arab terrorist certainly represents a danger to Western civilization as such, but he does not represent a specific danger to Western women. The fantasy presents the Arab as a naïf when it comes to the question of sexual enjoyment. The hypersexual and exotic Arab—the Sheik and his many progeny—has completely disappeared from the Western fantasy space.

The key to understanding this shift is examining a societal shift in our relation to enjoyment. The desexualization of the Arab coincides not just with the rise of concern over terrorism but also with a change how we perceive enjoyment. Whereas social authority has traditionally prohibited enjoyment, today it commands us to enjoy. This transformation from the prohibition of enjoyment to an imperative to enjoy has radically changed the nature of the social order. We now live surrounded by seemingly infinite images of enjoyment and inducements to enjoy. But the problem is that shift from prohibition toward an injunction to enjoy has made enjoyment all the more difficult. Despite the multitude of images of enjoyment that we see every day, enjoyment still seems out of reach. In fact, these images of enjoyment serve to remind us of our lack of enjoyment. The more the social order bombards us with pressure to enjoy, the more we experience our failure to do so. This dramatic social transformation facilitates a corresponding transformation in our fantasy life.

Historically, fantasies of the racial other allowed subjects to imagine and enjoy the untrammeled sexuality of the other that the limits of the social order would not allow them. The fantasy of the Arab man with his harem of women all ready to please him sexually is an exemplary case. One accepts the limit of a single wife and a monogamous relation with her as long as one can have recourse to the fantasy of the harem. The subject enjoys the fantasy, and this fantasy suffuses the would-be mundane reality of monogamy with enjoyment. In the wake of the emergence of the injunction to enjoy, however, the fantasy of the Arab man with the harem is no longer necessary. The Western male now has almost unlimited access to images of enjoyment on the internet, on television, and in the cinema. But this surfeit of sexual stimulation renders the stimulation less stimulating. Pornography that one can easily and stealthily access over the Internet loses its capacity to arouse, especially after the thousandth viewing. It is in response to this changed situation of the Western subject in relation to enjoyment that the fantasy of the Arab has undergone a complete reversal.

As a result of our changed social situation, the Western subject does not need fantasy in order to access images of excessive enjoyment because such images surround this subject on a daily basis. For such a subject, fantasy must find a way to render all of these images of excessive enjoyment enjoyable. The contemporary Western subject finds itself awash in images of enjoyment that it is unable to enjoy. Under the auspices of the imperative to enjoy, the provocative no longer provokes, the stimulating no longer stimulates, and the titillating no longer titillates. The image of the naïve Arab provides a source of eroticism for the Westerner caught up in the racist fantasy: for the naïve Arab, a miniskirt or a thong would be uncontrollably arousing rather than simply the indifferent material of everyday life. By fantasizing the Arab as a sexual naïf, those who take up this fantasy find a way to re-eroticize the images that have become commonplace and to recreate the possibility of scandal.

The Birth of the Arab Mind

The radical transformation of the fantasy of the Arab has occurred in our political and social discussion about Arab life and, even more prominently, in Hollywood's depictions of Arabs. Attempts to explain the actions of the September 11th suicide bombers expose the new fantasy structure clearly. In the aftermath of the attacks, the commonsensical explanation for the actions of the individuals involved was the reward of 72 virgins awaiting them in the afterlife. This idea informed the most infamous of the controversial Danish cartoons (which depicted Allah lamenting that he was running out of virgins because there were so many martyrs). The reward of 72 virgins for the Islamic martyr has little textual support in the Qur'an or elsewhere in Islamic thought. It was clear to everyone seriously analyzing the attacks that this reward was not the reason why martyrs blew themselves up. As theorist of suicide bombing Robert Pape notes, "Many, perhaps most, suicide terrorists fit the paradigm of altruistic suicide."[27] They view their suicide as a way of sacrificing on behalf of their nation or religion.

And yet, the image of the 72 virgins serves as perhaps the most widely repeated explanation in much of the West because it fits perfectly within the controlling fantasy structure of the Arab. Only a sexual naïf would sacrifice himself for the promise of virgins in paradise since, as many Western commentators have noted, virgins tend to produce subpar sexual experiences. Experienced Westerners know this while naïve Arab terrorists do not. In the racist fantasy, it is the sexual naïveté of the Arab that aligns him fantasmatically with the possibility of the ultimate sexual enjoyment. Unlike the cynical Western subject, the naïve Arab sustains the capacity for arousal. It is the idea of this capacity for arousal that also informs Western coverage of Arab woman and their dress.

Like all reporting, reporting on activities in Arab countries is not an empirical enterprise. Though well-intentioned reporters may carefully relay only the facts that they discover in the area they choose to investigate, fantasy determines where they will look and what they will look for. The contemporary fantasy of the sexually inexperienced and naïve Arab leads to media coverage of the repression of female sexuality in the Arab world. Though most Americans knew almost nothing about the customs and mores of Afghan society in the immediate aftermath of the September 11th attacks, they did know about the burqa, the item of clothing designed to cover the entire body of a woman. Emphasis on the Taliban's demand that women wear the burqa fits the fantasy of the Arab man as a sexual naïf who is unable to handle a confrontation with female sexuality. While Western reporters can justify their coverage of the burqa or the veil as a product of concern for women's rights, it receives a much warmer reception than reporting on the status of women's rights in the West insofar as it nourishes the predominant racist fantasy.

Perhaps the most astounding instance of the transformation of the fantasy of the Arab is the explosion in popularity of Raphael Patai's *The Arab Mind* after the September 11th attacks. Patai's book, written in 1973, contains a swath of generalizations and stereotypes about Arab society. No expert on Arab culture or society would find any useful insights in the book because Patai leaps too effortlessly from examples of particular behaviors to wild universal claims about Arabs. And yet, with the rise of a terrorist threat from Arab nations, *The Arab Mind* became an important text for the U.S. military in its preparation to deal with an Arab enemy. Colonel Novelle B. De Atkine testifies to this in the foreword to the 2002 edition of Patai's book, where he asserts, "At the institution where I teach military officers, *The Arab Mind* forms the basis of my cultural instruction."[28] De Atkine was not alone in his use of the text as a training manual. But equally important, the book informed neoconservative thinking about how to engage the Arab world.[29]

The image of the Arab mind that Patai propagates is not that of the traditional fantasy. Patai's Arab is not an overly sensual sheik, an image that he actually confronts as a misleading "stereotype." Instead, Patai's description of Arab masculinity focuses on its childlike quality. The Arab, as Patai sees it, lacks a sense of reality, is prone to extreme outbursts, spends a long time at the maternal breast, has no sense of time, and, perhaps most significantly, is sexually inexperienced. Almost every aspect of Patai's account of the Arab mind implicitly equates the Arab with a child, but this child is not Freud's child of polymorphous perversity. It is rather the child of sexual innocence. Patai recounts:

> the average Arab, unless he happens to live in a larger town where prostitutes are available, or where, as in Beirut, Western sexual mores have begun to penetrate, has no sexual experience with women until he marries. If we add the fact that the average Arab does not marry until his middle or even late twenties (what with the necessity of paying a bride price to the father of his chosen), we find that usually years pass between sexual maturation and the beginning of licit heterosexual activity.[30]

Here, Patai emphasizes what remains clear throughout his entire discussion of Arab sexuality: the Arab man is a sexual naïf, inexperienced and easily aroused. His book's popularity is indissociable from its commitment to this fantasy image.

Whether or not *The Arab Mind* played a crucial role in shaping the mindset behind the torture at Abu Ghraib, the form that this torture took emerges out of the same fantasy structure that the book proffers.[31] The torture did not take the form of excessive physical pain but that of sexual humiliation, especially in front of women. The torturers forced their Arab prisoners into sexual enjoyment because they believed that this enjoyment would be more disturbing than any physical harm that they might inflict.[32] The controlling fantasy animating the behavior of the torturers at Abu Ghraib was the fantasy of the sexually inexperienced and vulnerable Arab male that Patai insists on in his book. The torturers brought this fantasy to Abu Ghraib not necessarily because they read and internalized Patai's ideas but because this fantasy now provides the framework through which Western subjects relate to the Arab world.

The fantasy of the naïve and childlike Arab informs even those representations that depict the threat of Arab terrorism. In fact, the idea of the Arab terrorist in contemporary Hollywood almost corresponds by necessity with an image of Arab naïveté. This correlation manifests itself clearly in a couple of examples: Peter Berg's *The Kingdom* (2007) and Jon Favreau's *Iron Man* (2008). In each case, though Arab figures threaten American lives, they appear naïve and the threat that they embody is completely nonsexual.

The Kingdom attempts to present a complex portrait of Saudi Arabian life. Although the film focuses on terrorist violence, it also depicts a modern Saudi police official who befriends the American FBI agents and displays a genuine desire to fight Islamic extremism. He is a fully sympathetic character: not only does he act heroically by the side of the FBI agents, we also see him at home interacting with his family and taking care of his sick father. But ironically it is this figure, Colonel Faris Al Ghazi (Ashraf Barhom), who most betrays the film's investment in the new Arab fantasy. Al Ghazi recoils and upbraids American Adam Leavitt (Jason Bateman) when the latter curses. He places a partition dividing the cot set up for agent Janet Mayes (Jennifer Garner) from those of her three male colleagues, and he tells her that he had wanted to provide separate sleeping quarters altogether. When the agents meet a Saudi prince, Al Ghazi ensures that Mayes will have a coat to put over her T-shirt so as not to offend the prince with exposure to her bare arms. The film shows that Al Ghazi, though he is a modern thinking Saudi, manifests a profound innocence. As a result, he has the capacity to be aroused, unlike his cynical American counterparts.

In *Iron Man*, the Arab men who kidnap Tony Stark (Robert Downey Jr.) (while he is in Afghanistan demonstrating a new weapons system) initially appear as dangerous and sophisticated terrorists. They imprison Stark and force him to build the weapon that he developed for the American military for them. But while Stark is supposedly working on this weapon system, he actually creates a weaponized iron suit for himself that allows him to escape. Despite their surveillance cameras, the Arab captors do not notice what he is really doing until he has already succeeded in finishing the device. Stark then successfully escapes from the group of Arabs holding him, in the face of their overwhelming numerical advantage. Later, after he has become Iron Man, Stark returns to Afghanistan to defend a group of villagers against the terrorist gang that held him. Here, the film divides Arabs into the menacing terrorists (who would senselessly slaughter the innocent) and the pure victims. Iron Man quickly defeats the terrorists and saves the villagers, but the film soon makes clear that this terrorist threat is not the real threat. The villain of *Iron Man* is a white man, Stark's partner Obidiah Stane (Jeff Bridges), who manipulates the Arab group into kidnapping Stark and then easily steals the suit that Stark developed from them. As he kills the leader of the Arab group, he notes the Arab inability to understand technology. Although placing a white character in the position of the principal villain in lieu of an Arab group would seem to represent a departure from the typical fantasy of the Arab terrorist, it actually furthers the fantasy through its reduction of the Arabs to a childlike status.

The task of the fantasy of the Arab today is not so much constructing a terrorist enemy as creating an image of someone who has the ability to enjoy where the West became cynical. The oxymoronic figure of the naïve terrorist fills the fantasmatic role for the West. Through this fantasy, Westerners can imagine a capacity for enjoyment that they no longer have. In the aftermath of the September 11th attacks, the predominant fantasy of the racial other for about a decade or so became that of the Arab, but the function that it served was quite different from that of the lusty Black man or the greedy Jew. The Arab of the racist fantasy must be naïve enough to find the banality of Western inducements arousing.

As the memory of September 11th recedes, the handiness of the figure of the naïve Arab has diminished. The importance of the Arab version of the racist fantasy is no longer what it was during the early 2000s. It is still present in contemporary psychic life, but it is no longer the prevailing version. At any time, people might reactivate it and bring it back to prominence. But it is possible that it will no longer be required because another form of the racist fantasy will provide access to the mode of enjoying represented by the Arab man.

But even if it disappears entirely, the existence of the Arab version of the racist fantasy has much to teach us about the structure of the racist fantasy and its relationship to enjoyment. What this fantasy reveals is that figures of enjoyment can lurk within an image bereft of it. Enjoyment manifests itself not only in prodigious displays of excess but also in an absence. Through this alignment of the racial other with absence, the transformation of the Arab version of the racist fantasy points toward an opening beyond racism.

Racism and Modernity

"Not God but a Swastika"

The racist fantasy is not eternal. It has a moment of birth—and hopefully a moment of evanescence sometime prior to the heat death of the universe. As with the racism that this fantasy helps to promulgate, it comes into being with capitalist modernity. Racism separates modernity from premodern societies.[1] It emerges with the project of modern emancipation and interrupts this project before it can even begin to make headway.

Premodern societies are not without discrimination. But they discriminate on the basis of religious beliefs and practices, or they discriminate in terms of those in the society and foreigners.[2] This distinguishes them from modern ones, which discriminate primarily through racism. Despite its radical break from traditional identity, modernity invents racism, which is discrimination on the basis of identity.[3] The paradox of modernity is that at the same moment when identity begins to count for nothing—modernity is the uprooting of traditional identities—it becomes the privileged site for deciding who belongs and who doesn't. Racism emerges as paradigmatic through this paradox.

In the European Middle Ages, one belonged to the society on the basis of one's identity as a Christian. In this world, the fantasy of salvation was the ruling social fantasy. It portrayed the heretic or nonbeliever as a barrier to the complete enjoyment associated with eternal bliss. The heretic played the role of the obstacle in the fantasy. Those who didn't affirm Christianity or who questioned its doctrine did not belong. They faced discrimination or even death for their nonidentity. This structure reaches its brutal zenith with the Inquisition, which eliminated people for their supposed heresy. One died for one's lack of investment in the ruling fantasy.[4] Religion played this fantasmatic role in traditional societies around the world, not just in Europe. As modernity emerged, religion ceased to function as the primary social adhesive. Race replaced it.

We can see the radical break between traditional society and modernity through the different attempts to eliminate Jews from the social order. The pogroms of Medieval European society were fundamentally different than the Nazi Holocaust. Medieval authorities wanted to eliminate a religious alternative to Christianity. Their pogroms attacked Jews for their religious beliefs, whereas Nazism killed them for their racial identity. Conversion might allow a Jew to escape death in the Middle Ages, but the Nazis did not care whether Jews converted to Christianity or not. Their target was racial. In fact, they investigated nominal Christians in order to discover a conversion that was obscuring this person's Jewishness. The Medieval pogroms struck at Judaism, and Nazis struck at Jewishness.[5] Nazism is thus not a retrograde phenomenon but wholly part of the modern world that it lashes out against. Nazism's preoccupation with race aligns it with modernity.[6]

Modern philosophy begins in the 1600s with an egalitarian revolution that disdains any discrimination at all. At the beginning of the *Discourse on Method*, the paradigmatic modern work, René Descartes expresses a remarkably forward-thinking conception of cultural difference. As he details his own process of radical doubt about everything he has learned, he recognizes that his own thinking is a product of the society in which he was born and that he would think totally differently had he been born in another situation. Descartes' rejection of his own racial superiority is a thoroughgoing gesture of modernity. He writes, "I thought... how the same man, with the same mind, if brought up from infancy among the French or Germans, develops otherwise than he would if he had always lived among the Chinese or cannibals."[7]

Descartes has no illusions about racial difference rooted in biology. He knows that he is no different than anyone else biologically.

In response to the publication of his philosophy, one of Descartes' critics advances the idea that his proof for the existence of God, which relies on an innate idea of the divine, might not apply to members of purported "primitive races." Presented with this assertion of radical difference between races, Descartes firmly rejects this idea of racial difference and insists that everyone shares the idea of God, even if this idea appears in a different form for others than it does for the European.[8] The insistence on universal equality is integral to Descartes' vision.[9]

In addition to rejecting any notion of racial superiority or even racial difference, Descartes rejects the power of tradition. He begins his philosophy not with a bow to traditional ancient or scholastic authorities but with his own process of thinking. Instead of accepting prior authorities, he begins by doubting them, along with everything else, acknowledging no authority whatsoever except his own thinking. This is the process that Descartes describes in the *Meditations on First Philosophy*.[10] By denouncing allegiance to any traditional authority, he announces modernity's fundamental egalitarianism. No one has an intrinsic authority over anyone else, not even Plato and Aristotle. Without any authority to rely on, modernity leaves people on their own. There is no hierarchy, certainly none based on racial difference.[11]

Smelling Immanuel Kant

This is an idea that modern philosophy struggles to sustain. Even though Descartes gets modernity off on the proper foot, things quickly go awry. Modern European philosophy imbibes the racist fantasy time and time again. In *Against Race*, Paul Gilroy points out that racism accompanies the project of modern universal equality from the beginning, despite the fact that it undermines this project. He states, "Enlightenment pretensions toward universality were punctured from the moment of their conception in the womb of the colonial space.

Their very foundations were de-stabilized by their initial exclusionary configuration: by the consistent endorsement of 'race' as a central political and historical concept."[12] Modern Western philosophy's embrace of race as a concept marks the path through which it beats a retreat from the threat of universal equality. Racism is a respite from the radicality of this threat.

Racism becomes central to the modern project, as a look at figures from David Hume and Immanuel Kant to Gottlob Frege and Martin Heidegger reveals.[13] Hume and Kant believe in the natural superiority of whites, while Frege and Heidegger both fear a Jewish takeover of the world.[14] Soon after Descartes' insistence on the insignificance of racial difference, a number of key thinkers introduce race into their philosophy as a factor in how we judge subjectivity. The fact that this infects thinkers at the pinnacle of Western philosophy, like Immanuel Kant, indicates that it is not just a slight misstep. There is something about racism that modern thinking cannot manage to avoid without great difficulty.

This leads Charles Mills and others to contend that the modern project is inherently racist. Mills suggests that we replace the notion of the modern social contract with the idea of a racial contract, since racism plays a central role in the founding of all Anglo-European nations. He understands that racism enables modernity to hedge on its project of universal equality. As Mills sees it, in the modern world universal equality applies only to those who count as white. He writes that "the color-coded morality of the Racial Contract restricts the possession of this natural freedom and equality to *white* men."[15] Instead of a social bond that applies to everyone, philosophers constructed a Racial Contract that specifically tosses out everyone who isn't white. In their egalitarian polity, some are more equal than others.

The exclusivity of modern equality vitiates equality as a universal project. If equality is to be actual, modernity must extirpate the racism that undermines the ideal. The turn to racism flies directly in the face of pronouncements of universal equality, which is what these thinkers should have easily seen. The fact that they didn't—the fact that Kant laments that "all Negroes stink"—indicates that conceiving of universal equality did not immunize one from the most rebarbative inegalitarian prejudices.[16] Despite discovering a strict moral imperative that leaves no loopholes for one's private prejudices, Kant cannot recognize that it was he who stank rather than "all Negroes." That is, he is blind to how the other might perceive him, even though his egalitarian morality demands that we recognize the other as an end in itself and not simply in relation to ourselves. His racist fantasy colors his ability to see fellow subjects with an ethical status equal to his own. Kant's racist deviation from his theoretical investment in equality should force us to question the nature of this investment.[17]

It is tempting to separate Kant's racism (which appears in his anthropological speculation) from his egalitarian ethics (articulated in *The Groundwork of the Metaphysics of Morals* and the *Critique of Practical Reason*). This is the path that most followers of Kant choose.[18] It works to some extent: the ethical texts betray no hint of the exclusivity that appears in the anthropological thinking. But there is still an imperative to think them together, to refuse the easy gesture of keeping morality pure from any racist taint, since the apparently disparate ideas do belong to the same thinker. If we try to keep them distinct, we end up turning a blind eye to racism and repeat the repression that has historically allowed racism to flourish. Repressing racism is part of the racist program. Failing to think Kant's ethics alongside his anthropology, we miss the fundamental role that racism plays in modern thought. We need not throw out Kant's universalist ethics, but we must understand Kant in light of his turn to racism.

The exclusivity that racism establishes marks a clear retreat from universality. A universalist ethics can have absolutely no place for racism if it is to remain consistent. In this sense, racism is at odds with the basic project of modern philosophy. But this retreat from modern universality also explains why it happens. Racism deflects the would-be radicality of the modern political project. Modernity's promise of an end to inequality is both politically and psychically confounding. It strips away people's ability to sense who they are and where they fit in.

Without inequality and without the sense of identity that depends on inequality, one exists in a state of perpetual alienation. But accepting this alienation without the respite of identity and inequality is the challenge of modernity.

In the wake of the modern breakthrough, people lose their bearing as they lose their social identity. The idea of universal equality uproots the basis from which people would distinguish themselves. Equality leaves people without the traditional hierarchies that sustain authority. In the wake of modernity's egalitarian turn, all authority loses its authorization. As it becomes questionable, the displacement of authority forces people to recognize that they have nothing on which they can rely. In this sense, equality leads to a radical freedom, a freedom that is inherently traumatizing because it leaves us without any psychic or structural support for who one is and what one should do. Racism allows hierarchy to persist despite the promise of modernity. It restores a sense of authority in an epoch that uproots it.

Without the admixture of racism, the idea of universal equality has the effect of fundamentally disrupting the social order. It instantly calls into question all ways of ordering society. Without anyone to consign to the position of nonbelonging, it becomes difficult to conceive of how to constitute belonging to the modern social order. In this way, modernity inaugurates a crisis of belonging. The garden variety German in the 1930s has no secure sense of her identity as a German, no secure sense that she belongs to German society. This is what the figure of the Jew provides. Thanks to the racist vision of the Jew, the German can become certain of what it means to be a German. The racist fantasy provides an imaginary solution for the problem of modernity. The idea of universal equality precipitates this crisis of political belonging that racism counteracts. It reintroduces a hierarchy in which those who belong know that they belong because they know that others don't.

The catastrophe of modern racism—perpetuated through the racist fantasy—undermines the great breakthrough of modernity. The deracinating of traditional hierarchies created a universe of immense possibility. The inability to confront directly the radicality of this possibility produced the racist fantasy that obviated the possibility and promised a restoration of the surpassed hierarchies.[19]

Perhaps the chief challenge of modernity is ridding its political structure of the racism that sustains it—and the belief in the reality of race that follows from this racism. As Achille Mbembe points out, "Race contradicts the idea of a single humanity, of essential human resemblance and proximity."[20] To get rid of the stain of racism means insisting on a single humanity, a universal humanity defined by its alienation from all particular identity. This is the challenge of thinking universality without exclusivity. Genuine universality brooks no exclusions, but thinking it requires an embrace of universal nonbelonging, the shared failure to truly fit within any social order. The struggle with this defining failure is the struggle with universality. Without a race to stand in for this nonbelonging, everyone must constantly struggle with it. The elimination of modern racism is only possible through the abandonment of any dream of wholeness. This is the path that modernity has consistently rejected.

Racism shatters the liberal dream of total inclusion and mutual recognition. The persistence of racism reveals that inclusion always runs up against a fundamental limit—in order for some to belong, others must not belong. There is no way around the necessity of nonbelonging, no way to construct a society where belonging does not simultaneously entail nonbelonging. One knows that one belongs only by seeing those who don't. Belonging is a mark of distinction that resists any universalization.

This is why we must jettison the liberal consensus. Throughout the history of modernity, liberalism has tried and continually failed to eliminate racism. It doesn't see the structural necessity of nonbelonging entailed by the liberal dream of total belonging. The liberal project is inherently self-defeating. Only by giving up this dream and accepting our nonbelonging can we find a universal possibility. Unlike belonging, nonbelonging is universal. We fail to belong as a universal collective.

If we examine protests against racism, this possibility becomes manifest. Universal nonbelonging is not an abstraction imposed on our politics but a political act already in evidence. It is apparent in the strategy of all protesters. In demonstrations against racist police violence, the protesters do not call for their inclusion in the police or for inclusion in any form, which is how one knows that they are not liberal protests. Instead, they openly identify with the victim of the racist violence—saying things like "Hands up, don't shoot," "I can't breathe," or "We are George Floyd." The solidarity of the protesters is not that of belonging but of nonbelonging. They are not advocating more inclusion but align themselves with those who don't fit in, often explicitly. When protesters lie on the ground as if they were also victims of violence, they place themselves in the position of those who don't belong. The protest itself articulates the political path of equality. It is only through universal nonbelonging that modernity can actualize its ideal of equality.

Notes on the State of Thomas Jefferson

If we want to see how the racist fantasy can undermine the modern project of universal equality, Thomas Jefferson provides perhaps the unsurpassable example. Although he is one of the most learned thinkers of his time and invests himself in the Enlightenment ideal of universal emancipation, Jefferson cannot emancipate his own thinking from the trap of racism. Racism penetrates into Jefferson's thinking because of its power as a fantasy that organizes the way that he satisfies himself. Racist ideas play no part in Jefferson's philosophical conception of universal equality, and yet they penetrate fully into Jefferson's thought. All of Jefferson's learning cannot displace this fantasy. Its persistence in someone like Jefferson testifies to a psychic power that has the ability to completely overrun our conscious thought processes. When Jefferson stumbles, he stumbles on the racist fantasy and the image of Black enjoyment that this fantasy lays out.

Despite owning slaves himself, Jefferson's thinking on the issue of slavery is much more egalitarian than most of his fellow founding fathers and that of most whites of his day. There is a radicality to his original version of the Declaration of Independence, which includes a paragraph-long diatribe against George III of Britain for his role in the slave trade, which Jefferson excoriates. The original Declaration states,

> He was waged cruel war against human nature itself, violating it's [sic] most sacred rights of life and liberty in the persons of a distant people who never offended him, captivating & carrying them into slavery in another hemisphere, or to incur miserable death in their transportation thither. This piratical warfare, the opprobrium of INFIDEL powers, is the warfare of the CHRISTIAN king of Great Britain. Determined to keep open a market where MEN should be bought & sold, he has prostituted his negative for suppressing every legislative attempt to prohibit or to restrain this execrable commerce.[21]

Jefferson's statement here does not sound like that of a slaveholder. He inveighs against the British monarch for barbarism of the slave trade, which he describes in the most unequivocal terms. For Jefferson, the slave trade and slavery are an absolute blight on enlightened humanity. He includes this section of the Declaration to make clear the horror of slavery.

This language would have undoubtedly offended King George. But it was too radical for the Southern members of the committee responsible for the Declaration who demanded its excision. It would not survive this demand, despite Jefferson's desire to retain it. However, the fact that Jefferson originally writes it indicates his own sense that slavery is an unalloyed wrong, a belief that testifies to his universalist egalitarian thinking. Here as elsewhere in his writings, Jefferson makes clear that the evil of slavery violates the universal equality that he devotes himself to.

But this doesn't allow him to escape the racist fantasy, which leads him into the fundamental contradiction of his thought: he believes in universal equality and Black inferiority at the same time. This is the animating contradiction of Jefferson's thought and life. He has no way to explain this contradiction; it simply appears in his writings without any justification. For example, in his major work, *Notes on the State of Virginia*, Jefferson articulates his absolute abhorrence of slavery and insists unequivocally on emancipation. He understands that the enslavement of Africans is an unconscionable wrong perpetuated by the United States. And yet, in the same work, Jefferson gives voice to standard version of the racist fantasy when drawing up a comparison of races.

It is not just that Jefferson doesn't want to cede his position of power as a white man relative to other racial groups. His perceptions themselves become skewed. The role of the racist fantasy in shaping Jefferson's thoughts on blackness is evident when we examine his descriptions of different races. Jefferson believes in universal equality but cannot avoid the suspicion that those of African descent are less equal than Europeans and Native Americans because of the way that the racist fantasy structures them in his thinking.

Jefferson's contradictory thinking about racism reaches its apogee when he attempts to generalize about Black character. Here, he doesn't just articulate a belief in Black inferiority. Instead, he views blackness with the lens of a racist fantasy that highlights unrestrained Black enjoyment. The race problem for Jefferson is fundamentally the problem of Black enjoyment, as much as it is about the evil of slavery. Blackness connotes an increased capacity for enjoyment that outstrips that of white counterparts. Jefferson cannot find a way to square this excess of enjoyment with his conception of racial equality, and it leads him to sound just like a garden variety white racist, not a champion of universal emancipation.

Black enjoyment manifests itself in the activities that Jefferson sees on his plantation. Talking about Black people in general in *Notes on the State of Virginia*, he states, "They seem to require less sleep. A black, after hard labour through the day, will be induced by the slightest amusements to sit up till midnight, or later, though knowing he must be out with the first dawn of the morning."[22] Jefferson's belief in this resiliency when it comes to amusement emerges directly from the fantasy of the racial other's privileged enjoyment. While whites have to rest and restrict their enjoyment in order to avoid exhausting themselves, blackness, in Jefferson's version of the racist fantasy, involves no such limitations on the capacity for enjoyment.

This privilege also aligns the racial other with sensuality. Jefferson continues,

> They are more ardent after their female: but love seems with them to be more an eager desire, than a tender delicate mixture of sentiment and sensation. Their griefs are transient. Those numberless afflictions, which render it doubtful whether heaven has given life to us in mercy or in wrath, are less felt, and sooner forgotten with them. In general, their existence appears to participate more of sensation than reflection.[23]

Jefferson writes directly from the structure of the racist fantasy. Just as the fantasy attributes excessive sexual prowess to blackness, so does Jefferson. Likewise, every deficit that he associates with blackness in *Notes on the State of Virginia* has to do with the relation between blackness and enjoyment. He thinks about blackness from the perspective of the racist fantasy, not in the Enlightenment terms of universal equality. Jefferson's modernity falters when it becomes caught up in the racist fantasy because this fantasy is intrinsically linked to the radicality of the modern project. He cannot sustain the universality of equality, despite his utter conviction that universal equality inheres in our subjectivity. Universal equality would strip Jefferson of the security of identity, a security that his investment in the racist fantasy protects. This is why he invests himself in it.

Even though Jefferson sees blackness negatively, he nonetheless grants it a privileged relationship to enjoyment that whiteness does not have. Black sensuality stands out in his mind. While he does not consciously express his desire for this sensuality, it is lurking between the lines of what he writes. Its presence there is a direct result of his investment in the racist fantasy. Black enjoyment stands as an obstacle, in Jefferson's mind, to the achievement of full-fledged social equality. This obstacle is nonetheless also the site where he himself is able to envision access to this impossible enjoyment.

Here we see perfectly how the slaveowner can partake in an enjoyment that he appears to forgo for himself. Jefferson can tell himself that he is above Black sensuality while nonetheless indulging in it through the racist fantasy. What's more, Jefferson, like so many slaveowners, accessed this fantasized enjoyment through his sexual relations with his slave Sally Hemmings. Given what he says in *Notes on the State of Virginia* about Black enjoyment, one might postulate that she was appealing for him because she was a figure of illicit enjoyment. Perhaps all of Jefferson's prejudicial views about Black sensuality provided a path to enjoyment for him when he had sex with his slave. Blackness serves as an obstacle to enjoyment that enables white access to enjoyment. In this way, one could imagine that Jefferson was able to distance himself from this sensuality and immerse himself in it at the same time.

When looking back on a figure like Jefferson, it is tempting to see his clear racism as an indictment of the project of universal equality, as if the racism were the hidden truth of the fundamental values of modernity. But his betrayal of universal equality does not taint universal equality as a value. Instead, it indicates that one cannot envision equality without taking stock of how fantasy shapes the terrain on which we coexist. One must fight this fantasy in order to sustain equality. One must rethink equality through the distorting power of fantasy and the enjoyment that it produces. There is no social reality free of fantasy. But at the same time, we have the ability to move beyond the racist fantasy by recognizing that our universal equality exists not through what we have in common but through what we don't have. Accomplishing this demands that we give up our investment in biology as the unquestionable authority of the modern world.

The Living Bible

The turn from premodern religious discrimination to modern racist discrimination follows from a change in what constitutes the ultimate ground of society. For premodern societies, God or some deities provide the ground for the social order. The divine functions as the final authority, the court of last resort. In modernity, however, divinity loses this status. Though belief in God persists, God no longer plays a constitutive role for the social structure.[24] God gives way to biology, just as religious discrimination gives way to racism.

The authoritative role that biology plays in modernity underlies the turn to racism that characterizes the modern world. Differences rooted in biology—or pseudo-biology—come to the fore, while religious differences cease to be authoritative. From its origins as a discipline, biology has provided a scientific justification for racist attitudes. Although biology as a discipline is, of course, not inherently racist, it has historically enabled racists to believe that their attitudes are rooted in the way things actually are.

Even the relatively nonhierarchical classification of races that Carl Linnaeus proffers in his 1735 work *Systema Natura* contributes to modern racism. Although Linnaeus doesn't rank the races according to their biology, he nonetheless attempts to ground race in human biology, to use biology as a source for racial difference (and thus for racism). Johann Friedrich Blumenbach follows this up by dividing humanity into five distinct races in his 1775 work "The Natural Varieties of Mankind." This provides the major biological justification for racial classification. Blumenbach established genetic difference as the basis for these five distinct races in 1793. He grouped humanity into Caucasians, Mongolians, Malayans, Ethiopians, and Americans. The urge to think of humanity in terms of racial difference is not a neutral urge. It is racism that leads to the distinction between races, not the distinction between races that produces racism.

The production of race through acts of racism is what Karen and Barbara Fields call *racecraft*. They note that "through the transforming power of racecraft, an individual becomes a race."[25] Modern biology's attempts to discover and explain racial difference are indications of the massive retreat from modern universal equality. The threat that this universality poses to social hierarchies produces such retreats. We should see the racial speculation of modern biology as the primary front in modernity's promulgation of racism in response to its discovery of the trauma of equality.

Racism in modernity is not just a feeling. It is not just a visceral recoil that some experience in proximity to others. Throughout its history, it has an elaborate biological justification. From Christoph Meiners to Georges Cuvier to Arthur de Gobineau, thinkers attempted to give their racist conceptions of humanity a biological underpinning. This effort continues up to the present, with works such as *The Bell Curve* by Charles Murray and Richard Hernstein. Even less overtly racist researchers in genetics continue to employ race as a category despite its scientific nonexistence.[26]

Even as biologists now by and large insist on the nonexistence of race as a significant biological category, the turn to biology as a ground for thinking remains implicated in modern racism. While we should not obviously dismiss the insights of biology, we also cannot take them as the ultimate authority. Biology continues to play a major role in the ideological battle against equality insofar as it finds hierarchies written into our genetic code.[27]

In order to break from its racist tradition, modernity must eschew all authority, even that of biology or other sciences. Universal equality will only be universal when we get rid of our reliance on authority figures in whatever guise. The reliance on authority is incommensurate with equality because it elevates authority figures outside of the strictures of the polity that apply to everyone. We cannot square the exceptionality of the authorities with a thoroughgoing equality.

The modern world emerged through a break from traditional society. The racism that has characterized it is not a remnant of tradition but the result of the recoil from the radicality of the modern break. Another break is necessary, one that strips away modernity's reliance on the racism that betrays its most precious insights.

CSI Galápagos

If modernity produces the scourge of racism as its obscene shadow, modernity itself must have the tools to combat this shadow. These tools appear to reside in the developments of biology. Even though biology played a crucial role in the development of racism, today it seems to be safely on the opposite side, on the side of emancipation. Given the discoveries since Darwin, biology now appears to play a crucial role in the eradication of all racism. But biology has always functioned both to support racist ideas and to challenge them. It always works at cross purposes, which is why the struggle against racism cannot hang its hat on biological evidence.

Darwin himself came from an abolitionist family and saw himself as an opponent of racism.[28] On the one hand, the discovery of a single ancestor for all humanity (and all life) undermined one biological justification for racism, the notion of distinct origins for each race. If one traces descent back far enough, there can be no racial difference whatsoever. Biologists all agree that the idea of Eve, the first common ancestor, having a race would be nonsense. But on the other hand, the theory of natural selection gave ample fodder to those who defended a hierarchy of races based on their relative fitness. The notion that the best adapted survive and prosper played right into the hands of the most committed racists.

It is not just Darwin's followers (such as Francis Galton or Herbert Spencer) who turn the theory of natural selection into a justification for racist politics. Darwin himself, in *The Descent of Man and Sexual Selection in Relation to Sex*, gives in to this temptation as well. He sees imperial conquest as a manifestation of natural selection. He argues, for instance, "At the present day civilized nations are everywhere supplanting barbarous nations, excepting where the climate opposes a deadly barrier; and they succeed mainly, though not exclusively, through their arts, which are the products of the intellect."[29] The intelligence of superior races leads them to displace inferior ones. Darwin even sees courage and loyalty as traits common to superior peoples that will enable their political victories. His embrace of such unabashed racist speculation undermines the radical egalitarianism of his theory of the single ancestor.[30] As Darwin's own case reveals, biology is constantly pulling in opposed directions—toward servitude and toward emancipation at the same time.

From the racist perspective, admitting the truth of a single ancestor was the price paid for gaining access to a biologically justified hierarchy that could authorize extermination. At least this is how it played out in history through Nazism and other political projects based on a racial hierarchy. In a historical examining of the relationship between biology and racism, the verdict on the effect of biology is largely negative. It has done more to support the efforts of racists than it has to undermine them.

The breakthrough of the idea of a single ancestor for all humanity thwarted the possibility of conceiving different races as unrelated. After Darwin's promulgation of this idea, convinced racists could no longer assure themselves of their absolute difference from the racial other. Unfortunately, this discovery did not even produce a hiccup in the working of the racist fantasy. Darwin displaced absolute racial difference only to endorse the idea of natural hierarchies, which played directly in the racist fantasy.

The problem is that the theory of natural selection leaves intact the notion of hierarchy. It even provides racial hierarchy with a biological justification. As André Pichot points out, "Darwinism brings us very clearly into a hierarchical ranking of races according to their degree of evolution. This hierarchy has no need of an essentialist definition of species and race; it fits very well into a continuity of living forms, a gradation running from the least to the most evolved."[31] Pichot makes it clear that racists were not simply distorting Darwin's doctrine when they took it up as a justification for social hierarchies based on race. The doctrine does actually support such hierarchies because it sees struggle and hierarchy throughout the natural world. It also apotheosizes the adaptation that produces winners in life. Those who are less adapted as a result of their biological inheritance must perish. This is, for Darwin, the law of nature, and it is, for Pichot, the ideological justification for both capitalism and racism.[32] It even has a hand in justifying Nazism.

It is not a matter of condemning Darwin for the turn that his doctrine took after his lifetime. But we should pay attention to how ineffectual his turn to the single ancestor was in eliminating racism, in part because the implications of the theory of natural selection obviated the revolutionary impact of the idea of the single ancestor. The same struggle that we see in Darwin's own thought between the elimination of a biological justification for racial distinction and an investment in racial difference continues to resound in biology. Biologists no longer have an investment in a racial hierarchy, but they have not uniformly given up on the idea of racial difference rooted in biology.

The human genome project reveals a fundamental homogeneity among what used to be considered different races. The genome shows the insignificance of racial difference. In this way, it builds on Darwin's understanding of the single ancestor. As Dorothy Roberts points out in *Fatal Invention*, her work on biology's inability to overcome its investment in race, difference within racial categories outstrips difference between these categories. She writes, "The entire range of human variation for some genetic traits can be found on the African continent. A person from the Congo, a person from South Africa, and a person from Ethiopia are more genetically different from each other than from a person from France."[33] The insistence on a biological justification for racial difference teeters after Darwin's intervention and fully collapses after the discoveries of contemporary genetic research. But even this is not enough to put an end to the impulse toward looking to biology as a foundation on which to establish the truth of racial difference.

Despite the apparently incontrovertible evidence that racial difference plays no part in human biology, certain biologists nonetheless insist on using race as a basis for their research. This includes both racist researchers concerned with sustaining a racial hierarchy and antiracists committed to establishing racial diversity as an ontological principle. These latter are a significantly larger group. The advocates of racial diversity see this diversity itself as a virtue, an indication that humanity is inherently multiple rather than homogeneous. This multiplicity manifests itself in racial difference, a difference that we should affirm, not repress, they believe.[34]

Whatever position one adopts, biology will never provide a solution to the massive social investment in racism. Enjoyment has historically driven the appeal of racism and will continue to do so. Biology has historically served as a justification for racism rather than its cause. No matter what insights it comes up with, it will always remain in this secondary position. It cannot take the lead in the fight against racism, either by proving that race doesn't exist or by demonstrating that there is a diversity of nonhierarchically organized races.

The turn away from biologically justified racial hierarchy has had little effect on the extent of racism in the world. This is because racism is rooted in the unconscious—specifically, the fantasy that continues to adhere to the significance of racial difference. The absence of a biological ground for racism actually fuels the racist fantasy with even more enjoyment. This additional enjoyment stems from the fetishistic disavowal at work when this biological ground is absent. The fantasizing subject must disavow the knowledge that racial difference has no significance. One knows this but acts as if one doesn't by continuing to hold onto a racist fantasy. The sacrifice of one's knowledge through disavowal increases the libidinal power of the fantasy for the subject.

Without a biological ground, racism transcends logic and becomes inexplicable. People experience the significance of racial difference as a stubborn fact within the racist fantasy even when they know consciously it has no biological ground. The inexplicability of racial difference gives it a transcendent quality. It matters even more for people when they have no way of explaining it and when they know better. Indulging in the racist fantasy becomes not just a way of procuring an otherwise impossible enjoyment, it also becomes an avenue for undermining elitist knowledge. In this way, the biological abandonment of any racial hierarchy feeds the racist's enjoyment. By indulging in the racist fantasy, one now gains the added enjoyment of defying the experts. One must deny what everyone knows and continue to act as if one doesn't know it.

In the act of fetishistic disavowal, subjects evince a double attitude toward what they know: they know while disavowing this knowledge. In the case of the racist fantasy, on the one hand, they know that there is no racial hierarchy, that it has no biological justification. But on the other hand, they act as if it does exist. The actions defy their knowledge. In an essay on fetishism, Octave Manoni comes up with a famous formulation to describe this attitude. This attitude is: "I know well, but all the same …"[35] By accepting the existence of what one also denies, one is able to include the act of defiance within the fantasy. The investment in the fantasy becomes even more of a transgression when one knows better. One transgresses not just an external authority but also one's own knowledge. The falsity of the fantasy in this way contributes to its power to deliver enjoyment.

The struggle against the racist fantasy cannot proceed solely through an appeal to knowledge. One must also address the enjoyment that this fantasy produces. Doing so entails working through the fantasy and making clear how one can obtain the same enjoyment without the unnecessary detour through this fantasy. People remain stuck in their racism because they believe that giving it up would deprive them of an enjoyment that they could not find anywhere else. But the enjoyment that the racist fantasy provides is nothing but the subject's own form of enjoyment attributed to the racial other. Showing that this is the case diminishes the appeal of the racist fantasy. Racism is not an easy path to enjoyment but a roundabout one to get at an enjoyment that could be had with much less trouble.[36] One need not go through the trouble of the racist fantasy to have the enjoyment that it provides because this enjoyment is always that of the subject itself insofar as it necessarily doesn't belong. The subject enjoys its own nonbelonging through the nonbelonging that it attributes to the racial other in the racist fantasy. But people can do without this fantasy by taking responsibility for their own enjoyment rather than attributing to the racial other. The failure to take this step and to abandon the racist fantasy stems in large part because a capitalist economy requires it. For this reason, one cannot be fully antiracist without being at the same time anticapitalist.

The Racist Baker

One of the strongest arguments in favor of the capitalist system is that it punishes racism and prejudices of all sorts. This gives it the appearance of working in concert with modern egalitarianism, despite the massive inequalities that exist within the system. The logic of this argument is simple. If I discriminate at any point in the capitalist process, I fail to maximize my own profit, thereby opening the door to a less prejudiced rival that will seize on this chance to earn what I have refused to capitalize on my possibilities for earning. This works in both buying and selling. If I won't buy from a Chinese supplier due to my prejudices, a competitor will do so and thus be able to undersell me when we bring our products to the market. At the same time, if I refuse to sell to Chinese patrons at my business, here also a competitor would come along and make the money on these consumers that I have chosen to ignore. In this way, capitalism provides an economic sanction against the immorality of my racism.

This is an argument that Milton Friedman lays out in *Capitalism and Freedom*. In this work, Friedman contends that the morality of capitalism stems from the egalitarian politics that it promotes. Despite his popularity among conservatives, Friedman celebrates moments in the history of capitalism when the system ultimately eviscerated conservative attempts to single out certain groups on the basis of their identity or even their political beliefs. Capitalism accomplishes this because of its imperviousness to personal considerations. Freidman writes, "An impersonal market separates economic activities from political views and protects men from being discriminated against in their economic activities for reasons that are irrelevant to their productivity—whether these reasons are associated with their views or their color."[37] On the one hand, capitalism forges an unrestrained greed among its subjects—it demands that they believe greed is good, to put it in the idiom of *Wall Street* (Oliver Stone, 1987)—and it levies a considerable fine on those who allow their prejudices to impact the process of exchange.

While there is clearly something to Friedman's moral argument for capitalism's inherent antiracism, when one looks at the ability of racism to flourish throughout the history of the capitalist system, one cannot but conclude that the analysis misses the mark. It is not just that Friedman is right in theory but wrong in how capitalism actually works. What Friedman and all those who see capitalism as inherently antiracist miss is the central role that the racist fantasy plays in the perpetuation of capitalist subjectivity. It is true that those who refuse to serve the racial other might damage their profitability, but on the other hand, they feed the fantasy that enables millions of people to sustain their investment in capitalism despite its continued failure to deliver on the promises that it makes to them.[38]

Capitalist subjectivity involves an investment in the promise of an unlimited future satisfaction. This promise, linked to the idea of constant future accumulation, structures life in capitalist society. The commodity form, the structuring principle of capitalist society, contains in it the idea of infinite future accumulation and infinite future enjoyment. To accept the logic of the commodity form is to never have enough because one never arrives at infinity. This sense of not having enough is the motor that keeps the capitalist system running. If we already believe that we have enough to satisfy ourselves, we would not embark on the process of constantly accumulating more. No one who had enough could be a capitalist subject. Capitalist subjects accumulate with the idea of amassing enough money or enough commodities to allow them to enjoy without restraint, but this future of unrestrained enjoyment never arrives.

This is the basic psychic logic of capitalism, whatever its economic logic might be. The same logic also works with every commodity that I purchase. I'm seeking a commodity that will provide complete satisfaction. But the promise of complete satisfaction exists only as a promise that no commodity ever redeems. Once I have the commodity or have accumulated riches, I always find that I miss that complete satisfaction that the commodity initially promised. After purchasing the newest iPhone, I realize that it doesn't really offer that much more than the previous version, which forces me to look ahead to the next version for the satisfaction that I fail to receive from having the commodity. The commodity promises a future of unrestrained enjoyment that it never delivers, just like the capitalist system itself. Under capitalism, we enjoy in a future that structurally can never arrive.

The problem is that capitalism never permits anyone to reach the nirvana of enjoyment without restraint because this nirvana doesn't exist. One never reaches the goal of having enough because this point recedes in the distance the closer one gets to it, just like the green light that marks Daisy's house for Gatsby in *The Great Gatsby*. The more one has, the more one experiences one's lack of satisfaction. Rather than filling lack, excess ends up highlighting it. This is why those who win in the game of capitalist accumulation don't stop accumulating but become even more bent on accumulation than those who have hardly anything. The continued ruthless accumulation displayed by figures such as Bill Gates and Jeff Bezos makes sense only if one takes stock of the underlying psychic logic at work in capitalism. They experience themselves as more deprived than the most impoverished subject in the capitalist universe. That's how the logic of capitalism works.

Embarking on the project of accumulation, I want the unrestrained satisfaction that is missing in my daily life. The magic of capitalist accumulation works so that whenever I attain what I want, it soon becomes apparent that satisfaction entails a little bit more. This little bit more is intrinsic to each act of accumulating and renders it endless. Obtaining what I wanted, I find that I just missed it and must return to the project of accumulation. Thus, after obtaining what I previously desired, I desire more money, a newer phone, or a larger television.

Accumulating inevitably leads to the desire for additional accumulation rather than the sating of desire. Within the capitalist psychic economy, no one says I have enough because one never experiences what one has as enjoyable enough. There is always a more excessive enjoyment on the horizon that more accumulation would allow me to access. The experience of an excess cannot be as satisfying as its image promises that it will be. Excess is excessive insofar as we can never reach it, which means that it never delivers us from our lack.

Requiem for a Dream

But capitalist society must find a way to deal with all the dissatisfaction that derives from the commodity's incessant failure to deliver on its promises. Otherwise, the dissatisfaction would threaten the continued existence of the capitalist system. Marx would be proven right: workers would get together and overthrow the capitalists, and even the capitalists themselves might join in the revolt, if they too grasped the commodity's failure. This is where the racist fantasy comes to the rescue for capitalism. The racist fantasy offers a tidy explanation for why I fail to experience the enjoyment that capitalism promises to me as an obedient subject. The racist fantasy lets me know that the fault is not in capitalism but in the racial other, the one who takes the job that I should have thanks to affirmative action or obtains government handouts based on my tax payments or simply steals my possible sexual partners with illicit inducements. Once I succumb to the lure of the racist fantasy, I have a figure to blame that takes all the guilt off the capitalist system. Racism generates an unquestioning attitude toward capitalism by drawing our attention away from it.

Once my dissatisfaction with my lot in society becomes the responsibility of the racial other rather than the capitalist system, that system effectively insulates itself against revolt. This is the story of capitalism's history that remains hidden. Thanks to my investment in the racist fantasy, I don't join a union or collectively organize for a different socioeconomic system. I don't vote for leftist candidates who would promise to put up barriers to the unrestrained accumulation of capitalist overlords. I don't even reserve any enmity for the stock trader who is accumulating millions while my retirement fund disappears. Instead, because of my investment in the racist fantasy, I see the racial other as the figure responsible for all the ills that I suffer.

Because of the way it redirects animus away the capitalist system itself or its representatives, the racist fantasy provides protection for this system. The fantasy obfuscates the structure of exploitation so that one cannot recognize the source of one's dissatisfaction. One has a ready explanation for one's lack of material success, and this explanation points away from the structure of the capitalist economy itself. When I am ensconced in the racist fantasy, race colors every economic question and blinds me to the capitalist economy as a problem.

This works for both conservative and liberal policymakers. Conservatives imply that the racial other—most often, the immigrant—is responsible for the failures of the working class to gain wealth. Liberals, for their part, tailor their proposals to social problems separated from the economy. This is exactly what Touré Reed finds lacking in American liberalism after the Second World War. In *Toward Freedom*, he writes, "Liberals' tendency to divorce race from class has had dire consequences for African American and other low-skilled workers. Specifically, race reductionism has obscured the political-economic roots of racial disparities, resulting in policy prescriptions that could only have limited value to poor and working class blacks."[39] By targeting just the racial other without regard for class relations, policies end up exacerbating racist conditions and serving capitalist society. The end point of this liberalism is Hillary Clinton's broadside against the "basket of deplorables" that gave those invested in the racist fantasy a megadose of enjoyment but did nothing to counter capitalism's continuing onslaught against labor.

No capitalist entity can genuinely fight against racism. Corporate support for movements such as Black Lives Matter is always support given with the company's fingers crossed. Every corporation depends on the functioning of the racist fantasy in order to remain viable, no matter how well-intentioned those who run the show. Supposed woke capitalism cannot exist because the elimination of racism would eliminate the sustainability of the capitalist system.[40]

We can see compelling evidence for this in one of the most famous cases of woke capitalism—the behavior of the National Basketball Association (NBA) during games played amid the explosion of the Black Lives Matter movement and the Covid-19 pandemic. The NBA decided to play its games in a Covid bubble created at Disneyworld in Orlando, Florida. As part of the agreement between (almost exclusively white) owners and (predominantly Black) players, the league allowed players to wear social justice slogans on their jerseys in the place where names were usually located. Some of the slogans made radical statements: "Say Her Name," "Equality," "Anti-Racist," and even "Group Economics." But what stood out about these slogans were the ones that the NBA did not permit.

A substantial portion of the NBA's revenue comes from China. In order not to put this revenue at risk, the league banned slogans such as "Free Hong Kong" or "Free Tibet," which one might imagine that a few players would have chosen, since these slogans represent a contemporary political cause that directly concerns the actions of the NBA. This was a purely financial decision on the part of the NBA, a decision that reveals the fundamental impossibility of anything like woke capitalism. The league would only take its fight against injustice so far, only to the point where it did not endanger revenues. But a genuine fight against racism always endangers revenues. This is what capitalism cannot abide.

Capitalist entities reproduce themselves through the production of more today than they produced yesterday. They require consumers invested in the accumulation of more and more enjoyment. They require consumers with an outlet for the dissatisfaction that the process of accumulation necessarily produces. This outlet is the racist fantasy in some form or another. It is a fantasy that capitalism cannot live without.

Even though police violence is the most visible form of contemporary racism, the corporate investment in the racist fantasy is even more extreme than that of the state. Corporations, no matter how they try to paint themselves and no matter how critical they are of racist state violence, are never the friends of those invested in antiracist struggle. The capitalist order owes its continued existence to the racist fantasy. While a corporation might assist in fighting a more obvious manifestation of racism, no corporation in the world wants to do away with racism as such. Doing so would portend the end of capitalism. For every capitalist entity, this is an existential question, which is why there is no such thing as a nonracist capitalism, despite the dreams of Milton Friedman.

The other benefit of the racist fantasy for capitalist society is that it has the same function in reverse for those who are racial others. It works for both racists and the victims of racism in related ways, even though it places them in opposed positions within its framework. If one is a Jew in German society in the 1930s, for instance, the racist fantasy provides one with figures responsible for one's exploitation. One would turn one's focus to Nazism as the source of oppression and take it off capitalism. In this way, the prevalence of the racist fantasy hides the working of capitalism for the victims of racism just as it does for the oppressors.

One doesn't experience capitalism as the driving force of one's oppression. Thanks to how the racist fantasy shapes German life, Jews in the 1930s experience racism as the most tangible barrier to their unrestrained enjoyment. Capitalism fails to deliver on its promise to Jews just as it does to Germans who aren't Jewish—much more so—but the widespread existence of racism enables those who are Jewish in German society to attribute this failure to racism rather than to capitalism. One can become a fervent critic of racism and continue to believe in capitalism. Attacking racism while supporting capitalism requires not recognizing how capitalism survives through the racist fantasy.

Perhaps the most compelling depiction of the way that racism can distort the subjectivity of one forced into the position of the racial other occurs in Toni Morrison's first novel. *The Bluest Eye* describes the trauma of racism on a young Black girl, Pecola Breedlove. This trauma manifests itself primarily through Pecola's overwhelming desire to become beautiful, which for her means becoming white and obtaining blue eyes. After Pecola's father rapes her twice and she has a child who dies, Pecola notices that people begin to treat her differently. Rather than seeing this as a result of the violence she suffered, Pecola attributes it to the fact that she now has the blue eyes that she has always fantasized about.

Pecola's fantasy about blue eyes consumes her entire existence. It provides her respite from the suffering that the combination of capitalism and racism imposes on her. Blue eyes, in Morrison's vision, represent all the benefits of white society that racism precludes Black individuals from having. Blue eyes function as the fullest expression of the commodity. Because racism denies Pecola access to the kind of existence that whites have, she invests herself entirely in the logic of capitalism. Racism eliminates any room for her to question this logic. This is part of its trap.

The critique of racism combined with silence on capitalism is most evident among entertainers and athletes who take a political stand. These public figures deserve immense credit for speaking out when others stay silent in the face of obvious injustices. But their critique typically remains focused on racism (or sexism) and never touches on the capitalist economy.[41] Undoubtedly, this is due to the incredible salaries that they receive, but it does limit their political effectiveness.

For everyone, the racist fantasy lets capitalism off the hook for its inevitable betrayals. This fantasy drives us to see race, not capitalism, as the culprit for whatever oppression that we suffer. This is why capitalism cannot do without the racist fantasy. In the absence of this fantasy, capitalist subjects would have a direct experience of the dissatisfaction that capitalism produces. They would be able to link this dissatisfaction to the logic of capitalism itself. One cannot imagine capitalism without the racist fantasy because one cannot imagine everyone accepting the brutality of capitalist life without having some way to exculpate capitalism for its sins.

The racist fantasy sustains capitalist society at the expense of both the victims of racism and capitalism's laborers. While the racist fantasy produces occasional explosions of violence such as lynchings and police shootings, it usually has the effect of keeping capitalist society functioning without major upheavals. The problem is that the continued existence of the racist fantasy breeds the potential for an eruption of fascism. The continued existence of the racist fantasy within capitalist society leaves this society always on the verge of tipping over into fascism.

Fascism occurs when leaders attempt to construct a social order that responds to the racist fantasy. They attempt to counter the fantasized excesses of the racial other with policies that openly espouse authoritarian violence against this figure. We enter into fascism at the point where the reaction to the fantasy occurs on the level of the state. Fascism reorganizes the state in an effort to prevent the racial other from blocking access to the object. This effort can go from official censure of the racial other all the way to its annihilation, as was the case in Nazi Germany. Nazism represents the ultimate expression of the fascism and the end point of the racist fantasy.

Fascism represents a constant danger for capitalist society. Its reliance on the racist fantasy leaves it always on the verge of tipping over into fascism. When class division becomes exacerbated (as will tend to happen within capitalism), the turn to fascism becomes increasingly possible. This turn occurs when people begin to treat the racist fantasy as a reality that they need to aggressively combat. That is, they demand state solutions to the fantasized danger that the racial other represents. Capitalist society cannot do away with the risk of fascism because it cannot do away with its reliance on the racist fantasy.

The racist fantasy works hand-in-hand with the fundamental capitalist fantasy. Capitalism uses the fantasy of unrestrained enjoyment to encourage a relentless drive to accumulate. It motivates the subject's incessant competition with the other. Without this fantasy of future enjoyment without restraint, no one would embark on the project of accumulation to the extent that capitalism requires it. Even Adam Smith confesses this. He points out that the wealthy actually live miserable lives, but the fantasy that wealth brings complete satisfaction is a necessary one. Smith argues that this fantasy "rouses and keeps in continual motion the industry of mankind."[42] Such a fantasy operates as a crucial and necessary engine for capitalist productivity. If we don't believe in the fantasy of accumulation leading to an ultimate satisfaction, we will cease to accumulate. But this basic capitalist fantasy also requires the racist fantasy in order to explain why I do not achieve what this capitalist fantasy promises.

Many theorists of capitalism have commented on the intrinsic relationship between capitalism and racism. But what has not been sufficiently recognized is the dependence of the psyche of the capitalist subject on racism (and specifically the racist fantasy). Racism enables one to accept the dissatisfaction that comes with living in capitalist society and to redirect one's ire about this dissatisfaction. Without this backstop guarding against radical desires, capitalist society would simply be unable to survive in its current form. The racist fantasy keeps everyone's eyes on the capitalist prize and off the horrors of the system. For this reason, the fight against racism, in order to have a chance to succeed, must also be a fight against capitalism.

While the racist fantasy is available to everyone in modernity, Europeans and white Americans have been culpable for more racism than the rest of the planet put together. The worst racist abominations— from European colonialism to American slavery to the Nazi Holocaust— all stem from Europe and its descendants. It is not coincidental that Europe is also the birthplace of capitalism and that the United States is the nation in the world most committed to it. The white American investment in the racist fantasy is more fervent than that of any other nation because the United States is also the most unabashedly capitalist nation. The commitment to capitalism requires a commitment to the racist fantasy as a way of explaining capitalism's failure to keep its promises. Racism keeps the capitalist system running.

If modernity cannot do without its racist underside, this is due in no small part to the role that it plays within capitalist society. Modernity's struggle for equality must be a struggle against the specific form of capitalist modernity. Fighting racism requires also fighting the exigencies of capitalist society because one of those exigencies is the racist fantasy. It is impossible for capitalist society to function without its racist underside, which is why the opposition that capitalists display to racism can never be effective, even if it is sincere. An antiracist society must be a society that is no longer capitalist.

The Variegations of the Fantasy

Through the Looking Glass Darkly

While not every society relies on a foundational racist fantasy—at least, it's possible to imagine one without it—every society that has structural racism does. In a racist society, the foundational racist fantasy provides the matrix for how our perception works in society. As the fantasy organizes enjoyment for subjects, it also aligns perceptions with this enjoyment. Racism's insinuation into ways of fantasizing ensures that it will shape people's perceptions and make it impossible for them to develop nonracist ideas. Fantasy is not a secondary response to a dissatisfying situation but a primary way of apprehending one's situation.[1]

Subjects perceive through fantasy and its distortion of their senses. It colors every perception that they have. One doesn't first perceive someone and then subsequently categorize this person in the position of the racial other. The racist fantasy is not an appendix to social reality but the ground on which that reality exists. What's more, there is no clear and distinct opposition between reality on the one side and fantasy on the other. Instead, collectively shared fantasy is what creates the sense of shared reality that people have in common. One perceives the racial other directly because one perceives through the fantasy. This is why Jacques Lacan states that "everything we are allowed to approach by way of reality remains rooted in fantasy."[2] Fantasy establishes the psychic structures through which people know what counts as reality and what doesn't. The world of social reality has depth—it seems real—because they fantasize a background to everything that they simply perceive.

There is no such thing as an originally satisfying reality that occurs prior to the instantiation of a fantasy structure. In other words, in order to find reality satisfying, we first require a fantasy structure through which we can relate to reality. Fantasy tells us how to relate to reality and what to value in it. It even tells us what to regard as real. This is what a social order gives to its subjects as they enter into it: not just a shared reality but a shared fantasy.[3] The mediation of fantasy gives reality its satisfying hue because the fantasy frame creates the space in which a satisfying object may appear. Without the fantasy frame, there is no psychic space to accommodate the satisfying object.

When fantasy organizes enjoyment, it blinds people to the inequality that the distribution of enjoyment obfuscates through its ability to make this inequality enjoyable.[4] Fantasy does not necessarily have a conservative valence, but its role in organizing enjoyment makes it an important tool for societies seeking to dismantle potential threats to their structure. We can see this clearly in the working of fantasy within capitalism. If I invest myself in the fantasy of winning the lotto, my desire is not oriented toward challenging the dictates of capitalist society. The fantasy of great wealth always renders people docile and obedient, even if it leads them to break the law. The fantasy directs my enjoyment in a way that purchases my silence. This is even more true with the racist fantasy. By focusing on the racial other as the obstacle to enjoyment and channeling enjoyment through this figure, the oppressive structure of the social order goes unchallenged for the person caught up in this fantasy. The racist fantasy provides the basis for a distribution of enjoyment that keeps the racist society running.

Although there are many other manifestations of racism in society than the racist fantasy, this fantasy is important because it determines the enjoyment that racism produces. Racist institutions create brutal conditions for those living under them, but without the racist fantasy to support these institutions, those working to sustain them would lose their incentive to do so. Fantasy provides the payoff. This is why the struggle against racism needs to include a fight against the power of the racist fantasy. It plays a necessary role in sustaining the overall racist structure in the social order.

If political action doesn't intervene on the level of fantasy, it is not touching on why the foundation of the social order remains as it is. Because she sees the structuring power of fantasy for the social order, Molly Rothenberg claims, "the *politics* of social change is irremediably fantasmatic."[5] Rather than seeing fantasy as a supplementary realm that should be dismissed or gotten rid of, we should see it as the privileged site for politics. Political acts must intervene on the level of fantasy if they are to introduce a substantive change.

Fantasy plays a structuring role not just in the formation of an individual's sense of reality but even in our collective sense of reality. In addition to being individual, fantasy plays a collective role in shaping the significance of our social reality. Carl Jung was wrong to posit a collective unconscious, but there is a collective fantasy. A shared sense of reality with others in a society stems from a shared fantasy because fantasy provides the foundation that enables us to relate together with others to a world where we know what really matters.

When others share a basic fantasy structure with us, this provides the basis for what we collectively experience as reality. Evidence for this appears in all our instant judgments about what we witness in the world. For instance, we look at a woman holding a baby in her arms, and we believe that we see a loving mother. We watch a football player yelling at his girlfriend, and we believe that he is an overaggressive jock. We hear a group of teens complaining about their high school, and we believe that they are expressing ordinary teen alienation. These figures make immediate sense to us not because they themselves have an immediate sense but because they fit within a socially shared fantasy structure. These are obvious instances of people fitting within the fantasy structure, but this type of analysis extends to everyone that we encounter. Our very ability to encounter people depends on our ability to locate them within our shared fantasy space.

Although there are purely individual fantasies, there are also collective ones that enable societies to cohere around them. The racist fantasy is the primary example of a collective fantasy. It establishes a bond between members of the society by separating those who belong from those who don't belong through their mode of enjoying themselves. The racial others are the ones who don't belong, and it is the fantasy that asserts this nonbelonging as a site of unrestrained enjoyment, no matter what the actual condition of those who don't belong is. The enjoyment of those who strive to belong depends on their identification with the enjoyment of those who don't. Belonging is wholly dependent on nonbelonging, both for the sense of belonging itself and for any enjoyment this position provides. If we examine the racist fantasy, it becomes clear that the racist always enjoys through the enjoyment of the despised racial other.[6] The figures of the obstacle are the sites where unrestrained enjoyment appears possible.

The racist fantasy creates an avenue for members of the society to find enjoyment in a direction that doesn't threaten the structure of the society but instead affirms it. Because it is excessive and intrinsically violates limits, enjoyment is always a danger to the smooth functioning of the social order. But at the same time, every social order needs the enjoyment of its members as the fuel that keeps the society running. As a result, the social order must play a dangerous game with enjoyment— encouraging it on the one hand, while finding ways to dissipate its disruptiveness on the other. Despite the social tumult that it provokes, racism is one of the ways of dissipating enjoyment's disruptiveness. The fact that racism is always on the verge of producing a civil war indicates the power of the enjoyment that fuels it.

In order to contain its disruptiveness, the ruling order channels enjoyment into avenues that sustain this order. The danger that enjoyment poses to the social order lessens when it occurs through the organizing principle of the racist fantasy, which directs it down paths that help to keep the social order functioning. Even though we imagine that racism has deleterious effects on our bond with each other, that it harms the social order, the racist fantasy nonetheless can provide a social glue that holds a society together.

Through the shared enjoyment that comes from a mutual investment in this fantasy, members of the society that accept the racist fantasy have a clear connection to each other. The bond that derives from the racist fantasy is of a different order than the bond emanating from a shared investment in the positive traits of the nation, such as its commitment to human rights or its aid to the underprivileged. The shared investment in the racist fantasy gives all those who share in it a dirty secret that they have in common. The wrongness of this racism and the sense of transgression attached to it create a connection that trumps almost any other.

The most obdurate bonds derive from shared transgressions. The pact that forms around a crime is stronger than the one that originates in a good deed.[7] This is why the blue code of silence that protects violent police officers rarely breaks, while those who join together in a peaceful protest typically feel no lasting connection. The shared transgression gives members of the group something held in common that others cannot partake in or even know. The resistance to publicity, the secret of the sin, creates the bond.[8] The shared transgression separates and collectivizes through the separation.

The connection between racism and immorality is intrinsic. Racism emerges with the idea of universal equality that reveals the injustice of racism. There is no racism prior to the knowledge that it is wrong. This means that there are no innocent racists, no one who is a racist without a sense of its immorality, even if the knowledge of the immorality is unconscious. To be a racist is to revel in one's immorality along with others who share this position, even if none ever admit consciously to this reveling. As a racist, one knows that one acts in violation of the fundamental tenet of modernity—its insistence on universal equality. The shame of this violation ties one to everyone else who feels similar shame.

Those who don't share in the fantasy, however, exist outside of the bond and are inherently suspect as members of the society. They are members of the society but don't belong. Their lack of participation in the shared transgression bespeaks their position as outsiders who cannot be trusted. They are not just responsible for almost all social ills but are also a threat to reveal the hidden source of the shame that the fantasists share. Those who don't partake of the illicit shared fantasy might at any moment expose the racist subject's racism.

Although those invested in it usually have some conscious knowledge of the racist fantasy, the way that the fantasy organizes enjoyment is unconscious. Not even the most convinced racists have a conscious understanding of how racism organizes their enjoyment. Even though enjoyment itself is not unconscious, what is impervious to knowledge is the relationship between the racist fantasy and the enjoyment that it produces. The connective tissues—the psychic pathways that lead from the racist fantasy to the subject's enjoyment—are unconscious. As a result, racists experience enjoyment but do not know why they enjoy. The source of this affect remains mysterious. Although people may consciously want to put racism behind them, their unconscious desire clings to it as a source of enjoyment. The path to this understanding and redirecting this enjoyment runs through the underlying racist fantasy.

Light in the South

Perhaps the writer most committed to displaying the absolute priority of the fantasy frame is William Faulkner. This becomes apparent in his great novels of the 1930s in which he attempts to submit the reader to the fantasy structure of various characters. Through his formal experimentations, Faulkner makes it clear for his readers that fantasy has ultimate primacy in our perceptions. The most significant of the great novels, *Absalom, Absalom!*, reveals how the perceptions of Quentin Compson derive not just from his own fantasies but even more from the fantasies that his ancestors have imposed on him. In the novel, Quentin and his Harvard roommate Shreve recount (or construct) the history that his father and a woman from his hometown, Rosa Coldfield, have told Quentin. By mediating this history through narrators who are themselves expressing what they have heard from others, Faulkner highlights the importance of the fantasy frame. One gains more insight into the fantasies that shape the characters than into what actually happens.

The story itself focuses on racism in the American South. Thomas Sutpen is the primary figure. He starts out as a poor white peasant, born to abject poverty in West Virginia. The shaping event of Sutpen's life occurs when his father sends him on an errand to a plantation, and a slave refuses him entrance at the front door. This shunning—a direct result of his class position—drives Sutpen to leave his family and begin working on a plantation in the West Indies, where he defends a plantation against a Black revolt and marries the plantation owner's daughter. He accumulates a fortune in the effort to overcome what he views as an absolute humiliation. The humiliation derives from the racist fantasy, which transforms the instance of class oppression into an experience of a racial denigration. The fact that a slave forces him to go around to the back of the estate that he comes to visit becomes the source of the aggression in Sutpen's psyche. The fact that the wealthy owner of the estate insisted on this policy doesn't shape Sutpen at all. It is simply that a slave is the vehicle for his humiliation that so disturbs him. Sutpen dedicates his life to ensuring that this will never happen again. Like Sutpen, all of Faulkner's characters in *Absalom, Absalom!* exist within the structure of the racist fantasy. None of them ever gain any purchase on its hold over them.

Quentin Compson is exceptional in this sense. Through Quentin, Faulkner depicts a white character who sees the damage that the racist fantasy has imposed on him, even if he is ultimately not able to live outside of it. He recognizes how these fantasies have overwhelmed his existence. He says, "*I have heard too much, I have been told too much; I have had to listen to too much, too long.*"[9] Quentin suffocates on the fantasized version of the past that has been passed down to him.

In the case of Quentin, Faulkner shows that the fantasy governing his existence—and ultimately destroying his life—is the racist fantasy, a fantasy that includes an idealization of white femininity, which serves as the object of desire within this version of the racist fantasy. The novel is difficult to untangle because Quentin doesn't first experience events and then construct a fantasy. Instead, the fantasy provides the matrix through which Quentin perceives. As Faulkner depicts this fantasy, it is blackness and Black enjoyment that serve as the obstacle to enjoying the idealized white woman. The fantasized history that Quentin and Shreve narrate concludes with a struggle between Henry Sutpen (Thomas Sutpen's son) and Charles Bon, his half-brother who is in love with his sister Judith. Henry's father Thomas incites Henry to kill Bon when he reveals that his half-brother has a Black mother, not because the relationship with Judith would be incestuous.

What is crucial about the dynamic in *Absalom, Absalom!* is that Charles Bon, as a Black man in the racist fantasy, has access to the incestuous object, an object presented as absolutely desirable in the novel. This is what drives Henry mad with racist envy. Henry doesn't object to incest since this is what he wants as well. But the incestuous object has the value that it does through Bon's intercession. Bon functions as the obstacle to Henry's enjoyment in the fantasy structure that Quentin describes. He is an obstacle that provides access to an enjoyment that would otherwise seem impossible. Throughout the novel, Henry is unable to perceive anything outside this structure because it is the basis from which he experiences the world.

While the form of *Light in August* doesn't go as far as *Absalom, Absalom!* in depicting the experiential priority of the fantasy, it does show how the racist fantasy pushes characters to the most extreme acts. *Light in August* narrates the story of Joe Christmas, a man who doesn't know if he is Black or not. Stuck in this existential hinterland, Christmas constantly struggles with the question of his place (or lack of a place) within the society of the American South. He begins a sexual relationship with Joanna Burden, a white woman who is attracted to him specifically because of the enjoyment that she sees in his blackness. However, the relationship turns sour as Christmas begins to have sex with other women and as she becomes jealous of these affairs. Out of jealousy, Burden plans to murder Christmas and then kill herself. When Christmas kills her in self-defense, white society pursues him with murderous vehemence.

In some of the best moments in his entire corpus, Faulkner captures the lust that drives the white lynch mob in its pursuit Christmas. Their violent aggression has a thoroughly sexual flavor to it, as Faulkner's prose makes clear. His evocation of the sexuality of the lynch mob reaches its apex when the mob catches Joe. One of the members of this mob, Percy Grimm, takes it on himself to castrate Christmas. As he accomplishes this act, Grimm proclaims, "Now you'll let white women alone, even in hell."[10] These words that accompany Grimm's act reveal the ubiquity of the racist fantasy: lynching is an act of horrific violence, but this is a thoroughly sexual violence, a violence that attempts to access for itself the enjoyment that it identifies in the blackness of Christmas.

Percy Grimm, the castrator, has no experience of Joe Christmas outside of the racist fantasy. His perceptions derive from this fantasy, a fantasy that shapes the form of Christmas into that of a licentious figure of pure enjoyment. The lynching takes place because of the expansiveness of the fantasy. Even though the gruesomeness of this act disgusts the other white men present, no one tries to intervene to stop it. This scene shows how far the racist fantasy goes in determining what one perceives and how one acts on these perceptions.

Not only does Faulkner's narrative style reflect the experiential priority of fantasy for the subject. It also shows this at work in the specific case of the racist fantasy. Many of the characters in his novels begin from within this fantasy and never find their way out of it. But the narrative structure of Faulkner's novels permits the reader to share in this experience and thereby to gain some purchase on the primacy of this fantasy. Although Quentin Compson can only escape the racist fantasy through suicide, Faulkner's reader has other possibilities.

Without fantasy, we can have no sense of reality at all. In this sense, we are all Quentin Compson. It is not just brutal racists like Percy Grimm who find themselves in this position. Everyone who lives within the domain of the racist society cannot but partake in it, even if one finds oneself its target. Fantasy determines what counts as significant and what is insignificant. It provides a mapping of the social terrain. It gives our reality a framework of significance through which we navigate our daily lives, dictating what we should pay attention to and what we should ignore. What matters for the psyche is not the distinction between reality and fantasy but rather the libidinal investment that it has in the events that it experiences, whether they occur in reality or whether the psyche only fantasizes them. This libidinal investment is what fantasy provides. It causes some objects to appear as desirable and others to appear as odious.

People have a social reality in common with others insofar as they partake in the same basic fantasy that underlies this reality and gives it its consistency. What doesn't fit within the fantasy frame doesn't count as reality for them. The fantasy frames their social reality. People either find a way to integrate recalcitrant material into the fantasy frame or they reject it as external to their reality. It is not if it doesn't fit. If they cannot dismiss it as nonexistent because of its recalcitrance, their fantasy undergoes an existential crisis that leads them to unleash violence on the recalcitrant entity, precisely the kind of violence that Faulkner depicts emerging in *Light in August*.

The House Unamerican Fantasy Frame

The power of the fantasy frame to shape perceptions becomes apparent if we look back at midcentury American history. Americans in the 1950s and 1960s shared a fantasy of communism overrunning the United States. Although Americans ostensibly feared it, this fantasy had an incredible unifying power. The fantasy of the threat of communism had the effect of binding American society together in a way that had never occurred beforehand and would not occur subsequently. In fact, when people today lament the loss of a prior American unity, what they are lamenting is precisely the death of this fantasy frame. They don't know it, but they are lamenting the absence of the communist threat.

The fantasy of a communist overthrow of the United States created a life in common among those who identified with American society. At the same time, however, it had deleterious effects, giving birth to the nuclear arms race, McCarthyism, and the Vietnam War, just to name a few of its unfortunate products. All this destruction emerged out of the fantasy that communist nations were not just different than the United States but were an existential threat to it. Whether they actually were or not has no bearing on the libidinal investment in the threat. Communism played the role of the obstacle within the American fantasy. The United States might have confronted communism as an external threat and defended itself against this threat without integrating communism into the fundamental American fantasy. But this is not what happened.

Being an American meant accepting the basic anticommunist fantasy, even if one rejected certain excesses that it produced (like McCarthyism). Perceptions of reality occurred through the structure of this fantasy, so that Americans divided the world into the free and the communists. Because of the constitutive role of this fantasy in the American psyche, one simply could not be an American with any degree of sympathy to communism.

Anyone who failed to adopt a vehement anticommunism became immediately suspicious, no matter what the person's prior standing in American society had been. This dynamic became especially apparent when fervent anticommunists in Congress stepped up their political investigation of Hollywood in 1947. Led by Republican congressperson J. Parnell Thomas, the House Unamerican Activities Committee (or HUAC) had hearings about the membership of notable Hollywood figures in the Communist Party. They did so because of their fear that communist ideas were seeping into American cinema and thereby posing an ideological threat to American society. In October 1947, the committee famously called eleven unfriendly witnesses that they suspected to be Communist Party members. Only one witness, Bertolt Brecht, cooperated with the committee, and he left the country just after his testimony. The others, known as the Hollywood Ten, refused to answer the committee's questions by invoking their First Amendment rights under the Constitution. Despite this wholly American form of defense, the Hollywood Ten quickly lost the nation's support and gained the reputation for being traitors.[11]

This became evident when a group of Hollywood luminaries devoted to backing their colleagues flew to Washington in a show of support. This group, the Committee for the First Amendment, initially received a warm welcome all across the country. After all, everyone loves film stars. They touched down at several stops during their flight to Washington and greeted adoring fans that welcomed their efforts. The group's membership included famous stars such as Humphrey Bogart, John Garfield, and Lauren Bacall. This star power wowed people at first. It seemed as if the fantasy of the communist threat would buckle in the face of this enormous show of Hollywood glamour. But soon the power of the anticommunist fantasy overwhelmed even Bogart's star power (which was unequaled at the time). Almost overnight, he ceased to be an American hero and became a communist traitor.

The opprobrium was so intense that Bogart had to quickly retract his support for the accused and withdraw his membership in the Committee for the First Amendment. Before the end of 1947, less than two months after his courageous stand with the Hollywood Ten, he put out a statement proclaiming that he had been duped by communism and that he was now fully aware of its dangers. This apology, made public soon after his political stand, testifies to the power of the anticommunist fantasy in shaping the conditions of social reality. Even a star that had the status of Humphrey Bogart was not safe from social exile if he stepped outside the anticommunist fantasy that bonded the American nation.

The political retreat restored Bogart to his former status, and his transgression became nothing but the result of his political naïveté. According to the public perception of the events, he wasn't savvy enough to know the tremendous danger of communism. It was a mistake that he would not repeat. Bogart underwent a transformation from a real American to a traitor to a real American again without ever becoming a different person. As his case shows, one's status in American society depended on how one comported oneself within the anticommunist fantasy. Bogart's position in society was a reflection of his position within this fantasy, not the result of what he was in reality apart from the fantasy, since this did not at all change. This is because there was no social reality prior to the structuring anticommunist fantasy. The fantasy determined what counted as real.

The shared fantasy provides the foundation for how people in a society like that of twentieth-century America perceive their reality. But this is not a dynamic confined to the anticommunist American past. It is operative in every society, no matter how small or open it might be. In order to live together, we require a sense of what counts as real and what we give value to, and this is what fantasy provides for us. While the ruling fantasy need not be as nefarious as American anticommunism, there is no such thing as a true shared fantasy that avoids constructing a foundational lie. The structuring fantasy creates a shared fiction that establishes the social playing field. Every structuring fantasy creates a libidinal investment in certain aspects of reality at the expense of others. It always slants the playing field of the social order.

The fact that the anticommunist fantasy could function just like the racist fantasy—with communists taking the place of the racial other— reveals that there is nothing specifically about race that creates the racist fantasy. The racial other fits in a position in the fantasy, but any figure could occupy this position and function similarly. The fantasy could place communists in the position of the obstacle, and they would provide access to unrestrained enjoyment in the way that the racial other does. As long as the figure of the obstacle persists in the position of nonbelonging to the social order, any figure will do.

The racist fantasy plays a structuring role in capitalist modernity. It determines what can be perceived every bit as much as the anticommunist fantasy did for twentieth-century America. Through the racist fantasy, various forms of the racial other become figures of unrestrained enjoyment. To perceive the racial other as a racialized other is to perceive this enjoyment as illegitimate. This shared perception is the result of the dominance of the racist fantasy. Those who don't partake in it seem not to belong to the social order at all.

The Invention of an Answer

The enjoyment that the racist fantasy produces is an enjoyment associated with those who don't belong to the social order. All enjoyment is the enjoyment of nonbelonging, enjoyment that occurs through the limit that the social order poses. In this sense, enjoyment is the converse of desire. Subjects desire in response to the demands that figures of social authority make, and they enjoy through those consigned to a position of nonbelonging by these same figures. Desire is a response to social authority, while enjoyment emerges out of what authority rejects. Even though those rejected by social authority exist in a marginal position within the society, this position offers an access to enjoyment that those who believe that they belong to the society cannot have. This is why fantasy, including the racist fantasy, focuses on those who don't belong.

We learn how to desire through our interpretation of what the social authority desires. Desire is linked to the demands of the social authority. In contrast, we discover our mode of enjoyment through an identification not with the social authority but with the figure of social ostracism. Enjoyment emerges out of what has no place within the signifying order, out of what is absent.[12] This contrasting relationship to otherness informs how desire and enjoyment touch on racism. The racist fantasy brings together how we desire and how we enjoy in a specific calculus. The racist fantasy is an attempt to use the racial other's enjoyment as the solution to the problem of desire.

All speaking beings are desiring beings. The speaking being is divided from itself by virtue of the fact that it speaks, that it never achieves self-identity. Its speech is always in front of it and never allows it to coincide with itself. The satisfaction of the speaking being operates through this self-division rather than through its elimination. The speaking being enjoys what it lacks, but it fantasizes of an enjoyment without lack, an unrestrained enjoyment.

No matter how much I fulfill certain desires, I will continue to lack and remain a desiring subject. Realizing my desire for a nice house leaves me still desiring furniture to fill it, and when I obtain furniture, I desire a nicer house. My self-division leads me to always seek something else that would solve the problem of this divide. But the divide is constitutive. Every attempt to eliminate it leaves the speaking subject in the position of continuing to desire, which is itself an indication of the persistence of the divide.

Desire has an insatiability that contrasts with biological needs. Needs can be satisfied in a way that desires cannot. Food can satiate hunger, but it cannot realize my desire. If I realize my desire for apple strudel and eat a piece of it, for instance, I do not cure myself of desire, even though I may no longer be hungry. My desire attaches on to another object, like a piece of cherry pie, that would provide the satisfaction that the apple strudel did not. The object of desire fails in a way that the object of need does not. I can eat food that satiates my need for food or find an apartment that fills my need for shelter. But the same is not true of desire. My desire for the proper food and for the right lodging persists—and would persist even if I found the proper object.

Desire is insatiable because it is never just my desire but the desire of the social authority or the big Other.[13] Desire operates in relation to a social authority, even though the figure of this authority changes throughout the existence of the individual. It might begin as the parent, then become other children at school, and finally be popular opinion within society or colleagues at work. Social authority is not political authority. It is the group of popular teens at school rather than the school principal. Who the social authority is remains in flux, but at all points, some figure or groups of figures operate in this role for the subject. The social authority is the figure who creates the standard for what is desirable.[14] We learn to desire by trying to grasp what these figures of authority themselves desire. Desire is nothing but this quest to solve the problem of the social authority's desire that leaves us in a state of perpetual lack. There is no solution to this problem because there is no object that would realize desire and provide complete satisfaction.

The effort to solve the problem of the authority's desire always comes a cropper because the authority is split in the same way that the subject itself is. In other words, the social authority doesn't know what it desires any more than the subject does. It makes demands on the subject—wear these clothes, talk in this way, listen to this kind of music—but there is no hidden singular desire animating these demands. Instead, the authority waits for the subject to come along and decipher what it desires. All the authority's demands are attempts to rouse the subject into an act of interpretation that will retroactively identify a coherent desire. The social authority needs the subject to prop it up and identify what it desires. There is no desire of the authority outside of the subject's interpretation of this desire. This interpretation is how the subject defines itself.[15]

Desire exists through our inability to obtain just what we desire. This structure of impossibility creates an intractable barrier not just for individuals trying to relate to each other but also for every social authority trying to exert control over the members of society. Social authority must contend with the problem of desire that irrupts within every demand that the authority itself makes. The commands of a social authority are never simply taken at face value because they always include a desire that cannot be articulated. Desire is the gap within what a social authority tells us to do. But it would never emerge if we didn't misapprehend the structure of the authority.

Desire comes about when we mistake a social structure—the self-division of the social authority—for an epistemological problem. I start to desire because I don't know what the authority desires, but I fail to see that the authority's desire is also unknown to the authority itself. This initial mistake about the social authority is a necessary mistake because it has the effect of kickstarting the subject's desire.[16] To see through the authority and to recognize immediately that there is no mystery about the authority leave one without a way to begin desiring at all. That said, the social authority's desire is not a mystery with a solution but a fact of existence. I perceive the mystery that surrounds the authority as my own failure to know what the authority wants, when in fact the authority doesn't know what it wants.

Although the social authority does issue demands, its desire is distinct from what it demands, and my subjectivity emerges through the opacity of this gap.[17] The social authority proclaims that it wants a certain action—total devotion, say—but when it encounters this action, it finds that this is not what it desired at all. We never desire what we say we want but always something askew relative to our demand. This is why those who do everything that a teacher asks are rarely the teacher's favorites. The favorite is the one that interprets the desire of the teacher lying underneath and within the overt dictates. The desire of the social authority is never for strict obedience but for the appropriate form of transgression of the demand.[18] The key point is that there is no clear answer to the question of what the social authority desires. No matter what I do—conform a little or a lot—I never have any assurance that I have correctly interpreted the authority's desire because this desire has no concrete existence outside my interpretation of it.

This is where the racist fantasy comes to the rescue. It provides the missing assurance about what the social authority desires. It gives one a clear sense of what the authority desires through the narrative of racial enjoyment that it envisions. The social authority desires the enjoyment of the rejected racial other. The social authority desires what it cannot officially accept. Fantasy imagines an illicit response to desire because desire is always desire for what doesn't properly belong within the social order.

This is the fantasmatic answer to the question of desire that the racist fantasy provides. This fantasy then functions as a social guidebook. If the authority's desire is the novel *Ulysses*, fantasy is the crib sheet directing one through its variegations, describing the narrative, revealing the central themes, and so on. This crib sheet provides a path of interpretation that gives the subject a sense of where it stands relative to this desire. It produces a way of making sense of this desire that enables the subject to tame the threat that it poses to the subject's identity.

Fantasy, especially the racist fantasy, lets the subject know where it stands. Within this fantasy, one learns to orient one's desire around the racial other's enjoyment. By providing this fantasmatic answer, the racist fantasy not only solves the problem of the social authority's desire for the subject but also points out how it can enjoy. Whereas desire always remains on this side of enjoyment, seeking without finding, the racist fantasy actually facilitates the enjoyment of the object through the racial other.

The Master's Tools

Access to an otherwise transgressive enjoyment becomes apparent when looking at the role of sexuality in slavery. The enslavement of Africans brought untold economic benefits to the white masters. But in addition to these economic benefits, it also brought enjoyment benefits. As Sheldon George notes, "Slaveholding became an access route to economical bliss and the surplus *jouissance* of fantasy."[19] With slave women, the white master is able to transgress the rigid sexual morality that governs his relations with his spouse and discover the enjoyment forbidden to those who try to belong to Southern society with its rigid moral code. Sex with the slave enables the master to partake at night in what he gives up during the day.

The slave narrative of Harriet Jacobs, *Incidents in the Life of a Slave Girl*, highlights the role that the master's sexuality plays in the horrors of slavery. Jacobs points out that the female slave exists in the constant fear of sexual assault. White masters have an absolute right to the slave's sexual being, as the slave woman provides a site of enjoyment for the white master. When he attacks the slave woman, the master is able to transgress all the limits that he respects with his spouse.[20]

Through the fantasized racial other, the white master can access the carnality that the moral code of the US South demands he give up while in white society. The repression of carnality returns in the master's dealing with the slaves, to whom he fantasmatically attributes an excess of carnality. This is a process that Frantz Fanon notices at work in American racism. In *Black Skin, White Masks*, he states, "For the majority of Whites the black man represents the (uneducated) sexual instinct. He embodies genital power out of reach of morals and taboos."[21] What Fanon doesn't add—but what Jacobs shows—is that this same fantasy holds for Black women. The excesses of morality professed by Southern white men manifest themselves in the horrific sexual violence visited on slave women, who are the fantasized site of licentious sexuality repressed in dealings with fellow whites.[22]

Much of the first part of Jacobs' narrative details her efforts to avoid succumbing to her master Dr. Flint's sexual predations.[23] She chronicles the constant sexual exploitation at the hands of Dr. Flint. She writes that for the slave girl, "there is no shadow of law to protect her from insult, from violence, or even from death; all these are inflicted by fiends who bear the shape of men. The mistress, who ought to protect the helpless victim, has no other feelings towards her but those of jealousy and rage."[24] Jacobs points out that ultimately the slave girl has no choice but to submit to these predations, since the master holds the power of life and death over the slave. The master is free to realize the racist fantasy and to treat the slave girls or women as sites for finding an enjoyment that would otherwise be proscribed for him.

There is no defense for the female slave, not even the moral code that supposedly rules the white South, nor its most ardent representatives, the white women. The morality of Southern white women doesn't lead them to play a protective role for female slaves. For the most part, they do not see themselves as the defenders of these women. Jacobs herself notes that white women would appear to be the natural allies of the female slaves. When male masters use female slaves as their sexual tools, they betray their spouses at the same time as they assault the Black women. One would expect, Jacobs posits, that the outrage of the white women would lead them to act as critics of the husbands and defenders of the female slaves. But this is not what predominately happens. The white women envy the enjoyment that they fantasize the slave women experiencing with their spouses. Rather than allies, they become enemies.[25]

Some white women in the position of mastery go even further. Because they participate in the same racist fantasy as their husbands, white women under slavery seek out the Black man for the unrestrained enjoyment that they fantasize in him. This is a phenomenon described by Stephanie Jones-Rogers. In her essay on the role of white women in the sexual violence of slavery, she notes the poisonous combination of "the sexual relations between white slave-owning women and enslaved men in tandem with the exploitative acts of sexual violence that white men perpetrated against enslaved women."[26] Although it didn't occur as often as sexual violence perpetuated on slave women, male slaves also had to endure sexual assaults. One lived in constant fear of sexual violence because of the position that one occupied in the master's racist fantasy.

Jacobs eventually flees the sexual aggression of Dr. Flint and escapes to the North. The escape requires her to spend seven years of her life hiding in small crevice above the shed attached to her grandmother's house. This hideout indicates metaphorically the position that the racial other occupies in a racist society. Hiding out in this small crevice, Jacobs occupies the position of nonbelonging. She is confined, and yet this confinement marks the only site of freedom within racist society.

To be a slave in the American South was to exist in a constantly sexualized state. White masters could examine one's body at any time and engage in whatever kind of sexual experimentation they could imagine. This sexual exposure provided an unending reinforcement for the racist fantasy. To the white masters, blackness appeared to embody a heightened sexuality because these masters placed their slaves in sexualized situations.

Sex with a slave enabled the white master to escape the rigid sexual morality at work in the American South. One could submit to this morality precisely because one had the ability to reach outside it with slaves. The racist fantasy transformed the typical Black subject into a figure of unrestrained enjoyment, an unrestrained enjoyment that the white master could access at any time. This fantasy underwrote the slave system and organized the distribution of enjoyment within that system. The racist fantasy allowed white people to be upright citizens and absolute degenerates at the same time. They could strive to belong to their moral society while partaking in the thrill of nonbelonging.

This is the matrix that the racist fantasy always enacts. It constitutes the source of its lasting appeal.[27]

The racist fantasy continues to appeal well beyond the bounds of slavery due to the access that it promises to those who don't belong. This fantasy distorts the racist subject's perceptions, allowing this subject to see nonbelonging as a position replete with unrestrained enjoyment. This distortion in perception gives subjectivity an orientation toward enjoyment that it otherwise wouldn't have. Fantasy provides an enjoyable answer to an otherwise unanswerable question.

Conformity with Something Extra

The enjoyment in the racist fantasy stems from those who don't have the social authority's recognition, those that don't belong to the social order. At the same time as it offers recognition for those who capitulate, the social authority ostracizes others. Social recognition is always limited in this way. Without the contrast between those who belong and those who don't, its recognition would be completely worthless. Only by looking at those whom I know don't belong can I be sure that I do belong, which is why all belonging is faked and hides a real universal nonbelonging. Ostracism—the creation of a part of the social order that doesn't belong—is essential to the constitution of any social order. Belonging acquires value through the creation of a group that doesn't belong, and this is what the racist fantasy accomplishes. It effectuates the distribution of belonging at the same time as it distributes enjoyment.

The racist fantasy attributes unlimited enjoyment to those who don't belong—to the figure of the racial other. This enjoyment exists only in fantasy. It is the "satanic joy" that Hitler imagines that he sees in the Jewish youth out to seduce young German women. No one actually manages to enjoy fully without any lack. No one ever experiences real satanic joy. But the fantasy distorts the real nonbelonging of people and transforms it into the complete avoidance of lack. This distortion of social nonbelonging into a site of an enjoyment privilege prepares the way for racist violence.

Rather than seeing the violence done to the racial other and having compassion for people in this position, someone ensconced in the racist fantasy looks on these figures with envy. This is the envy that consumes the white suburbanite listening to hip hop songs about exciting Black life in the city, or that of the sports fan who screams racist epithets at the player from the opposing team. Only by taking stock of the racist fantasy is it possible to make sense of this bizarre phenomenon—people from a socially privileged group becoming consumed with envy for those who don't belong.

The actions of the racial other cannot ameliorate the nefariousness of the racist fantasy. Once one is caught up in the racist fantasy as the racial other, there is no change in comportment that can alter the fantasy. This is what Ibram X. Kendi is getting at in his history of racism in the United States. He points out the failure of attempts at "racial uplift" as a solution to the problem of racism. Kendi states, "The more Black people uplift themselves, the more they will find themselves on the receiving end of a racist backlash."[28] For Kendi, the success of individual Black figures doesn't cause the structure of racism to teeter but rather reinforces it. This occurs because racists interpret these success stories not as evidence that their racism is mistaken but through the racist fantasy. The result is that, to follow Kendi's example, any Black success in America gives the racist even more to envy, not less. From the perspective of the racist fantasy, the racial other's success doesn't eliminate the nonbelonging that holds the key to the racial other's enjoyment. It just adds to the enjoyment advantage that the racial other has.

The racist fantasy operates through the misinterpretation of the racial other's nonbelonging. It envisions nonbelonging as the avoidance of lack. From the perspective of the racist fantasy under Nazism, the Jew who doesn't belong appears as a nonlacking figure and thus as a figure of unrestrained enjoyment. But even though nonbelonging doesn't escape lack, it is nonetheless an indication of an authentic relation to the social order that those who believe themselves to belong do not have. No one actually belongs because there is no consistent authority that can confer belonging. Nonbelonging is the fate of everyone. This is what those invested in the racist fantasy miss: they don't see their own nonbelonging and thus the possibility of enjoying it.

The key to understanding social recognition is understanding that one can never obtain it. Neither the diligent worker nor the criminal nor the CEO of a tech company achieve social recognition. The barrier to recognition lies in the absence of any entity that could bestow it on the subject. If there is no social authority, every attempt at gaining recognition will fail. It ends up depending on an outsider, a figure of nonbelonging, whose nonbelonging convinces the subject that it belongs and obscures the universality of nonbelonging. To be an insider means to be completely dependent on the outsider who stands as the proof that one is really an insider. This is why popular teens are constantly mocking the unpopular: it is only in this way that they can assure themselves of their belonging. Each act of mockery helps to secure their belonging, but the mockery can never stop because, as an illusion, belonging can never become entirely secure.

People opt for belonging, and yet they never feel like they really belong (because they do not and cannot). My search for recognition founders on the nonexistence of the social authority who could define the boundaries of belonging. Fantasy ameliorates my inability to properly belong to the social order and attain recognition. Fantasy makes up for the failure of recognition. But it does so by enabling those who choose belonging to parasitically enjoy through those who don't belong. Fantasy structures an access to enjoyment for those who abandon enjoyment for the sake of belonging to the social order. It is the point at which those who believe that they belong can touch the outside, like Truman (Jim Carrey) at the end of *The Truman Show* (Peter Weir, 1998), when he leaves his sheltered existence for the first time.

No one lives without fantasy. But for those who have a recognized position within a social order, fantasy has a precise role. It gives the subject access to the enjoyment that is otherwise denied to it as a member of the social order. Fantasy is the compensation doled out to those who conform. Frantz Fanon notices this dynamic at work in the colony. Building on this idea, David Marriott points out, "blackness, as a stereotype—idea, affect, fantasy—functions as a source of traumatic energy in the ideological life of the colony. Negrophobia and its fantasies appear to have taken over people's minds."[29] The conformist racists find in the fantasized racial other a fount of traumatic energy or enjoyment. They miss out on the enjoyment of nonbelonging because of their attempt to belong, but through fantasy they can identify with this enjoyment and thereby partake in it for themselves.

Fantasy gives those who capitulate a taste of the enjoyment that belongs to those who are unrecognized within society. This taste of enjoyment keeps the social order going, even though the enjoyment is itself a threat to the stability of the order.[30] Every society survives by channeling the enjoyment that threatens it into a fantasy that sustains it. Those who try to belong use their fantasies to feed on the enjoyment of those who don't belong, which is why, for instance, white Americans devote themselves so assiduously to Black sports stars and entertainers.

This allows us to see the radical edge of fantasy. It marks the point where those who strive to belong actually abandon their commitment to belonging for the sake of enjoyment. Fantasy is the site of an enjoyment that has the potential to disturb even as it performs a domesticating function. But by transforming the partial enjoyment of nonbelonging into a complete enjoyment that overcomes lack, fantasy performs an ideological function. Rather than recognizing their own nonbelonging within the fantasy, subjects envision a foreign nonbelonging attached to the other, a foreign nonbelonging that harbors unlimited enjoyment. The radical core of fantasy, however, lies in its relationship to nonbelonging, a relationship evident even in the most ideological of fantasies, the racist fantasy.

Every subject confronts the insoluble problem of the social authority's desire. No one can tell me how to interpret this desire without simultaneously raising the question of how I should interpret this advice. There is no unambiguous answer because there is no metalanguage that could talk about desire without occasioning another question of desire. The racist fantasy intervenes to provide a solution, although this solution can only exist as a fantasy and can never be realized. In response to the question of what the social authority desires, the racist fantasy introduces the racial other's enjoyment. In the racist fantasy, the racial other's enjoyment is the realization of the desire of the social authority, which seeks what is beyond its strictures.[31] The positioning of the racial other outside the strictures of the social order is precisely the source of the enjoyment that the racist fantasy delivers.

We can see this in the example of the welfare queen, famously attacked by Ronald Reagan in the 1980s. Although Reagan never mentioned the race of the welfare queen, he implied the blackness of this figure. In the fantasy scenario that he painted, she lived the high life on the public dole, enjoying on the back of the white working class that was paying for her cigarettes, liquor, ice cream, and children. By invoking this fantasy scenario, Reagan ensured his own popularity among lower class whites—the famous Reagan Democrats—because he explained that their lack had a clear cause in the excesses of the welfare queen rather than the variegations of the capitalist system. This version of the racist fantasy allowed them to see that they were laboring for her enjoyment, and they took action to remedy this situation by voting for Reagan.

The welfare queen was a figure of enjoyment without lack. She didn't do any work and thus didn't have to sacrifice at all for her enjoyment. This is exactly what the working-class whites who supported Reagan themselves believed that they wanted to be doing. They wanted to partake of this perfect enjoyment without suffering—an impossible enjoyment, since enjoyment requires suffering—that they fantasized in the welfare queen. The image of the welfare queen lying around without having to work gave them an image of enjoyment with which to identify. Their opprobrium for the welfare queen was the vehicle for their enjoyment of the excesses that they imputed to her.

Fantasy transcends the confines of desire by solving the problem of lack. The enjoyment that fantasy envisions for the subject is located beyond the social authority, in the figure of the other that the social authority does not recognize. The unrecognized other is the site of enjoyment in fantasy. This unrecognized other is the fantasized solution to the problem of desire. Because it relies on this figure of otherness, even the most ideological fantasy—like the racist fantasy—houses a potential disturbance to the functioning of the social order that it supports.

Enjoyment appears at the point of social ostracism, the point beyond social constraint. This is what Joan Copjec is getting at in *Imagine There's No Woman*, when she notes that "jouissance flourishes only there where it is *not* validated by the Other."[32] Even the enjoyment that sustains the social order must occur beyond the constraints of this order. It cannot have the sanction of the social authority and remain enjoyment. The racist act produces the site of enjoyment at the limit of society that fuels the racist fantasy, which allows those within the society to access this enjoyment. Racist society survives on the enjoyment imputed to those it condemns to a visible nonbelonging.

Although racism denigrates and demeans the racial other, it locates enjoyment in this figure. The denigration creates an otherness in relation to the social authority that opens up an image of enjoyment. In this sense, racism creates a self-perpetuating loop in which the more the racial other is consigned to the position of nonbelonging the more enjoyment the racist fantasy posits in this other. In other words, every increase in racism makes the racist fantasy all the more enjoyable.

The subject of the fantasy experiences this racial other as a dangerous figure of enjoyment who has access to what the subject does not. In the racist fantasy, the racial other threatens to swallow the subject in its teeming enjoyment—the satanic joy of the Jew, the opulent lifestyle of the welfare queen, and so on. But the threat is at once a possibility for enjoyment that the subject would otherwise not have. By encountering this threat, the subject can experience the fantasized enjoyment that is inaccessible for it outside the fantasy. By facilitating identification with this enjoyment, the racist fantasy enables the subject to enjoy through the other. The racist fantasy solves the problem of desire for the racist subject by asserting the racial other's enjoyment as the answer to this desire. Desire asks, "What does the subject want?" The racist fantasy responds, "The enjoyment housed in the racial other." This response readies the racist for an outbreak of violence.

5

The Violent Issue

Hitting the Bottom

Fantasy forms the basis of social reality held in common, but when our social reality begins to drift too far from or come too close to the constitutive fantasy, our sense of reality breaks down. In order for reality to feel like reality, it must more or less align with the fantasy. The "more or less" is crucial. Despite the necessary role that fantasy plays in constituting what counts as real, reality is not just a reflection of the fantasy. Reality is rooted in the fantasy but also distinguishes itself from its fantasmatic origin, which is how we can engage in reality testing. We know that objects are real insofar as they represent our fantasies without too perfectly corresponding to them. The social reality must be distinct from the fantasy, but if it becomes too distinct or too close, it ceases to be real.

For example, the reality of the slice of pizza that I eat derives from the distance between the pizza that I eat and the perfectly satisfying slice that exists only in our fantasy. If I eat the perfect piece of pizza, I would know that it wasn't real. Or one knows that one is having sex with a real person because this person sweats, has odors, and doesn't orgasm at the proper time. The imperfections attest to the reality of the piece of pizza or the sexual partner. These imperfections allow one to distinguish between the fantasy and the social reality. But if the failure to align with the fantasy goes too far and social reality becomes too distinct from the fantasy, the sense of reality collapses for the subject. If the piece of pizza begins to taste like cardboard, it ceases to seem real. Or if the sexual partner doesn't resemble the fantasy at all, the sense of reality disappears, and sex becomes just a mechanical procedure. These occurrences are what occasion outbreaks of violence. Although few people engage in violence when their pizza doesn't taste right, reality drifting too far away or too close to the racist fantasy is another matter altogether. Confronted with the breakdown of their fantasy because of reality's changed relationship to it, they engage in a violent outburst that attempts to destroy the object and reestablish the coherence of their social reality.

When social reality and fantasy come too close together, we begin to lose the distinctness of the fantasy. It seems as if we are becoming lost in the fantasy world. If this happens, the fantasy can no longer provide enjoyment since the enjoyment derives from the break from reality that occurs in the fantasy. In contrast, if the social reality doesn't resemble the fantasy at all, the social reality effaces the fantasy. In this way, we lose touch with the fantasy, and social reality becomes unreal. Either way—whether reality gets too close to the fantasy or becomes too distant—this represents a threat to the fantasy's ability to deliver enjoyment to the subject.

Violence attempts to bring social reality back to its proper distance from the constitutive fantasy. It occurs when people lose their bearing in society, when the path to enjoyment appears blocked or even eroded by a recalcitrant reality or a reality that ceases to appear distinct from the fantasy. This is what happens when people confront an object that no longer fits in their fantasy structure or a reality that mirrors their fantasy structure completely. They lose the security of their fantasy structure because the difference between reality and fantasy becomes too great or too narrow. As a result, reality comes to appear as a completely foreign terrain, or it merges with the fantasy world. It is as if one moved to a foreign country overnight or never could awaken from one's dreams.

Violence is an attempt to restore the sense of reality that breaks down in order to preserve the fantasy as a vehicle for enjoyment. Violence tries to preserve the fantasy by keeping it at a distance from reality. The sense of reality and its underlying fantasy deliver enjoyment to members of a society while simultaneously keeping this enjoyment at bay. That is, our social reality continues to exist in a way that portions out a steady stream of enjoyment that remains at a low level. The society's collective form of enjoyment depends on sustaining the fantasy as the support for reality. Violence erupts at the moment when reality no longer seems informed by the fantasy—the point when one can no longer enjoy the reality. It works at conserving the social order's basic fantasy and the organization of enjoyment that follows from this fantasy.

With this in mind, let's return to anticommunism in the 1940s and 1950s. In the 1930s, communism was a viable alternative in the United States. Franklin Roosevelt posed the New Deal as a way of staving off the communist threat. Despite its role as the producer of America's ideological fantasies, Hollywood was not immune to the allure of communism, especially during the 1930s. But the attempt by Congressperson Martin Dies to investigate communism in Hollywood during the late 1930s fell completely flat. No one except Dies had any enthusiasm for excising communism from Hollywood, even though communism was at this time a genuine possibility for the United States.

By the time the House Unamerican Activities Committee began its much more damaging campaign against Hollywood after the Second World War, communism had ceased to be a threat. This investigation prosecuted the Hollywood Ten and led to the formation of the Blacklist that successfully policed Hollywood's politics until 1960. HUAC's aggression against Hollywood gained acceptance where that of Martin Dies did not because it appeared at a time when the social reality had become distant from the underlying fantasy. The communist threat had basically died out. Edward Dmytryk's *Crossfire* (1947) instigated the hearings about Hollywood, but it was nothing but a tame liberal critique of anti-Semitism, as far from advocating American communism as one could imagine. In the late 1940s, the anticommunist fantasy was sputtering on a lack of actual communists and would wait until 1950 to have them in the form of Julius and Ethel Rosenberg. Before their arrival on the scene, HUAC acted to bring the fantasy and the reality back into alignment—to persecute the communists into existence.

Violence emerges when our reality ceases to correspond to what our fantasy says it should be. Violence tries to realign fantasy and social reality.

Lynching follows the same logic as the anticommunism of the twentieth century. This violence becomes most pronounced when the racist fantasy—excessive Black enjoyment—fails to manifest itself in the social reality. The social reality seems bereft of Black enjoyment, which causes the racist subject to lose its bearings. Racist violence erupts when the social reality no longer seems to confirm the racist fantasy, when fledgling moments of equality break out, such as during Reconstruction. This violence attempts to create the figure of the racial other at the precise moment of its evanescence.

The paradigmatic instances of racist violence occurring in response to the social reality growing distant from the racist fantasy in the United States were the Wilmington Race Massacre of 1898 and the Tulsa Race Massacre of 1921. These acts of horrific violence that resulted in hundreds of Black deaths and the destruction of many Black-owned businesses attempted to eliminate the proof that Black society was no different from white society. In both cases, a Black professional class had emerged, despite the society's racism. And in both cases, whites lashed out against the markers of Black social success that gave the lie to the underlying racist fantasy. By destroying the markers of Black social success and killing successful Black subjects, the racists behind this massacre destroyed the social reality that no longer resembled the racist fantasy. The image of successful Black business owners did not fit the racist fantasy, but the violence reestablished the ground of the fantasy by consigning blackness again to the position of the social other. The Wilmington Race Massacre and the Tulsa Race Massacre show that even at the moment when some Black individuals win in American society, they lose, precisely because their social triumph violates the determinants of the racist fantasy. Those invested in the racist fantasy attack the racial other for confirming the fantasy and for violating it. There is no behavior that can guarantee the avoidance of bloodshed when one is in the position of the racial other.

Let's consider white men watching a Black boy relating to a white woman. If the boy expresses indifference, he violates the racist fantasy by revealing it to have no relation to reality, but if he shows any interest at all (perhaps going so far as to smile at the woman), the fantasy would overrun the social reality for the white onlookers. The smile of the Black boy literalizes the fantasy of Black sexual enjoyment that has the ultimate seductive power of white women. Because the white men are looking on through their racist fantasy, either act could cause their sense of reality to collapse. If it does, an outburst of violence would result.

At this moment, violence is the only recourse that the white racist has, short of abandoning the racist fantasy altogether (which means giving up one's racist enjoyment). Through the act of violence, the white racist reintroduces the alignment between the social reality and the racist fantasy. Violence provides another form of enjoyment that both satisfies the subject's libidinal urges and stifles the threatening enjoyment in the other. The violence toward the Black young man or child both establishes him as a sexual threat and eliminates that threat—by castrating, killing, and burning him. Before it gets rid of the threat of the racial other, violence first of all must erect it. This is its primary social function.

The connection between the racist fantasy and violence remains invisible to those invested in the fantasy. This is what Frank Wilderson documents in *Afropessimism*. He states,

> What if you belonged to a race of people with a private army under the command of their fantasies? Reason would have to go to war with your regime of violence before your conditions would be ripe for you to reconsider the phantasms you had projected onto the world. Imagine the resources of a violent structure that can deputize the whims of an entire race.[1]

As Wilderson sees, fantasy leads right into racist violence. It creates the conditions of possibility in which violence appears as the logical result.

Fantasy depends on its confirmation in reality. It must find echoes in reality, but it cannot manifest itself directly as real. Only insofar as it is evident as the support for reality can fantasy continue to provide a structure of enjoyment for those invested in it. Violence in the wake of the growing distance between fantasy and reality—or their overproximity—attempts to restore this path to enjoyment.[2]

Kriminals

The racial other is often figured as a criminal.[3] In the traditional American version of the racist fantasy, the association of blackness with illicit sexual enjoyment provides the lens through which Black men appear as inherently criminal. Black criminality is not a social fact but the result of the racist fantasy that demands it. Or, it appears as a social fact when people look at society through the frame of the racist fantasy. Criminality helps to explain how the Black man bests the white man in the competition for white women. Without resorting to his inherent criminality, the Black man would not be able to beat out the white man on the terrain of sexual competition. In the fantasy, sexual prowess alone is usually not enough. Criminality often comes in support.[4]

In the racist fantasy, the Black man illicitly seduces white women or even rapes them to achieve the enjoyment that white men cannot. Thus, in addition to having the inherent advantage of greater natural sexual prowess, in the fantasy the Black man gains an additional advantage by not obeying the social restrictions of that the white man heeds. The law is not enough to hold the Black man at bay because he evinces no respect for it.

The criminality of the racial other is not just a barrier to the subject's enjoyment. It is also the way that the subject enjoys itself. By attributing this criminality to the racial other, the subject can view itself as law-abiding and upright while all the time enjoying the psychic benefits of criminality by identifying with the racial other's enjoyment. In this way, the racist fantasy enables the subject indulging in it to experience the delights of criminality without ever having to consider itself a criminal.

The promise of fantasy is always eating one's cake without paying the price for it with added pounds.[5]

The inherent criminality of the racial other points to an additional figure in the fantasy. The third party in the fantasy is the figure of authority that the racial other dupes in order to enjoy the object. In the fantasy, the racial other gets around the barrier that the authority poses in a way that the subject cannot by breaking the law or using subterfuge to evade the constraints that govern everyone else. The ability of the racial other to evade the restrictions of the law has a direct link to this figure's lack of morality. Even though the fantasy portrays the racial other as lacking the intelligence of the subject, this figure nonetheless has superior skills in manipulation.[6] The figure of authority successfully controls the activity of those who are in the same boat as the subject of the fantasy but cannot overcome the wiles of the racial other. Within the fantasy, the fecklessness of legal authority against the racial other's stratagems requires extraordinary measures.[7]

This is the justification in American society for the intervention of an extralegal force to contain the racial other. Entities such as the Ku Klux Klan arise directly from this fantasy formation as a response to the image of a Black evasion of official authority. According to the racist fantasy, the bungling white sheriff cannot prevent the Black man from surreptitiously absconding with or raping white women. The Klan sees itself as a necessary expedient for disciplining the Black enjoyment that the white legal structure cannot succeed in taking care of on its own. Because the fantasized Black man brooks no moral constraint, the law does not represent enough of a brake on his actions. From the perspective of the racist fantasy, law is never enough to stop the excess that Black enjoyment represents. Within the American version of the racist fantasy, legitimate authority cannot successfully police illicit Black enjoyment.[8]

The Ku Klux Klan shed horrific amounts of actual blood. But the group grew in response to the racist fantasy that held sway over its members, not in response to any actual events. The Klan fought an excessive Black enjoyment that occurred only in its own fantasy. The supplemental army of whites that came together as the Ku Klux Klan saw itself as the sole force that could bring this excess back into the confines of the social order through their disciplining mechanisms, including the extraordinary measure of lynching. The Klan was a supplementary police force that targeted unrestrained Black enjoyment.

The inadequacy of the official authority figures speaks to the vast difference that separates white and Black in the racist fantasy. Official authority effectively contains white enjoyment because it operates within the socially defined limits—there is no need for a Klan to contain the danger that it represents—but the extreme sexuality and criminality of blackness place it beyond the reach of the normal functioning of this authority. The extraordinary status of a group like the Klan testifies to the extraordinary nature of Black enjoyment. But this enjoyment exists only within a racist fantasy that posits its existence. Without this underlying racist fantasy and the outsized part that it grants to the Black hijacking of the enjoyment that should properly belong to whites, the Klan would be unimaginable.

The Delights of Lynching

In America after the Civil War, the phenomenon of lynching broke out in response to the egalitarian pretensions of Reconstruction. White racists resorted to lynching in order to keep what they viewed as a flood of Black enjoyment at bay and simultaneously keep their own form of enjoyment alive. Racists experienced their hallucinations of Black male encounters with white women not as innocent interactions but as the collapse of their social reality. Lynching occurred because the whites convinced themselves that the very fabric of the social reality of the time was threatened insofar as it no longer resembled the racist fantasy that grounded it. This explains how it could be possible for otherwise ethical people to partake in or even turn a blind eye to such grotesque horrors. Typically, lynching took place when social reality grew too far removed from its fantasmatic basis and thus began to founder.

Lynchings can occur when someone confirms the racist fantasy, when whites see a real case of Black enjoyment, but more often they take place when the social reality doesn't confirm the fantasy. The case of Emmett Till shows the horrific power of the racist fantasy when the social reality doesn't correspond to it. Emmett Till was a fourteen-year-old boy. Nonetheless, whites saw in Till a sexual threat to themselves when he supposedly evinced interest in a white woman. It is unclear what Till actually did, but this lack of clarity is to the point. As all accounts of him confirm, Till was emphatically not a threatening boy. But the racists who lynched him did so because of the distance between the fantasy and his reality. No matter what he did, whites wrapped up in the racist fantasy would posit sexual prowess in him, despite his young age. The fact that Till was only fourteen did not mitigate the imagined enjoyment but only heightened it. By brutally killing him, the white men acted to confirm that he did really correspond to the foundational racist fantasy despite his appearance. In this way, they restored their sense of reality. This act testifies to the fundamental role that the racist fantasy of unrestrained Black enjoyment that impinges on white enjoyment plays in their psyche.

In a courageous political act, Till's mother insisted on an open casket for her boy. By displaying Till's young body for the public to see, she exposed the extent to which he did not correspond to the racist fantasy. The open casket showed not just Till's body but also the racist fantasy that had to be draped over that body in order to kill him. Revealing the distance between the body and the racist fantasy was a political gesture, a way of fighting back against the racist murderers. The distance between Till and the racist fantasy was precisely what motivated his murder, a murder that attempted to create a menace where one didn't exist.

The phenomenon of lynching enables us to see how fantasy relates to social reality. On the one hand, fantasy informs the structure of our social reality. We produce this reality through our fantasy and see it through a fantasy frame. But at the same time, social reality can drift away from the underlying fantasy that supports it and create a loss of the sense of reality. I know what is real by recognizing the fantasy being confirmed in reality. The test of reality is the confirmation for the social fantasy.

In the case of the primary racist fantasy, this becomes clear when lynching causes this fantasy to appear in reality. The racist fantasy paints the racialized other as a threat to the racist subject's enjoyment. In the American South, typical white racists viewed every Black person that they saw as potentially embodying this threat, as figures of illicit enjoyment. The consistency of their social reality depended on seeing the racialized other in this way. They knew that what they were seeing was real because they saw Black people enjoying and threatening their own enjoyment.

The practice of lynching is perhaps the most extreme response to the fantasy figure of the enjoying racial other. Lynching is an extralegal practice, occurring primarily in the American South in the seventy years following the Civil War, that functioned as a compensation for the supposed inadequacy of legal authorities in the face of the threat of Black enjoyment. According to the logic of the racist fantasy, the Black man, as an embodiment of the racial other, had an ability to enjoy that official law and authorized policing could not contain. This enjoyment threatened the relationship that white men had with white women. It threatened to block their access to the fantasy object by monopolizing it. Lynching most often targeted Black men who were believed to have engaged white women in some measure of sexual relationship—from acts as innocent as a desiring glance to accusations of rape.[9] Whether the Black men actually engaged in any sexual activity or not was immaterial. All that mattered was how their actions registered in the racist fantasy. The fantasy was not only more important than what really happened. It actually created the reality.

White society propagated a constant barrage of images of Black enjoyment to ensure that enough whites would be ready to attack when necessary. In *Caste*, Isabel Wilkerson describes how American popular culture prepared the way for the lynching party on an everyday level. She writes, "In America, a culture of cruelty crept into the minds, made violence and mockery seem mundane and amusing, built as it was into the games of chance at carnivals and county fairs well into the twentieth century."[10] Whites become accustomed to seeing Black enjoyment and to seeing Black enjoyment punished in games such as "Son of Ham," where participants could pay for the thrill of throwing a baseball at a Black person's head.[11] These games prepared the way for the more extreme violence of the lynching party.

Whenever Black enjoyment was at work, according to the racist fantasy, the official law was inadequate. The law was not able to punish Black enjoyment that expressed itself in an ogling look, despite the danger manifested in this look. From the perspective of the racist fantasy, this look was not against the law, but it represented a lethal menace to the white capacity to enjoy. And even though rape was illegal and punishable by death, this punishment did not come swift enough or was not thorough enough, given the magnitude of the peril that the racist fantasy saw in this act. Both extremes of Black enjoyment, the innocent and the violent, required lynching to come to the aid of the official authorities in order to snuff it out and discourage any further manifestations of this enjoyment. Lynching is the ultimate expression of the racist fantasy.

The extreme brutality displayed by the lynching party—they would go so far as to castrate Black victims and burn them alive—acted as a signal to anyone else who might evince an interest in white women. The emergence of the extralegal practice of lynching testifies to the measure of the threat that the American version of the racist fantasy attributes to blackness. The extreme nature of lynching and its horrific barbarity reveal that Black enjoyment stood as a fundamental challenge to the entire American social structure. Whites had to have recourse to this practice because their investment in the racist fantasy was so thoroughgoing that it demanded it.

But lynching does not just eliminate the threat of Black enjoyment. At the same time that it destroys the Black man's capacity for sexual enjoyment (through castration and murder), lynching provides a means through which the perpetuators can themselves partake of the illicit enjoyment that they fantasize in the racial other. Lynching is first and foremost a manifestation of white sexual enjoyment. The brutal violence of the lynching is a thoroughly sexualized violence, which is why it targets the Black genitalia. During a lynching, Black enjoyment is the means through which the fantasy produced enjoyment for whites. While lynching is an act of barbaric violence, it reveals how the racial other's enjoyment serves as the source of enjoyment for those invested in the racist fantasy.

The perpetuators of lynching themselves feed on the enjoyment of the racial other that lynching attempts to destroy. In the act of destroying the racial other's fantasized enjoyment, the lynch mob enjoys the violence of this destruction. Although we imagine lynching as a hidden activity done under cover of the night by masked men, it is in actuality a quasi-public ritual whereby racist white society shares in the Black enjoyment that threatens it. During a lynching party, whites nourish themselves on the Black enjoyment that they destroy. Lynching parties really are parties, attempts to organize enjoyment around the act of violent destruction.[12]

The festive celebrations that often surrounded a lynching manifested the enjoyment of the victim. The violence didn't dampen the atmosphere of the lynching but actually created it, as perhaps the most gruesome lynching in American history attests. The lynching of James Washington in Waco, Texas, in 1916, occurred after his conviction for the rape and murder of a white woman.[13] A lynch mob cut off Washington's fingers and castrated him before burning him to death over a period of two hours.

During this time, a crowd that included 10,000 people participated in the event and drew on the enjoyment that the racist fantasy attributed to Washington. Although it is not clear whether or not Washington committed the crime, the extremity of the event reveals that the racist fantasy, not a concern for justice, drove the participants to act. Washington's guilt or innocence—in fact, the crime itself— was entirely beside the point. The participants were concerned above all with enjoying themselves, which is why the party lasted for so long and drew so many participants. The celebratory atmosphere surrounding the event testified to the enjoyment that it provided for those involved, as do the souvenir charred body parts that many kept and the picture postcards that commemorated the day for the white crowd. The barbarism of the whites nourished itself on the enjoyment of the racial other. Lynching parties like this one reveal the truth of Sheldon George's claim that white enjoyment has its counterpart in Black trauma. The horror of Washington's trauma was the occasion for a sickening outburst of white enjoyment.

The violence of lynching called to mind the actions of the Black man being punished for those involved in it and enabled them to relive these actions in the guise of punishing him. The lynching enabled the perpetuators and spectators to access this sexual enjoyment through their violence. Despite the difference between sexuality and violence, they come together in the act of lynching, which translates fantasized sexual enjoyment into a form of violence. The violence provides a way for the lynching party to approximate the lawlessness that it imputes to Black sexuality. Lynching allows one to act in the way that the Black man does within the racist fantasy—that is, to enjoy without restraint.

Lynching is a way of transferring the enjoyment that the racist fantasy imputes to the racial other to the racist subject. All of the extremes acts that take place during a lynching bespeak this enjoyment. The sexualized enjoyment of the racial other becomes the violent enjoyment of the white persecutors. But this violence retains the sexual character from the racial other in the fantasy. This is why castration is so important in lynching. Even if no actual castration takes place, every lynching attempts to appropriate the enjoyment attached to the Black sexual organ.

In one American version of the racist fantasy, Black enjoyment hinders any realization of white desire. The fantasy envisions the Black man doing what the white men refrained from doing—enjoying women without the constraints of marriage or propriety. Within the racist fantasy, all kinds of lasciviousness are open to the Black man in his relations with the white woman because the Black man respects no constraints on his sexual appetites. The Black man enjoys in the stead of the white man and does so in a way that the white man himself cannot—at least not openly.

The role that castration plays in lynching is revelatory on this count. Almost all lynchings involved castrating the victim. Sometimes, the aggressors would castrate the victim and then place the man's sexual organ in his mouth. This excessive act reveals that lynching is all about the sexual enjoyment that whites attribute to their victims. Castration is even more important than death in the ritual. It reveals that the point is not just punishing a criminal or sending a warning to other potential criminals. Instead, lynching aims at destroying the sexual enjoyment of the Black man and cutting off his ability to please white women. The act of castration takes aim at a fantasized sexual superior, but in the act of destroying this enhanced capacity for sexual enjoyment, lynching allows the lynching party to touch and view the source of unrestrained enjoyment—the Black man's sexual organ.

Black sexuality horrifies the white racists who engage in this practice, but it is also integral to their own enjoyment. Castration bespeaks the sexual enjoyment of those doing the castrating. They see castrating the Black man as a way for themselves to avoid castration, that is, to circumvent their status as lacking subjects. The extremity and horror of the punishment that these whites dish out testify to the psychic forces driving it. The image of a Black man being sexually involved with a white woman drives their own unconscious sexuality. When they castrate the Black man, they experience the thrill of this sexual activity and the sadistic joy of annihilating the site of the racial other's enjoyment. The racial other's enjoyment provides the vehicle through which the racist subject can enjoy itself.

The festival of lynching is the end point of the racist fantasy because it represents the subject's triumph over the racial other. Lynching promises access to the enjoyment that the racist attributes to this other. The rituals of lynching are not anomalies in the landscape of racist society. They are the result of the way that racist society imagines its possibilities for enjoyment. The popularity of lynching as a social ritual reveals the centrality of the racist fantasy in structuring the social order.

The Underside of the Nation

Fantasy is a setting that provides the pathway through which our desire can channel itself. Without fantasy, desire would remain aimless and indistinct. Desire does not emerge as desire until a fantasy structure provides a scene through which to arouse it. As Jean Laplanche and Jean-Betrand Pontalis point out in their epochal account of fantasy, "fantasy is not the object of desire, it is the scene. In the fantasy, the subject no longer in effect aims at the object or its sign but figures itself taken up in a sequence of images."[14] By establishing a scenario in which desire can appear to have a path to its realization, fantasy creates the groundwork for our desire.

I first start to desire a specific fantasy object before my desire becomes detachable from the fantasy scenario. Fantasy teaches the subject how to desire by showing it what to desire and giving it a path to that object. But fantasy is always in the background. While we can become conscious of certain figures and elements of our fantasies, the way that they provide enjoyment for us must remain unconscious. I cannot simply articulate my fantasies even to myself without encountering resistance that would distort them into a completely alien form. This is especially true in the case of the racist fantasy, which encounters the most distortion when one tries to bring it to consciousness. Because it involves such socially unacceptable desires, the racist fantasy remains almost entirely unconscious. As a result, the best vehicle for apprehending the racist fantasy structure is the examination of works of art.

The work of art offers a public version of a private fantasy, translating the unconscious private fantasy into a public one that everyone can enjoy.[15] Popular works of art have the merit of enacting ideological fantasies (such as the racist fantasy) in a way that more critical artworks do not. For instance, while *Citizen Kane* (Orson Welles, 1941) might expose the falsity of the capitalist fantasy of accumulation, a film like *Pretty Woman* (Garry Marshall, 1990) more clearly sucks the audience into falling for this fantasy. The same is true for racist fantasies. *Une Noire de…* (*Black Girl*, Ousmane Sembène, 1966) and *Bamboozled* (Spike Lee, 2000) reveal what racist fantasies hide, but their critical edge doesn't seduce spectators into the racist fantasy. The point of these films is to avoid doing so. This is what risible films such as *The Birth of a Nation* (D. W. Griffith, 1915) and *Forrest Gump* (Robert Zemeckis, 1994) manage to achieve by submitting spectators to the racist fantasy without reprieve. In this way, we can learn something from Griffith about the racist fantasy and the violence that it produces that Lee's masterful attack on racism does not show.

The Birth of a Nation depicts the history of the United States from just before the American Civil War until the end of the post-war Reconstruction era. It shows this history by juxtaposing the melodrama of the fictional Cameron and Stoneman families with actual historical events. The families are relatives from the South and North, respectively. We see historical events like the Civil War and the assassination of Lincoln through the perspective of the families' participation in them. Griffith uses the family narrative to up the stakes of the historical events. When Elsie (Lillian Gish) and Phil Stoneman (Elmer Clifton) witness Lincoln's assassination in the Ford Theater, their presence augments the trauma of the shooting. Likewise, seeing Tod Stoneman (Robert Harron), Duke Cameron (Maxfield Stanley), and Wade Cameron (George Beranger) die in battle triggers the spectator's investment in the costs of the war. During Reconstruction, the film shows the rise of a Black threat to Southern white society, emboldened by white Northern leadership. The climax of the film occurs with the formation of the Ku Klux Klan, an act that Griffith attributes to Ben Cameron (Henry B. Walthall)—who has the idea when he sees Black children afraid of a white sheet blowing in the wind—and the pitiless defeat of the Black threat. At the end, the surviving brothers in each family, Ben Cameron and Phil Stoneman, become romantically attached to the sisters in the other family, Elsie Stoneman and Margaret Cameron (Miriam Cooper).

Critics laud *The Birth of a Nation* for its technical mastery and its innovative visual storytelling.[16] The film established several important filmic conventions that subsequent filmmakers would take as paradigmatic, such as the use of crosscutting to create a suspense sequence.[17] But the film also lays bare the racist fantasy like no other work of art. The skill with which Griffith structures the film enables him to present the fantasy in its most compelling form, a form that other baldly racist works fail to attain. At the core of *The Birth of a Nation* lies the excessive Black subject whose unrestrained enjoyment threatens the structures of civilization (which is explicitly white civilization). This figure represents the heart of the racist fantasy.

The family's presence in the narrative heightens the power of the racist fantasy that the film employs. Griffith uses the family to highlight the fantasmatic threat that the racial other poses to the subjects of the fantasy, represented by the Camerons and the Stonemans. This threat becomes palpable after the Civil War ends and Reconstruction empowers the Black minority. As the film recounts it, Reconstruction is a time of unalloyed violence directed at defenseless Southern whites. It forces them to endure humiliation, violence, and even the threat of rape.

What is fascinating about *The Birth of a Nation* is how it deploys the spectacle of enjoyment. Although there are pleasant scenes of idyllic Southern life before the war and a pleasant double marriage at the end of the film, the film primarily confines its depictions of enjoyment to Black characters—and to white characters acting violently against Black characters. Even as Griffith conceives it, white life is basically dull except for the energy that it obtains from its interaction with blackness.

The first episode of Black enjoyment occurs when the visiting Stonemans tour the Cameron plantation and see slaves dancing and singing during their dinner break. The contrast between this dance scene and the white one that takes place later is striking. Whereas the Black characters dance freely, the white characters all dance alike according to rigid dance steps. Although Griffith depicts the Black

characters stereotypically, he does so in a way that highlights their
enjoyment. They might be unintelligent in his reckoning, but they
certainly know how to enjoy themselves. There is no question where
the greater enjoyment lies when examining these two scenes. It is as if
Griffith has taken to heart Jacques Lacan's claim that "if the master is
from the beginning engaged in risk, it is because he leaves enjoyment to
the other."[18] Although here Lacan is talking about the master's failure to
enjoy within Hegel's dialectic of the master and servant, his point holds
for the depiction of the joyless masters in Griffith's film. Furthermore,
in the rest of the film, Black characters are the only ones that appear
sexual. Whiteness is coextensive with asexuality, even in the case of the
young white men.

This hypersexualization of the Black characters points to the heart
of Griffith's racism. His film locates Black inferiority in the refusal or
inability to accede to symbolic restrictions of sexual enjoyment. It is
through the acceptance of such restrictions that one belongs to the
society. By depicting the flouting of social restrictions, Griffith identifies
blackness with a failure to belong to the social order. This is the sense of
the otherwise extraneous depiction of the South Carolina State House
of Representatives in 1870, where Black House members show their
lack of belonging by drinking during an open session, taking off their
shoes, and, most significantly, looking lasciviously at white women. In
the midst of highlighting Black ostentatious displays of enjoyment in
the chamber, Griffith cuts to the white minority heeding the rules of
decorum that follow from symbolic restrictions, as they look on the
scene from above. The positioning of white and Black in this scene is
indicative of their relationship to sexuality. The whites are above it while
the Blacks are down in it. This contrast emphasizes why, according to
Griffith, the Black individuals do not belong either in the statehouse or
in civilized society.

What's most important about this scene is that it does nothing to
advance the narrative of *The Birth of a Nation*. It is a narrative non
sequitur. But it plays a crucial role in furthering the racist fantasy
that the film imagines. The extraneousness of the scene underlines its

fantasmatic importance: Griffith goes out of his way to include Black excessiveness because it testifies to Black inferiority. As the racist fantasy has it, Black individuals are not advanced enough to be lacking as whites are. The excessive enjoyment that they display is the mark of their inability to lack. This image of blackness is the central plank of the racist fantasy. Consciously, it assures whites of their superiority, while it gives them an unconscious avenue to enjoy through identifying with this site of excess.

The depiction of Black enjoyment reaches its high point with Gus (Walter Long) and his sexual attraction to Flora Cameron (Mae Marsh). Gus, a Union soldier allowed to roam free in the subjugated South, enjoys his pursuit of Flora and the prospect of sex with her. This is also the point at which the film arouses the spectator through the racist fantasy. Griffith uses Gus's chase after Flora and her death to stimulate the spectator and create the desire for avenging her, which is what Ben accomplishes when he and the Ku Klux Klan lynch Gus. This vengeance is the only point at which the white characters show the kind of enjoyment that we see in the Black characters.

Gus represents the height of Griffith's racism. He is a figure straight out of the racist fantasy—a racial other driven to do nothing but enjoy the ultimate object of desire, the virginal white woman. The stereotypical depiction of Gus derives entirely from his role in the racist fantasy and his monopoly on enjoyment. He is a threat because he enjoys without restraint.

Through the figure of Gus, racist spectators are able to enjoy the prospect of sexually enjoying Flora while denying it to themselves. The film enables one to condemn Gus's lasciviousness while at the same time enjoying it. The racist fantasy that the film employs gives spectators access to an enjoyment that they don't have to acknowledge as their own. They can even tell themselves about their moral opposition to it.[19]

Although the Black characters ultimately play the part of a threat to the enjoyment of the white characters, it is not at all clear that the latter would enjoy themselves if this threat were removed. Unbeknownst to Griffith himself, the film reveals what the racist fantasy attempts to hide. We see that there is no white enjoyment without the threat that Black enjoyment poses to it. The threat that figures such as Gus and Silas Lynch (George Stiegmann) represent has the effect of stimulating white enjoyment into existence by endangering it. Without the threat of the racial other, neither the white families in the film nor the spectator watching it would have access to their own enjoyment. The threat threatens white enjoyment into existence.

The location of enjoyment in *The Birth of a Nation* is instructive. The film does not depict those who belong to the social order, like the Camerons and the Stonemans, as the privileged ones when it comes to enjoyment. They obey the rules and thus receive recognition, but they do not enjoy. Obviously, Griffith views their repression as the proper position, but he does show its psychic cost. Enjoyment is the province of those who don't belong to the society—the Black characters. The only time that any white enjoyment appears in the film is when Ben Cameron and the Ku Klux Klan arrive in response to Black enjoyment. Even here, however, it is Black enjoyment that has priority. The whites have to enjoy while wearing hoods over their faces and while responding to the outbreak of Black enjoyment.

The whites enjoy through the enjoyment of the racial others whom they destroy. In the film, white enjoyment always plays second fiddle to Black enjoyment. This is always true in the racist fantasy, which locates the racial other as the source of enjoyment. Although Griffith makes one of the most racist films in the history of cinema, the film gives an absolute priority to Black enjoyment. This does not testify to Griffith's evenhandedness but to his complete investment in the racist fantasy in which Black enjoyment is the primary social—or antisocial—fact.

The immense popularity of *The Birth of a Nation* at the time of its release and after testifies to the appeal of the fantasy it presents.[20] By constructing a narrative that tapped directly into the American version of the racist fantasy, Griffith gave spectators an avenue for their enjoyment. They could access the enjoyment of the racialized other that repulsed them, while at the same time keep their distance from it through the vehicle of the Ku Klux Klan. Fantasy enables individuals to transgress the social barriers and enjoy through the other, but it protects them from this enjoyment as well. One can experience the transgressive enjoyment of the other in the racist fantasy without losing the security of the social hierarchy and one's place within it.

Shooting at an Excess

Police shootings of unarmed Black individuals have been a recurrent trauma in American history. Social media began to bring mass awareness to these shootings in the 2010s, but the incidents predate this awareness and stain the entirety of American history. These shootings are commonplace. Police shoot far more Black individuals than white because of the position that Black individuals occupy within the racist fantasy that underwrites American society. Because they view Black individuals through the racist fantasy, the police shoot threats to the enjoyment of the object, not actual Black individuals. The prevalence of the fantasy enables them to fire without compunction, often many more shots than would be necessary to subdue even the strongest person. From the perspective of the racist fantasy, there is no such thing as excessive force.

The racist fantasy tells the police officers that what is excessive is not their use of force but the criminality of the Black man. This fantasized criminality leads directly to mass incarceration, which is not a fantasy. In *The New Jim Crow*, Michelle Alexander points out that today incarceration plays the same role that slavery and subsequently Jim Crow laws once played. She states, "Although this new system of racialized social control purports to be colorblind, it creates and maintains racial hierarchy much as earlier systems of control did. Like Jim Crow (and slavery), mass incarceration operates as a tightly networked system of laws, policies, customs, and institutions that operate collectively to ensure the subordinate status of a group defined largely by race."[21] What is distinct about mass incarceration, however, is that its fantasmatic justification derives from the image of the

Black criminal, which emerges as a figure as legal barriers to equality disappear.[22] The police officers see their violence as simply a legitimate response to an actual threat due to the power that the racist fantasy has within the society. Were it not for the dominance of this fantasy, these acts of extreme violence would be bewildering for their very extremity.

In one of the basic American racist fantasy scenarios, the Black man plays the role of the racial other. By virtue of this position, he represents an enjoyment that threatens those who occupy the position of the subject in the racist fantasy. He is a barrier to the possible enjoyment of these subjects because he monopolizes the enjoyment of the desired object. This threat exists in the person of the Black man, which is why, when the police confront the Black man, the presence or absence of a firearm is immaterial. Just by standing awash in illicit enjoyment, the Black man is a danger. The person looking at him sees a figure from the fantasy and treats the Black man as such a figure.

This fantasy is what authorizes the use of deadly and excessive force. What stands out in so many of the police shootings of unarmed Black men is the number of rounds used to subdue the apparent threat. In almost every case, the force is wildly disproportionate to the threat. For instance, Los Angeles County Sheriff's Department officers shot Ryan Twyman with over thirty bullets on June 6, 2019. This degree of excess is not the norm in such shootings, but some type of excess is a constant. The police involved in these shootings almost never use one bullet but invariably fire many more than is necessary to subdue the victim. This is because they are not aiming at just another suspect but at the excess that exists outside the social order's control.

The police officer's excessive shooting occurs in response to the fantasized excess of the Black man. Even though this Black man may be doing nothing at all threatening, his status as a Black man—as the society's internal exile—constitutes him as a threat. As a Black man, there is simply nothing that one can do in this situation. One is a danger to the white police officer due to the fantasy frame through which the officer perceives. One's lack of bad intentions cannot prevent the officer from seeing the threat of an illicit enjoyment associated with blackness through the fantasy. No matter how innocently the Black victims act, once they are caught up in the racist fantasy, their situation is hopeless. This is why Philando Castile could carefully tell officer Jeronimo Yanez that he was opening his glove compartment to show Yanez his licensed firearm and Yanez nonetheless fatally shot him without receiving any legal repercussions. Such incidents testify to the power of the racist fantasy to determine life and death.

Being shot by a police officer is a leading cause of death for young Black men in American society. This fact alone bespeaks the incredible power of the racist fantasy and the damage that it inflicts. A Black man has a 1 in 1000 chance of dying at the hands of the police, far greater than the odds for white men. These odds are the direct result of the predominance of the racist fantasy in American society and the investment in it among the police force.

We can see this at work in Michael Slager's shooting of Walter Scott. On the morning of April 4, 2015, Slager pulled Scott over for a faulty third brake light. (Such low-level traffic violations are often the prelude to police shootings and also testify to the power of the racist fantasy, which sees obscene enjoyment in such insignificant violations of the law.) It is likely that Slager would not have pulled over a white motorist for a similar violation. After stopping his car, Scott began to flee on foot. Rather than just allowing Scott to escape for what was only a minor traffic violation, Slager pursued him. This decision reflected the extent to which the racist fantasy colored Slager's perception. When one looks from the perspective of this fantasy, the broken brake light of a Black man and his subsequent flight signal the presence of a dangerous felon.

After his pursuit of Scott, Slager ended up firing eight bullets at him, one of them fatally. From the perspective of the racist fantasy that informed Slager's interaction with Scott, the eight bullets were necessary to subdue the excessive enjoyment that Scott possessed and that threatened Slager. When explaining this inexplicable act of violence, Slager insisted that he felt threatened, even though he had no evidence that Scott was armed or represented any kind of actual danger. He made no aggressive move whatsoever. All that he did was drive with a broken brake light and flee. The fantasy of the danger led to Scott's death. Slager felt his own enjoyment at stake, which is why he acted so violently.

When one reads the details of a shooting like that of Scott, it seems bewildering. One searches for a hidden fact that would make sense of the incident—an overlooked weapon, a brief flash of resistance, or evidence of a greater crime. But in almost every case, there is nothing but the wildly disproportionate use of force. The disproportion can only seem proportionate when one takes into account the racist fantasy that figures the Black man as an overriding threat to all white enjoyment. One shoots not at a single Black man but at an amorphous menace that threatens to completely overcome white civilization.

There are no longer lynchings in contemporary American society. Officer shootings have replaced them. Unlike lynchings, they seem not to involve the entire community. But in fact everyone is able to participate in them virtually, as people eagerly watch the news reports of the latest episode of police violence. Whereas the whole community felt its involvement with lynching, officer shootings enable people to participate virtually while assuring themselves that these shootings have nothing to do with them. In this sense, officer shootings represent an ideological advance on lynching. They give the spectator a degree of deniability that lynchings do not.

The visibility of police violence is politically ambivalent. On the one hand, as the widely diffused murder of George Floyd in Minneapolis on May 25, 2020, revealed, such horrific spectacles can galvanize mass opposition to racist society. But on the other hand, spectators who watch the video repeatedly are, albeit without awareness, enjoying the contemporary lynching.[23] The only difference between attending the lynching of James Washington and repeatedly watching the murder of George Floyd is that the latter activity allows one some psychic distance.

Officer shootings provide those who fantasize themselves as nonracist with the assurance that an extralegal force is policing the excessive enjoyment of the racialized other. This is why activists who claim that the coverage of these events functions as a form of pornography are on the right track. News organizations cover the shootings in order to give everyone a taste of the access to and policing of illicit enjoyment that they reveal. But they also serve as a clear warning to Black individuals who believe in their own equality as citizens. By emphasizing the nonbelonging of Black individuals and the price paid for this nonbelonging, news coverage of police shootings has the effect of reinforcing the basic racist fantasy in the guise of exposing the horrors of racism.

If one doesn't take the racist fantasy into account, it seems as if the Black victim must have done something to provoke the police officer. This conviction prompts constant suggestions to Black men about how to act with the police in order not to get shot. These suggestions are offensive because they bespeak the blindness of the person offering them to the racist fantasy. When society is structured around this fantasy, there is nothing that one can do to make it through intact. One is completely at the mercy of the subject of the fantasy. Rather than trying to help Black individuals survive encounters with the police, energy would be better spent trying to undermine the power of the racist fantasy that makes such encounters so dangerous.

Biopowerless

Grasping the priority of fantasy in the psyche allows us to rethink the contemporary emphasis on power as a schema for analyzing the social order. The prevailing way of talking about racism today is through the lens of power. From this perspective, racism is a problem because it involves one group dominating another, not because of the way that it distributes enjoyment. This domination is the source of racism's injustice. According to this way of thinking, racism is wrong not because it violates universal equality but because it involves a power imbalance. The victims of racism find themselves stripped of power and thus missing the opportunities that the privileged perpetuators of racism have.

The primary exponents of the claim that racism is a manifestation of power are the biopolitical theorists. Led by Michel Foucault, these theorists put all their chips in the analysis of power, believing that power represents the primary problem in contemporary society. In this way, they break from Marxism's insistence that socioeconomic exploitation constitutes the primary evil of capitalist society.[24] This focus on power leads the biopolitical theorists to see the state, not capitalism, as the principal site for critique. As the basis for the exercise of power in the contemporary world, they claim, the state is what we must contest.[25]

According to Foucault, biopower represents a new form of power that no longer threatens subjects with death but instead makes them live.[26] The shift from the regime of punishment to that of biopower eliminates the threat of death hanging over everyone's head. It portends the end of public spectacles of execution, which it replaces with check-ups at the doctor's office and watches that constantly monitor our vital signs. These are the expressions of a new form of power that surveys and enforces our continued vitality. But there is one area where the state remains lethal.

This area marks the point at which the critics of biopower take on the problem of racism. Given this emphasis on the violence of state power, it's not surprising that the critics of biopower focus their critique of racism on the Nazis. They represent an exemplary case of state power being used to propagate and enforce racism. The lecture series *"Society Must Be Defended"* concludes with an analysis of the role that racism plays in Nazi Germany. As Foucault sees it, Nazism attempted to create a vital social body. But the creation of Aryan vitality required the elimination of the racial other. In other words, in order to make some live, other must die. Or as Foucault articulates it, "Once the State functions in the biopower mode, racism alone can justify the murderous function of the State."[27] Racism thus plays an exceptional role within the biopolitical regime.

Whereas every other aspect of the regime focuses on life, racism harnesses all the regime's negativity. The racial other cannot exist within the biopolitical imperative of life because it must function as the external threat that keeps everyone in line and committed to the project of life. In order for Germans to be forced to live, Jews must die. Racism enables us to divide the biological field between those forced to live and those who must die. It quilts the social field by determining its external limit.

When we analyze racism in terms of power, it becomes a cleansing mechanism. Racism aims at cordoning off or eliminating the race that threatens the vitality of the body politic. The racial other takes on the form of bare life so that citizens can recognize what they are not. In this sense, racism is integral to the logic of biopower, a regime of power that controls a population through measures that ensure its health. To remain healthy, the social order must avoid racial degeneracy. The social body requires an immunotherapy, and this is what racism provides. As theorist of biopower Roberto Esposito states, "Racial hygiene is the immunitary therapy that aims at preventing or extirpating the pathological agents that jeopardize the biological quality of future generations."[28] The murderous dimension of this logic reaches its end point in the form of the Nazi Holocaust, but it informs the less eliminationist forms of racism that characterize contemporary capitalist society.

According to this analysis, racism ensures the border between inside and outside that is necessary for a healthy body politic. Its fundamental task is one of exclusion and annihilation. The victims of racism have no role to play within the social order anymore. Power serves to exclude them and thus to be done with them, which is why Nazism's literal elimination of the racial other is paradigmatic for Foucault and Esposito (and Giorgio Agamben).

The problem with understanding racism in terms of a power imbalance is that it does not have the explanatory power that it first appears to have. When one initially hears about theorizing racism as a disproportionate allotment of power, it makes incredible sense. One concludes immediately that, of course, this must be right, especially when one contrasts how the dominant race lives with the oppressed group's way of life. But it is precisely the commonsensical status of this interpretation of racism that renders it most questionable. It seems correct because it remains on the level of conscious willing.

Understanding racism as an expression of domination frames it in a way that completely sidelines the role of the unconscious. The unconscious does not concern itself with power. Our will to power, to the extent that it exists, is in no way unconscious because it does not violate the logic of consciousness. The point of the unconscious is not simply that it is not known, that we are not conscious of it. The unconscious operates according to a different logic than that of consciousness.[29] Its functioning is not just not conscious but irreducible to consciousness. Ultimately, there is no way to translate the unconscious into consciousness because of this different logic.

We can see the role of the unconscious in the Nazi genocide if we pay attention to how Nazis figure Jews in relation to their movement. Nazis target Jews not to have power over them but because they view Jews as an obstacle to their enjoyment. That is, Jews figure in the unconscious of the Nazis. In the definitive account of the politics of Nazism, Arno Mayer claims, "Unlike all the other civilian victims of retaliatory terror, the Jews were demonized and turned into scapegoats not for real or alleged acts of hostility against specific German targets but for incarnating the nemesis of the Nazi pretense."[30] The Nazis are not trying to defeat a real nemesis but an unconscious, fantasmatic one. Power cannot be their motivation.

The will to power is different than unconscious desire. Our will to power may be unpleasant to think about if we consider ourselves ethical people, but it is in no way irreducible to consciousness. In fact, the will to power is an expression of the logic of consciousness. Corporate leaders have no problem articulating in no uncertain terms their allegiance to the will to power. We consciously strive to exert power over ourselves and over others. This is what Nietzsche gets when he states that "our drives can be reduced to *the will to power.*"[31] The problem with Nietzsche's formulation is that he doesn't restrict this will to power to consciousness. He sees our drives—our unconscious—in these same terms. This is what Freud breaks with when he discovers that the unconscious operates according to a different impulse.[32]

Unconscious desire, as Freud theorizes it, satisfies itself through disempowering us.[33] It is an anti-will to power, a force that undermines our conscious seeking after power. Because of the determining role of our unconscious desire, our power plays always run aground. Rather than gaining satisfaction through the exertion of power over others, we find ourselves constantly thwarting our own efforts. We find satisfaction in thwarting our will to power. Or, unconscious desire trumps conscious will to power. As a result, no matter how much power we obtain, it is never enough. When we obtain power, we are actually serving our unconscious desire by providing it with more opportunities for subversion.

During the Nazi Holocaust, the theorists of biopower claim that the Nazis killed the Jews by reducing them to bare life. The Nazis stripped the Jews of their political being, transforming them into nothing but life itself. As Giorgio Agamben famously puts it in *Homo Sacer*, "the Jews were exterminated not in a mad and giant holocaust but exactly as Hitler had announced, 'as lice,' which is to say, as bare life. The dimension in which the extermination took place is neither religion nor law, but biopolitics."[34] That is, the Holocaust is a pure act of domination, an expression of absolute power. What Agamben's statement elides is the factor of enjoyment, a factor that hinders any possible reduction of someone to bare life.[35] Agamben misses both Jewish enjoyment—what the Nazis are trying to extirpate—and Nazi enjoyment—what they experience while doing this.

Neither Foucault nor Agamben offers any theory about why the Nazis pursued the Final Solution. For both, the answer is obvious and lies in the determinations of power. But despite Hitler's claims, the Nazis didn't kill the Jews "like lice" at all. They performed horrific experiments on them and submitted them to every kind of brutal humiliation. They killed the Jews like figures of a threatening enjoyment rather than like lice.

Six million Jews died at the hands of the Nazis because they occupied a precise position within the Nazi racist fantasy. In this fantasy, their obscene enjoyment posed an absolute threat to the German nation and the enjoyment of that nation. In *Mein Kampf*, Hitler highlights this danger as the source of his onslaught against the Jews. He writes, "*the Jew today is the great agitator for the complete destruction of Germany.*"[36] Destroying Jews offers Nazis a path to eliminate this fantasized threat and simultaneously to partake in the enjoyment that they imagine Jews to be monopolizing. Backed by the ability of the racist fantasy to mobilize enjoyment, the genocide becomes an actual orgy of death. But we don't see the sexuality of the killing when we examine only in terms of biopower.

The analysis of racism in terms of biopower views it as an act of exclusion. The social order excludes the racial other in order to immunize itself. But this way of thinking radically short shrifts the role that racism plays in psyche of the racist. Racism does not simply exclude—and, actually, it does not exclude at all. The racial other doesn't belong to the society but is not excluded. This figure must remain part of the social order as its own excess in order to provide a source of enjoyment for those who belong. The nonbelonging of the racial other is not exclusion. If it were excluded, this figure could not act as society's enjoyment source.

The theory of biopower misses the continued need for the racial other because it envisions a social order of pure power relations where enjoyment, along with the unconscious, has no place. If power were the primary factor in the functioning of the social order, we could administer it much more effectively than we do. It would be easy to manage the equal distribution of power as long as there was no unconscious lurking to subvert the workings of power. But the fact that things never just work out shows that power cannot be the final word, despite how much we wish that it were so.

While teaching a class in 2019 at the University of Vermont, I noticed the constant expressions of near-absolute moral relativism by the students. I wanted them to express unqualified moral outrage at some horrific behaviors, but they stayed firm in their relativism. For them, morality was completely subjective, dependent solely on the beliefs of the individual. I noticed one exception to the insistence on relativism, which is why it was near-absolute rather than absolute. On the question of racism, the students to a person—there were sixty of them—were convinced that it was simply a moral wrong regardless of someone's personal morality. Racism was the one exception to their relativistic philosophy.

I decided to highlight this contradiction and ask them to reconcile it for me. For a few moments, they were all befuddled and disturbed, until one of the cleverer of them came up with an ingenious solution, a solution that fit perfectly within the contemporary interpretation of racism through the lens of power. This student claimed that the moral wrongness of racism stemmed from the uneven distribution of power that underwrote it. The students, she claimed, believed in moral relativism only to the extent that everyone shared equally in power. An unequal distribution of power—what racism clearly displayed—was intrinsically immoral because it precluded the possibility of acceding to moral relativism. That is, the great immorality of racism consisted in its effect of blocking the possibility for one to engage in relativism on an equal plane of power with everyone else.

This was a very contemporary—and revelatory—solution to the question. Racism was an evil not because it violated our sense of universal equality but because it evinced an uneven distribution of power. As the student herself admitted, the analysis presupposed the possibility of a world without any power imbalance at all, in which we could interact on a completely level playing field. But such a field cannot exist. Even if we could temporarily construct a society of even power relations, we would instantly undermine it in order to forge a path for enjoyment. Enjoyment occurs through the subversion of consciousness and its will to power. No matter how rigidly we focus on keeping power free of unconscious desire, this desire will always infiltrate the structures of power and disturb their equilibrium.

The emphasis on power in the critique of racism has other deleterious effects. One of the most common ways that the critique of racism in terms of power manifests itself is in the denunciation of "white privilege," which is the benefit that accords to those not found in the position of the racial other. The concept of white privilege emerges from the liberal critique of racism, which aims at eradicating all racism's manifestations on a case-by-case basis. But the problem with this line of critique is not simply its liberal individualist focus, nor is it the strange perspective that sees being part of an oppressive dominant group a "privilege."[37] Of course, not being shot by the police is an advantage when others are shot. But on the whole, whiteness places one as a subject in a position of blindness relative to the social structure, which is in no way a privilege.

But the liberalism of this position is not its primary failing. Instead, the problem inhering in the attack on white privilege lies in its failure to understand that the basic vehicle for racism today is a fantasy that places the racist in the privileged social position and the racial other in the position of nonbelonging. As a result, the attacks on white privilege actually feed racism rather than undermining it, which is why liberal whites are so often eager to criticize their own privilege. When they do so, they actually augment their enjoyment that occurs through the fantasy of the racial other. On the level of fantasy, symbolic privilege corresponds to an enjoyment deficit. For those invested in the racist fantasy, the more that they point out their social privileges, the more that they posit their lack of enjoyment and highlight the racial other's enjoyment advantage. In this way, they miss the site where their racism produces the enjoyment that sustains it. Enjoyment is located in the site of social ostracism, not social privilege. It is located in nonbelonging to the social order, not belonging. By pointing out one's white privilege, one enhances the fantasmatic image of the unrestrained enjoyment of blackness. The language of "white privilege" affirms the positions that white and Black already have in the racist fantasy, which is why it tends to affirm rather than challenge the racist fantasy.

If we leave the fantasy untouched, racism will continue unabated. Seeing racism in terms of an uneven distribution of power that excludes the racial other misses the role that this other plays in the enjoyment of those who have the power. Racism functions through the enjoyment of the racial other, an enjoyment that makes no sense as long as one thinks in terms of the distribution of power. Power is blind to the effects of enjoyment, but as critics of racism we cannot be. Rather than fighting against power for its complicity with racism, we should use power to fight against the racist fantasy.

On the Other Side of Fantasy

We Got the Beat

Seeing the ubiquity and recalcitrance of the racist fantasy can easily produce a feeling of defeatism. Fantasy accounts for much of the staying power of racism around the world, and it seems difficult to imagine how to defeat a fantasy. Its lack of material reality is its strength. One constant temptation in the struggle against the racist fantasy is the cynical gesture—throwing up one's hands and ascribing this fantasy to the nature of human relations. And yet, the fact that racism has a historical origin proves that it cannot be eternal. It must be possible to challenge and transform the power of fantasy. This requires both understanding how fantasy works and recognizing how to intervene into fantasy's distribution of enjoyment.

Attacking the racism of the racist fantasy requires abandoning one's investment in the possibility of unrestrained enjoyment. The investment in this possibility holds the key to the staying power of the racist fantasy. It also holds the key to the staying power of capitalism, which is why the struggle against racism must always also be a struggle against capitalism. Today, legal changes and the transformation of the public sphere have challenged overt displays of racism around the world. But these shifts have not done away with racism. They have brought the power of the racist fantasy to the fore. It has remained a powerful force in contemporary society around the world. Although there are nations where the problem of racism is more pronounced than others, no one has developed an immunity to it. Doing away with racism requires altering the law and revolutionizing what counts as acceptable in public, but it also involves changing people's relationship to the racist fantasy. Overcoming the racist fantasy involves taking responsibility for one's own enjoyment rather than continuing to enjoy through the racial other. This is the fundamental antiracist gesture: enjoying one's own nonbelonging instead of the nonbelonging of the racial other.

Although only a very few save lynching picture postcards today, the racist fantasy that led to such a practice has not undergone a fundamental change. Ritual enactments of the fantasy may be harder to come by, but the fantasy itself continues to predominate. As the public acceptance of racism has diminished, the unconscious power of the racist fantasy has not. The fact that the racist fantasy works unconsciously is the key to the power that it has over people psychically. The crucial step in the struggle against this fantasy is to recognize where it's operating without being noticed. While it's easy to see the racist fantasy at a Nazi rally, it's more difficult to see it at a sporting event or a concert. But until it loses its power in these arenas, it will remain in force.

We can see the continued prevalence of the racist fantasy in American society through the ongoing association of blackness with enjoyment, which has not abated since the time of widespread lynching. The outsized role that Black athletes and Black popular musicians have testifies to the structuring power of a fundamental racist fantasy that privileges Black enjoyment. Although American society's racist structures largely keep Black individuals out of top business and political positions, top positions in entertainment and sports are available because these positions, unlike the leadership of a massive company, fit into the prevailing racist fantasy.[1]

The figure of the Black athlete fits perfectly into the racist fantasy.[2] Athletic ability indicates sexual prowess and creates a powerful allure. Frantz Fanon makes a note of this already in the 1950s when he writes *Black Skin, White Masks*. He describes how white women respond to the queries of psychoanalysts concerning their sexual fantasies. He writes, "There is one expression that with time has become particularly eroticized: the black athlete. One woman confided in us that the very thought made her heart skip a beat."[3] The Black athlete exists in the fantasmatic position of pure enjoyment, which is why everyone so readily accepts this figure. But if the Black athlete aspires to a leadership role in sports, this completely changes the deal and challenges the fantasy structure.

This is why the National Football League in the United States has so much trouble promoting Black coaches and general managers. The players in the league are roughly 75 percent Black, but there are only a handful of Black head coaches and general managers. Despite explicit attempts at affirmative action such as the Rooney Rule (which compels teams to interview at least one minority candidate for head coaching vacancies), the NFL remains a bastion of white rule. The owners and the public have no problem envisioning Black players, but they cannot accept Black leadership, except on an exceptional basis. Black players fit within the racist fantasy and function as sites of enjoyment. But as coaches or general managers, Black individuals do not. Fans watch players from the perspective of the racist fantasy— seeing their violent activity on the field as an instance of the racial other's excessiveness. A head coach does not fit the fantasy and thus is less acceptable.

The clearest example of the association of the racial other with enjoyment is the reception of contemporary hip hop music. Hip hop music is the dominant musical genre among American teens, no matter what their ethnicity or geographic location. The dominance of this predominantly Black genre among white teens, even overtly racist white teens, indicates how well it speaks to the underlying societal fantasy. It is not an indication of a lack of racism in those who listen to it. Michelle Alexander links the violent misogyny of contemporary hip hop and rap to the tradition of the minstrel show. She argues that, like minstrelsy, these genres are designed to appeal to whites invested in a fantasy about blackness. She writes, "Like the minstrel shows of the slavery and Jim Crow eras, today's displays are generally designed for white audiences. The majority of consumers of gangsta rap are white, suburban teenagers."[4] The music plays directly to the racist fantasy, which underlies its great popularity.

The popular success of any musical genre depends on its ability to fit what fantasy requires. Hip hop could not make inroads into white suburban America if there were not a fantasy space there to accommodate it. Suburban white teens find an enjoyment in hip hop music that the drudgery of suburban American existence lacks. Hip hop allows them to indulge in the logic of the racist fantasy with a clear conscience about their absence of racism. They can know that they aren't racist because they appreciate Black musicians, but it is precisely this appreciation that indicates their investment in American society's racist fantasy.

In the beginnings of rock and roll, the relationship to the racist fantasy was more obscure but nonetheless at work. Early rock stars like Elvis Presley and the Rolling Stones themselves tapped into predominately Black musical forms. Rhythm and blues seeded rock music, which subsequently repressed this parent form. White fans could listen and partake of a fantasized Black enjoyment while disavowing any link to this origin. Today the link has become much more explicit.

The affection that suburban white teens have for hip hop music shows the ability of the racist fantasy to allow people to energize themselves on the enjoyment of the other. The marginalization of hip hop stars is absolutely essential to the esteem that their white audience has for them. If they did not display their social nonbelonging in their songs, they would not be popular. They sing about what their white listeners cannot themselves even speak without earning the ire of their parents and teachers. The extreme misogyny and violence of some of the more popular hip hop songs are not a reflection of the conditions in which the artists that produce them live. Their audience demands this graphic enactment of prohibited enjoyment. The toll that it takes on the artists themselves—many are gunned down at an incredibly young age—bespeaks the role of the racist fantasy in doling out life and death. Though they often occur at the hands of other young Black men, these deaths are the product of the racist fantasy that demands their unrestrained enjoyment.

We can see the enjoyment at work in hip hop by looking at a popular example, the remix version of "Da Real Hoodbabies" by Lil Gotit. The lyrics drip with an enjoyment that completely defies the social norms of contemporary American society. In fact, it is astonishing that there is no outraged feminist parent leading the charge to have such music pulled from popular music distributors. Tipper Gore has clearly fallen down on the job. In the first verse, the song proclaims a violent sexual enjoyment: "Hit it from the front, then I grab her by the neck / Nutted on her face, yeah, Gotit left a mess / Then she let the shit drip down to her chest." The second verse compounds the violence, contending, "If she don't give me head, I'ma cut off her neck." The song transgresses social norms about brutal misogyny, norms that are the heart of the contemporary social expectations.[5] It posits an enjoyment at the precise point where the social order restrains it. It offends both conservative moral sensibilities and liberal feminist ones. The extreme nature of the transgression that the song envisions corresponds with the status of the hip hop musician. This musician sings from the position of nonbelonging that enables him to violate social norms with impunity. The song plays into the fantasy of an enjoyment that is not subject to the restrictions that govern the society as a whole, an enjoyment made possible by the position that the hip hop musician occupies as a racial other.

Songs such as "Da Real Hoodbabies" are popular among suburban American teens because they enable them to access a fantasized enjoyment that would otherwise remain off-limits to them. They can fantasize about this enjoyment without ever living it. The popularity of these songs stems from their place within the underlying racist fantasy structure that locates transgressive enjoyment of nonbelonging with blackness. The fact that what the song portrays is not really enjoyable is not significant. If no one really enjoys grabbing women by the neck or ejaculating on their faces, this does not detract from the power of the fantasy. The song works because it fits into the fantasy structure. Teens listen to it and take part in this extreme enjoyment because the song aligns so perfectly with the society's underlying racist fantasy. One can listen and enjoy this fantasy without ever for a moment considering oneself a racist. The fact that the singer is Black enables listeners to experience themselves as utterly nonracist, which is what makes the racist fantasy so much more appealing than open displays of racism. Even though listening to hip hop music is a less toxic form of enjoyment that participating in a lynching, it is nonetheless involved in the same pathology because it relies on the same racist fantasy.

The role of Black artists in constructing American popular culture stands out. In *Race Matters*, Cornell West notices the strangeness of this dynamic. He says, "One irony of our present moment is that just as young black men are murdered, maimed, and imprisoned in record numbers, their styles have become disproportionately influential in shaping popular culture."[6] What West doesn't add is that there is a clear link between these two phenomena: they both reflect the position of young Black men within the prevailing racist fantasy. The cultural drivers in American society are those that this same society places in a position of nonbelonging. The fact that young Black men are disproportionately jailed and are disproportionately shaping American culture is not a coincidence. It attests to the predominance of the racist fantasy.

There are many hip hop songs that directly challenge the racist fantasy rather than perpetuating it in the way that "Da Real Hoodbabies" does. They confront white listeners with the brutality of contemporary racism and force them to address their own racism. This is the case with hip hop star Meek Mill. His songs, such as "Championships," challenge the association of blackness with enjoyment. They show that guns and drugs represent a capitulation to the logic of capitalist society, not a rebellion. Insofar as it makes people aware of Meek Mill, the racist fantasy that leads some people to listen to hip hop actually challenges racism. Figures such as Meek Mill demonstrate that the political charge of hip hop music is up for grabs.[7] But for many white consumers, it functions like attendance at a lynching, with similar baleful consequences.

The point is not to listen to Meek Mill instead of Lil Gotit. Instead, the way out of an investment in the racist fantasy requires taking responsibility for one's own enjoyment, seeing this enjoyment as one's own rather than that of the racial other. Whenever one is enjoying, one has responsibility for this enjoyment, no matter where it might seem to emanate from. This path also entails giving up the idea of an unrestrained enjoyment located in the racial other. Taking responsibility for one's own enjoyment includes the recognition that enjoyment is always lacking. It is only when one imagines the enjoying other that unrestrained enjoyment seems possible. The challenge of giving up the promise of this enjoyment is the fundamental challenge of the fight against racism. It requires viewing one's own limitations not as what must be overcome in fantasy but as sites of enjoyment on their own. It requires listening to hip hop without the racist fantasy functioning as the streaming device.

With Antiracists Like This

Films that attempt to depict interracial healing promise their own solution, a solution that is part of the problem. They promise a path out of racism but actually thrust people deeper into it. Whereas genuine antiracist films highlight the effects of racism instead of trying to heal them visually—*Sorry to Bother You* (Boots Riley, 2018) is an exemplary case of this—interracial healing films depict racism as a problem that experience can enable us to overcome. In this sense, instead of functioning as antiracist films, they actually play a key role in the perpetuation of racism. This is because they inevitably resort to the racist fantasy, which gives the lie to their expressions of healing. Any expressions of interracial healing that fail to challenge the foundations of racist society—including the racist fantasy—are nothing but bricks in the edifice of racist society's ideological structure.

Nowhere is this dynamic clearer than in John Lee Hancock's *The Blind Side* (2009).[8] This film shows a white Tennessee family adopting a young Black man who the mother, Leigh Anne Tuohy (Sandra Bullock), picked up walking alone on the street in the cold. After this bit of assistance, Leigh Anne decides to turn the young man into her project. By taking Michael Oher (Quinton Aaron) in and making him part of her family, Leigh Anne saves him from the life on the streets. In addition, she provides pivotal instruction for his budding football career, telling him to protect the quarterback as he would his family. Thanks to Leigh Anne's tutelage, Michael goes on to the University of Mississippi and ultimately to play professional football.

On the one hand, *The Blind Side* is a typical white savior story, in which the wealthy white woman saves the poor young Black man from a life of desperation.[9] But the film's popular success stems from its investment in the racist fantasy that goes far beyond the white savior. For his part, Michael does not play into the racist fantasy at all. He does not evince any enjoyment that would threaten the white family, despite fears from their friends that his enjoyment poses a direct danger to their daughter Collins (Lily Collins). At no point in the film does Michael even look at Collins as a desiring being. Instead, his only wish is to protect everyone in the white family. He is not a figure of threatening enjoyment, which is how the open racists within the film see him.

Michael exists to prove that the film is nonracist. In order to depict Michael as nonthreatening, the film must strip him of all sexuality. He never enjoys himself. Through the figure of Michael, the film assures us that there can be a Black man that we need not fear. But the film also makes clear that Michael is an exception, not the rule. One rule of racist conduct is that racists are always content to make exceptions to the racist rule, and *The Blind Side* is itself no exception to this rule.

Every other Black character in the film is awash in dangerous enjoyment and represents a threat to the social order. Michael's mother is a drug addict with no hope for escape. The gang in his old neighborhood threatens Leigh Anne with sexual taunts when she goes there to research Michael's life. There is a menacing Black enjoyment throughout the filmic world of *The Blind Side*, save in the character of Michael. Through the contrast between these figures of unrestrained illicit enjoyment and Michael, the film paints Michael as worthy of recognition. His desexualization bespeaks his acceptability as someone who avoids the enjoyment associated with blackness, both in the racist fantasy and in the logic of the film.

The spectator can enjoy *The Blind Side*, just like the listener can enjoy "Da Real Hoodbabies," thereby indulging in the racist fantasy while avoiding any open displays of racism. The acceptance of the nonthreatening Michael Oher proves the absence of any racism, while the scorn for the figures of the enjoying other—his mother and the neighborhood gang taunting Leigh Anne—derives from the racist fantasy that underlies the film. Michael escapes this fantasy only at the point when he proves that he doesn't enjoy but only wants to protect.[10] The film depicts him as worthy of acceptance insofar as he abandons the enjoyment that the film, following the racist fantasy, associates with blackness. Spectators can know that they are not racists because they accept Michael Oher, but they can indulge in their racism at the same time by cheering the ostracism of the racialized other that enjoys.

With antiracist films like *The Blind Side*, we no longer need overtly racist films like *Birth of a Nation*. It is even possible that the consequences of *The Blind Side* are even more flagitious than that of the Griffith film because *The Blind Side* pretends to an antiracism that *Birth of a Nation* does not. Be that as it may, the central point is that *The Blind Side* represents an important plank in the fantasmatic thrust of contemporary racism. It nourishes the racist fantasy rather than trying to take it on. Not only does it employ a white savior and thus exculpate whites from any complicity with the racism rampant in American society, it also depicts the Black enjoyment as a threat that even the Black man must navigate. As the film has it, Leigh Anne Tuohy is a hero because she saves Michael from this threat, not because she confronts and defeats a racist fantasy structure. The results of the kind of antiracism that *The Blind Side* attempts to practice are doleful. It is the product of a racist antiracism, an antiracism that cannot find a way out of the psychic determinants of the racist fantasy.

Antiracism does not demand that we stop listening to hip hop or that we refrain from watching *The Blind Side*, just that we abandon the association of this music and the characters in this film with the unrestrained enjoyment of the racial other. Rather than attributing this excessive enjoyment to the racial other, subjects must confront their own nonbelonging and the enjoyment that comes with it. It is only in this way that one takes responsibility for one's own enjoyment and disturbs the power of the racist fantasy. Until the association of the racial other with unlimited enjoyment breaks down, racism will continue to have a structuring role in the social order and anyone thrust into the position of the racial other will remain in danger from the contemporary version of lynching parties.

Why Race, Not Class

For many critics of contemporary society, the ideal solution to the problem of the racist fantasy would be to replace it with a class fantasy. This ideal touches on one of the enduring mysteries of modernity: Why hasn't a fantasy involving class ever emerged in the place of the racist fantasy? The racist fantasy has to attribute enjoyment to those who often evince rampant suffering more than enjoyment, given the position that they occupy in the society. On first reflection, it seems that it would be easier for the fantasy construction to employ society's wealthy as the figures of illicit enjoyment, since one can see this enjoyment much more evidently. This seems like a promising avenue for creating an alternative to the racist fantasy—a ruling class fantasy. They live in their mansions, travel in their private planes, relax in their yachts, dine in expensive restaurants, and drive luxury cars. The enjoyment that accompanies wealth is impossible to miss, whereas the racial others' enjoyment must be conjured up out of banal activities like the sound of their laughter or their mode of dress or the smell of their cuisine. The fact that a racist fantasy developed rather than a class fantasy should strike us as much more bizarre than it does, even if we aren't Marxists.

The absence of a class fantasy that locates illicit enjoyment among the wealthy is apparent in the form that populist movements have taken throughout the last century in contrast to the movements of the late 1700s. In the eighteenth century, the French and Haitian Revolutions targeted the wealthy as the thieves of the people's enjoyment. French revolutionaries placed the heads of aristocrats on pitchforks because they fantasized that these aristocrats were awash in the enjoyment that properly belonged to themselves. Haitian revolutionaries killed white plantation owners because they understood them as the source of their oppression.[11] The fantasy of the aristocratic elite hoarding enjoyment for themselves propelled both the French and the Haitian revolutionary movements. But this fantasy rarely persists for very long.

Perhaps the most convincing depiction of a fantasy of the libidinal depravity of the upper class occurs in Stanley Kubrick's *Eyes Wide Shut* (1999). The film follows the sexual adventures of Dr. Bill Harford (Tom Cruise) one night after his wife Alice (Nicole Kidman) recounts her fantasy of a sailor that she once saw. Spurred on by the jealousy that the fantasy triggers, Bill finagles the password (*Fidelio*) to a top secret orgy of the wealthy held at a local mansion. After he disguises himself, Bill manages to gain entry into the orgy and walk around before being exposed as an intruder. As he investigates, Bill sees masked men and women performing various sexual acts throughout the mansion, while others watch from their different perches. It is clear that Bill's entrance into this orgy puts his life in danger because it threatens to reveal the secret enjoyment of wealth to the public world. After the authorities of the event unmask him, Bill promises to keep the secret when he recognizes that his life is at stake.

Through this elaboration of the fantasy of the sexual enjoyment that accompanies extreme wealth, Kubrick indicates that there is a danger attached to the widespread dissemination of this fantasy.[12] The stability of the existing class relations depends not just on this activity remaining a secret, but also on restricting the emergence of the fantasy of this activity. Other than *Eyes Wide Shut*, very few films lay out the fantasy of the debauchery that wealth generates. There seems to be a censorship surrounding this fantasy. But regardless of whether films feel free to indulge in it, the class fantasy never gains much traction.[13]

When films do depict this fantasy, they show it in a way that encourages us to imagine ourselves as wealthy rather than as those left outside the wealthy's enjoyment. This is the case with Martin Scorsese's lamentable *The Wolf of Wall Street* (2013). The film chronicles the career of Jordan Belfort (Leonardo DiCaprio), who rises from being a penny-stock trader to a multimillionaire thanks to his unscrupulous trading practices. After his rise to incredible wealth, we see him and his colleagues engage in all sorts of debauchery: they participate in wild orgies, snort cocaine constantly, throw wild parties, and even construct a game out of throwing short people at a target. They do all this with money that they obtain through conning common people out of their savings by proposing dubious investments. Although their thievery and obscene enjoyment comes crashing down when federal agents finally arrest them, Belfort and his colleagues nonetheless represent an appealing model of enjoyment for the spectator.

Scorsese clearly intends for his film to function as a warning against Belfort's business practices and lifestyle. He surely made the film with the best of intentions. However, *The Wolf of Wall Street* runs into the same problem that bedevils Scorsese's films about the mafia: the intention of producing a critique ends up going totally awry, and we are left with a film that shows how appealing life with the moral turpitude of the stock trader really is. One watches the film fantasizing about how one might follow in Jordan Belfort's footsteps. In this sense, *The Wolf of Wall Street* does nothing to undermine the spectator's investment in wealth. It fails to place the wealthy in the position of the enjoying other that has monopolized enjoyment for itself. Instead, the film offers the spectator a position to partake in the wealthy's apparent enjoyment, which is why the film is an error.[14] The class fantasy continues to wait on its artistic champion.

The wide dissemination of this class fantasy could conceivably act as fuel for leftist political activity. If the lower classes of society fantasized that the wealthy were experiencing such untrammeled enjoyment at their expense, one might except that they would rise up and demand a part of it for themselves. Whereas the class fantasy actually makes a great deal of sense and targets those who have all of society's material benefits, the racist fantasy leaves those who have all the society's material benefits safe in their having and targets who don't belong. Nonetheless, the class fantasy that envisions the wealthy enjoying illicitly does not take. The failure of this fantasy to become widespread tells us something very important about the nature of enjoyment.

The class fantasy usually dies out quickly not for the reason that one would initially suspect. The problem is not that it dies as a fantasy because it's actually true and fantasy must contravene reality (though fantasy does gain psychic power insofar as it must deny reality). But in fact it is not the case that the wealthy really are enjoying in the stead of the rest of the society. We cannot fantasize successfully about the wealthy's transgressive enjoyment because they actually have more constraint on their enjoyment than any other group. Class status is an index of repression.[15]

The class fantasy doesn't take hold because the indulgences of the wealthy all occur within the confines of social propriety. The pleasures of the rich are never excessive enough to constitute an enjoyment worth fantasizing about. Even in the fantasy scenario that Kubrick dreams up in *Eyes Wide Shut*, the wealthy are primarily present themselves as observers of the enjoyment of those they pay to have sex at their orgy. We cannot fantasize about the enjoyment of wealth because obtaining wealth requires an investment in the social demand that militates against the ability to enjoy through what the social order lacks. To become wealthy is to capitulate, full stop.

This capitulation is what makes it possible for lower and middle-class people to identify with the wealthy. We can identify with the wealthy because their transgressions, no matter how extreme, never go too far. They never call into question the constraints of the social order itself. To do so would be to risk their class status, which is what the wealthy never do. This is why their eccentricities are actually bereft of enjoyment, despite what they try to tell us.[16]

Instead of a class fantasy that envisions the wealthy as the thieves of our enjoyment, we use the image of the wealthy's enjoyment as a site for symbolic identification. That is, we identify with the symbolic position of the wealthy rather than fantasizing about their enjoyment. This is what happens in *The Wolf of Wall Street*, which otherwise seems to reveal the possibility of depicting the wealthy awash in enjoyment. Psychic identification is not the same as fantasy. Both are unconscious processes, but they serve different ends. While fantasy stages and underwrites our desire, identification secures our symbolic identity, enabling us to have a sense of who we are in our society and to convince ourselves that we really have a place within the society through identification with them.

Even though we know that we will never attain it for ourselves, we identify with obscene excesses of immense wealth—the yachts, the mansions, the exquisite dinners, the fine clothes, and the opulent jewelry. No matter how excessive these debaucheries are, they are never excessive enough because they belong to the symbolic identity of the wealthy. One purchases them to impress others with one's belonging, not to enjoy one's failure to belong. The wealthy don't use their symbolic status in order to enjoy but enjoy for the sake of asserting their symbolic status. This distinction is crucial. The wealthy purchase yachts in order to display their wealth and provide others with a symbolic status that they can identify with. This identification plays an important role in the perpetuation of capitalism. People don't envy the excesses of the rich. These excesses, in direct contrast to the excesses of the racial other, do not occur at the subject's expense. Instead, they provide points that enable people to situate ourselves as proper subjects within the society.

This is why statements that left-leaning politicians make about getting rid of billionaires often damage their electoral prospects. While their followers might consciously believe that billionaires have no place in the egalitarian society that they aspire toward, the billionaire as such nonetheless plays an important psychic role for most subjects. We identify with the billionaire as a figure of excess within the social order. Even those of us who despise this inegalitarian figure of excess cannot help but identify with the billionaire's exalted symbolic status.[17]

To threaten to do away with this figure is much more threatening to the society than to mount the barricades and throw bricks.

The contrast between the billionaire and the racial other returns us to the basic difference between desire and enjoyment. Billionaires realize the desire of the social authority. By obtaining all that one can obtain in contemporary capitalist society, billionaires reach a point at which desire becomes exhausted. They can literally have whatever they want. They are in the position to buy every possible source of enjoyment— sexual partners, drugs, clothes, cars, boats, food, or animals. But the realization of desire still leaves enjoyment elsewhere. The fact that billionaires continue to pursue more indicates that they have not yet found the enjoyment that they seek, despite having realized desire as much as possible.

Billionaires exist at the point of full recognition within the social order, the point at which the social order exerts a maximal constraint on the subject. One seeks billions with the conscious idea of escaping social constraint altogether, but ironically, because this pursuit is nothing but strict obedience to the social demand, those most successful at it find themselves most constrained by it. Extreme wealth is constraining rather than freeing. Possessing extreme wealth ensconces one fully within the prison of the social order and its demand. Despite all of the elaborate displays of enjoyment that accompany extreme wealth, there is no enjoyment here. That is why the collective fantasy about it never lasts for very long.

It is the figure of nonbelonging who has access to enjoyment that the billionaire doesn't. This access stems from the ostracism that places this figure outside the system of recognition that constrains the billionaire. Billionaires exist at the point of full recognition, the point at which there is nothing within the social order lacking to them. The figure of nonbelonging is an anonymous subject with no symbolic status, while everyone knows the names of society's prominent billionaires. They have the highest social status. There is nothing that they cannot purchase—except for enjoyment, which has no price. It is the province of those who don't belong, a position that no amount of money can buy because money is the index of belonging. When billionaires purchase sports teams, they are trying to buy enjoyment, but they never sacrifice enough of their fortunes for this to be possible.

By fantasizing the racialized other as the figure of enjoyment in place of the wealthy, the racist subject is able to sustain an identification with the wealthy that a fantasy of the wealthy as the enemy would obviate. The combination of this identification and the racist fantasy works to secure the subject's position within the symbolic structure while providing an enjoyment that the symbolic identity itself cannot provide. When we wonder why people act against their own interests by falling for racist appeals while ignoring class-based critiques, we should look to the relationship between identification and fantasy.

The End of Inclusion

It is only through emancipation from the power of the racist fantasy that modernity can actualize the equality that it promises. This cannot be achieved through additional inclusion. The attempts to produce a society of equals through liberal or communist inclusion have all failed. Efforts at inclusion have always generated an opposition between those who belong and those who don't. No amount of inclusion can ever go far enough to erase the distinction between the friend and enemy, a distinction that provides the basis for the racist fantasy.

Conservative political philosopher Carl Schmitt claims that the distinction between the friend and enemy is constitutive for the political field. He sees liberal inclusivity as a danger to the continuance of this distinction and of politics as such. As Schmitt puts it in *The Concept of the Political*, "Political thought and political instinct prove themselves theoretically and practically in the ability to distinguish friend and enemy. The high points of politics are simultaneously the moments in which the enemy is, in concrete clarity, recognized as the enemy."[18] Without this recognition, Schmitt believes, a catastrophe ensues. We lose politics altogether, and the world sinks into an undifferentiated mass. Contemporary leftist champions of political struggle, from Giorgio Agamben to Chantal Mouffe, find Schmitt's position appealing because they see, despite the political gulf that separates them from him, the problem with the liberal attack on political antagonism.[19]

But if Schmitt is right, then there can be no universal equality. The project of modernity must founder on the distinction between friend and enemy or belonging and nonbelonging. Schmitt is not the last word, however. While he does apprehend the necessity of enemies to constitute a political group—the necessity of nonbelonging for belonging—he fails to consider the possibility of universal nonbelonging. It is only through rejecting the lure of inclusion that we can realize the modern ideal of universal equality. Equality can only be equality through the collective failure to belong. Nonbelonging does not require the distinction between friend and enemy, but it doesn't do away with political struggle, as Schmitt fears when one abandons this distinction. We cannot get to universal nonbelonging directly.

It is through fantasy that the enjoyment of nonbelonging becomes visible. Fantasy feeds off the enjoyment of nonbelonging. This is apparent even in the most risible fantasies, such as the racist one that this book has examined. No matter what it's content, every fantasy seeks out the structural position of nonbelonging in order to find the enjoyment that it accesses. This is the great formal lesson of fantasy.

By learning the formal lesson of fantasy while turning away from its content, we can turn away from the insistence on belonging, an insistence that necessarily produces racism. The racist fantasy has sustained the betrayal of equality in modernity, but it is only through the form of fantasy that we can see an alternative. Universal nonbelonging is the position that René Descartes points to at the beginning of modernity, a position that we have yet to actualize because we have remained stuck in the racist fantasy. Descartes could not yet conceive the importance of universal nonbelonging because he lacked a theory of fantasy. Fantasy both seduces subjects into a misrecognition of nonbelonging and enables them to grasp its structural importance for how they enjoy.

Breaking the hold of the fantasized figure of the racial other requires distinguishing between the real enjoyment that derives from nonbelonging and the image of enjoyment that fantasy attributes to this position. This move is the key to defeating racism because it enables us to discover a form of enjoyment that is more durable than that which the racist fantasy produces. The problem with the enjoyment deployed in the racist fantasy is not just its horrible destructiveness. It also fails to deliver on its promises. We imagine that we access an unrestrained enjoyment through the hip hop song, but listening to it never really brings us this. Lack persists.

This is because all enjoyment derives from lack. This is true of even the most powerful form of enjoyment known to subjectivity—the sexual encounter. One enjoys sex not because one achieves wholeness with one's partner but through one's sexual desire, which is one's lack. A nonlacking subject would not be able to have sex and would thus miss out on this enjoyment. One enjoys when one doesn't have it all, through what one doesn't have (like the sexual partner).

There is no subjectivity without lack, no one who achieves wholeness. The absence in the signifying structure—the position of nonbelonging within the social order—provides the enjoyment of lack that we misidentify, through the racist fantasy, as a complete enjoyment. The racist fantasy causes us to see an absence of constraint where there is actually an enjoyment of absence. This confusion is the lifeblood of the racist fantasy. Unraveling it must be at the foundation of any antiracist project.

The real enjoyment of nonbelonging is the enjoyment of lack. This is the enjoyment that occurs not when one is sure what Frantz Fanon is saying but when one struggles with his meaning. It is the enjoyment that comes from the struggles of the team that one roots for, not their boring successes. It is the enjoyment of confining oneself to watching just one episode of *The Wire* each night rather than trying to binge an entire season in a day. Enjoyment is always limited. Avowing the necessary limit on enjoyment deals a lethal blow to the racist fantasy. It permits the subject to enjoy its own nonbelonging rather than seeking out an unlimited enjoyment in the racial other.

This enjoyment is available to everyone, as long as everyone accepts the ramifications of nonbelonging. It is only in the racist fantasy that racial others have a monopoly on nonbelonging. In fact, even those whom the social authority designates as belonging—even the most privileged in society—can refuse this path and accept their nonbelonging. At any time, Jeff Bezos could give up his millions and confront the fact of his failure to belong. This is the choice of lack and the acceptance of enjoyment through lack rather than through overcoming it, which is what Bezos now appears bent on doing. Nonbelonging carries with it an enjoyment of lack that anyone can access. The embrace of lacking enjoyment is the basis of an antiracist existence. This is an enjoyment that one can avow as one's own. In doing so, one breaks the bonds of the racist fantasy.

The embrace of lacking enjoyment entails taking a fundamentally different view of one's satisfaction. Instead of portraying satisfaction as the overcoming of all obstacles standing in the way of attaining one's object, one must conceive of the obstacle as central to satisfaction. One must view one's obstacle as one's thing—that which both bars the object and at the same time renders it desirable. This reconception of the obstacle necessarily thrusts the racist fantasy aside. This fantasy imagines the obstacle as a threat that one must eliminate on the way to a complete enjoyment. With the acceptance of the partiality of satisfaction and the desirability of the obstacle, the racist fantasy loses its appeal. Once one sees through its promise of complete enjoyment, it loses whatever power that it once had.

Toni Morrison's novel *Sula* shows how it is possible to live after giving up the image of unrestrained enjoyment associated with the racist fantasy. Even though the novel focuses on the relationship between two Black women, Nel and Sula, it nonetheless depicts Nel dealing with the fantasy of the enjoying other who blocks her own enjoyment, which is a version of the racist fantasy. Nel, along with most of the townspeople in the Bottom, views Sula as a figure of obscene enjoyment who hoards all enjoyment for herself. Although Nel and Sula are friends, this resentment, mediated through fantasy, shapes their relationship. Sula has sex with many men of the town but never desires them. She turns to sex not for arousal but because it reminds her of her loneliness and solitude. Her enjoyment is lacking, despite how others see her. By highlighting the lack that persists through Sula's enjoyment, Morrison undermines the power of the fantasy that others attach to her.

We gain insight into the failure that is integral to how Sula enjoys. When she finally feels a connection to someone, she discovers that even this involves a misrecognition rather than a successful encounter. After Sula learns that her lover Ajax is actually named A. Jacks, this new knowledge disrupts her enjoyment. Sula says to herself, "I didn't even know his name. And if I didn't know his name, then there is nothing I did know and I have known nothing ever at all since the one thing I wanted to know was his name so how could help but leave me since he was making love to a woman who didn't even know his name."[20] This disappointment reveals that the image of Sula enjoying herself without restraint is simply a fantasy. By including such insights into Sula's psyche, Morrison makes it impossible for a reader to sustain the position that Nel has relative to her. Morrison completely undermines those who take the high ground relative to Sula, such as her friend Nel. Nel is convinced of her own morality and Sula's lack of the same. But the end of the novel gives the lie to this conception of things.

After Sula dies, the town loses its primary fantasy figure and relations among the townspeople deteriorate. Many end up destroying themselves at the moment they believe they are liberating themselves from white oppression. But at the conclusion of the novel, Nel undergoes a change. She recognizes her dependence on Sula as a figure of enjoyment while also grasping the lack in that enjoyment. The changed relationship to her fantasy enables Nel to become free for the first time, even though the price of this freedom is entering what Morrison calls "the circle of sorrow."[21] It is only by acceding to the fact of nonbelonging that she can take up a new position relative to the fantasy, which is the way of emancipation.

The path of nonbelonging is the only way out of racism. In this sense, one must adopt the symbolic position occupied by the racial other. This does not mean following the model of Rachel Dolezal, the white woman who gained notoriety when the public became aware that she was passing as Black. Dolezal passed because she believed in a nonlacking Black enjoyment that she wished to access. Such acts of passing confirm the racist fantasy rather than challenging it. The attitude that informs this type of passing misses the path of nonbelonging, which involves recognizing how the racial other lacks and enjoys only through this lack. Nonbelonging is evident in the case of the racial other, but since nonbelonging is a symbolic position—the point of absence within the symbolic structure, the point where there is no signifier—anyone can turn toward it. Passing for Black or marrying a Jew or darkening one's skin is not a shortcut to it. The fact that the racial other becomes identified with this position is simply a reflection of the predominance of the racist fantasy in our social order.

Destroying the ground on which the racist fantasy arises means destroying one's own sense of belonging. An antiracist practice thus undermines the symbolic position of anyone taking it up. It necessarily costs one one's sense of belonging to the larger symbolic community. Belonging itself is the heart of the problem. It is not just that belonging always produces those who don't belong. It is more that the compulsion to belong always produces the fantasy attached to those who don't belong. Nonbelonging, on the other hand, does not require its racial other because it is itself a position in which one enjoys lack. The enjoyment of lack—what taking up the position of nonbelonging enables—is the only genuinely antiracist possibility for us.

The problem is that the social order constantly bombards us with the blandishments of belonging. It feels good to feel like I belong. I walk into a room and experience that I fit with the others around me. It is only when I step back and pause that the emptiness of all belonging becomes apparent. I can come to see that those who would confer belonging on me themselves don't belong. With this insight, the appeal of belonging loses its shine. It is only at this point that I am prepared for the struggle against racism. But this is not the tack that many theorists envision for this struggle. For certain political thinkers, it is universal belonging—the fruit of mutual recognition—that holds the key to the elimination of racism.

The proposal to fight against racism by advocating mutual recognition has its basis in a belief that we can create a society in which everyone belongs. Mutual recognition equals universal belonging. The advocates of mutual recognition see it as the only possible solution to the scourge of racism, a scourge that works, they believe, through the denial of recognition for some and the hoarding of recognition by others. This hoarding is what the term *white privilege* signifies.

The chief exponent of the doctrine of mutual recognition is Jürgen Habermas. Habermas theorizes a morality that has its basis in the structure of signification, a structure that he aligns with mutual recognition. Mutual recognition already exists in the form of what Habermas famously calls an ideal speech situation.[22] The ideal speech situation underlies every speech situation. In it, we use arguments to convince each other in lieu of force and coercion. Ideally, the best argument wins, not the strongest. But the important point for Habermas is that in this situation every participant recognizes every other participant. It is a scenario of mutual recognition.

For Habermas, mutual recognition, established on this basis, is the sine qua non for a moral and just society. He contends that our morality "must emphasize the inviolability of the individual by postulating equal respect for the dignity of each individual. But they must also protect the web of intersubjective relations of mutual recognition by which these individuals survive as members of a community."[23] Through mutual recognition, we transform our society into a community in which everyone belongs. In this way, we realize the equality inherent in the ideal speech situation, an ideal that leaves no one out and that gives everyone a voice.

This project is in no way confined to the thought of Jürgen Habermas. While other proponents of mutual recognition do not locate its genesis in the ideal speech situation, thinkers such as Judith

Butler and Robert Pippin nonetheless see it as a solution to all forms of social violence, inclusive of racism. By mutually recognizing each other, we accept the other without forcing the other into our way of thinking. Mutual recognition creates the best of all possible worlds: I'm allowed to continue with my own private way of life while the other does the same. The only adjustment that this policy requires is that I validate the other's choice by not disparaging or rejecting it.[24]

Mutual recognition appears to be a cure for what most ails our society. Butler sees in recognition the possibility for transcending our violence and destructiveness. In *Undoing Gender*, Butler claims that "recognition is a reciprocal process that moves selves beyond their incorporative and destructive dispositions toward an understanding of another self whose difference from us is ethically imperative to mark."[25] The virtue of mutual recognition, as Butler sees it, is that it includes a respect for difference while at the same time including everyone. No one is left out, but no one feels coerced into joining. The belonging seems intrinsic.[26]

Recognition militates against the acceptance of nonbelonging. Social recognition brings with it the allure of belonging. Through recognition, we gain the sense that we belong to the social order. The problems with the project of mutual recognition begin with its necessary failure. Mutual recognition attempts to cast a wide enough net to include every member of society, but recognition is only valuable so long as it is exclusive. The nonrecognition of some is the price paid for the recognition of others. Without figures of nonbelonging that receive no recognition, we would cease to value recognition at all. Recognition would suffer the fate of the participation trophy given out for youth sports. Everyone wins a trophy just for participating in the sport, but the consequence is that even the kids themselves grasp the worthlessnesss of the trophies. A trophy is valuable—recognition means something—only insofar as we can look at those who don't receive it and see our difference.

Far from being a panacea for racism, extending recognition to those who are not now recognized entails widening the racist fantasy that underwrites our belonging to the social order. Belonging requires fantasmatic support to energize itself with enjoyment. There is no pure belonging without some version of the racist fantasy. It may not be racist, but it will include some form of ostracism. The only way to avoid such ostracism is by giving up the project of belonging altogether. The belonging that mutual recognition promises cannot form the basis of an egalitarian society. If we try to combat racism (and the racist fantasy) through the project of mutual recognition, we will obviate the possibility of embracing our nonbelonging and thereby end up strengthening the power of the racist fantasy.

Embracing one's nonbelonging involves seeing the nonbelonging that one attributes to the racial other in oneself. Rather than giving the racial other responsibility for one's own enjoyment, one takes responsibility for it oneself by giving up the enjoyment of the obstacle. To make clear how this process of taking responsibility for one's own enjoyment works, let's turn to a final joke. A golfer is having a terrible round of golf, the worst of his life. Tired and frustrated at the end of the round, the golfer lashes out at his caddy and proclaims, "You must be the worst caddy in the world!" Rather than take offense, the caddy responds, "No, that would be too much of a coincidence." In the fashion of the racist fantasy, the golfer tries to turn the caddy into the obstacle to his own enjoyment, which he identifies with a good round of golf. The golfer actually enjoys through this obstacle because it is the difficulty of golf, the failures, that makes it an exciting game to play. The golfer cannot avow himself and his own failure as the source of his enjoyment, so he blames the caddy. But the caddy's response flips the tables and forces the golfer to recognize himself and his own failure as the source of his enjoyment. Golf is an enjoyable sport not because it doesn't frustrate the golfer but because it does. The absurd difficulty of the game is the source of its enjoyability, not a barrier to this enjoyability. The caddy's response demands that the golfer take responsibility for his own lack and for the enjoyment that this lack produces.

Taking responsibility for one's own enjoyment is what Christina Sharpe has in mind when she analyzes recent racist acts of violence. This is precisely what the racist act refuses but what antiracism must insist on. In *In the Wake*, Sharpe proclaims that "Michael Brown is Darren Wilson's projection, as the unknown Black man in Susan Smith's case is hers."[27] When Darren Wilson shot Michael Brown, he was shooting at his own form of enjoyment, not that of the racial other. And when Susan Smith invented a Black kidnapper of her children, she was conjuring up the threat that she posed to them (that resulted in their deaths). The consistent refusal to take up enjoyment as one's own is the major stumbling block for the antiracist project.

The enjoyment that fantasy delivers emanates from the position of nonbelonging. All the liberal efforts to increase belonging, to include everyone, will always run aground on the fact of universal nonbelonging and the enjoyment that nonbelonging produces. The political difficulty involves avowing the link between nonbelonging and enjoyment. Everyone consciously wants to belong, to feel like a success. But enjoyment depends on failure, not success. One enjoys the struggles at golf, not the great successes. Or the great successes provide pleasure only in light of the struggles, which nourish the underlying enjoyment. To recognize the enjoyment of nonbelonging is to give up the fantasy that others somehow have more capacity for enjoyment than I do. Antiracism means taking responsibility for one's own enjoyment.

Notes

Introduction

1   The first thinker to theorize the psychic importance of enjoyment is
    Jacques Lacan, who uses the French term *jouissance* to describe this
    phenomenon. For Lacan, enjoyment is what keeps people going, the
    fuel that the psyche uses to reproduce itself. Its status is thus much more
    fundamental than pleasure, which one can do without for extended
    periods of time. In his account of jouissance, Nestor Braunstein takes
    pains to distinguish it from pleasure, claiming that it is "now an excess
    intolerable to pleasure, now a manifestation of the body closer to
    extreme tension, pain and suffering." Nestor A. Braunstein, *Jouissance:
    A Lacanian Concept*, trans. Silvia Rosman (Albany: SUNY Press, 2020),
    14. There is no enjoyment without suffering. One always suffers one's
    enjoyment because enjoyment takes one beyond the terrain of the merely
    pleasurable.

2   The film's openly critical attitude toward racism led to a ban on its
    exhibition in South Africa and in certain Southern states in the United
    States.

3   *South Pacific* uses color filters and Vaseline on the lens to create a sense
    of enjoyment during the scenes that involve what happens on Bali Ha'i.
    As spectators, we are seeing into a psychic world beyond the social reality
    depicted in the rest of the film (without filters and Vaseline).

4   In her analysis of another Rodgers and Hammerstein musical, *Flower
    Drum Song* (Henry Koster, 1961), from the same period, Anne Anlin
    Cheng points out that this film shows how assimilation with the
    retention of difference—the professed American ideal—has the effect of
    erasing desirability. The Chinese American woman striving to assimilate
    in American society while maintaining her Chinese identity ceases to
    be a site of enjoyment in the film. The character of Helen Chao (Reiko
    Sato) seems to walk the line between the two cultures perfectly, but it
    is precisely her success at this that eliminates her as a romantic object.
    As Cheng points out, "Helen is the category celebrated as culturally

desirable throughout the movie but is in the end undesirable, because this is a world that is finally not very interested in witnessing the fulfillment of racial integration." Anne Anlin Cheng, *The Melancholy of Race: Psychoanalysis, Assimilation, and Hidden Grief* (Oxford: Oxford University Press, 2000), 60. To lose the sheen of radical otherness is to leave the terrain of enjoyment, which the racist fantasizes existing beyond the limits of the social structure.

5   See W. E. B. Du Bois, *Black Reconstruction in America* (New York: Free Press, 1992); Eric Williams, *Capitalism and Slavery*, 3rd ed. (Chapel Hill: University of North Carolina Press, 2021); Cedric Robinson, *Black Marxism: The Making of the Black Radical Tradition* (Chapel Hill: University of North Carolina Press, 2000); and Charisse Burden-Stelly, "Modern US Racial Capitalism: Some Theoretical Insights," *Monthly Review* 72.3 (2020): 8–20.

6   Cedric Robinson, *Black Marxism*, 237.

7   Achille Mbembe, *Necropolitics*, trans. Steve Corcoran (Durham: Duke University Press, 2019), 60.

8   Jean-Paul Sartre, *Being and Nothingness*, trans. Hazel E. Barnes (New York: Washington Square Press, 1956), 578.

9   Mahzarin Banaji and Anthony Greenwald, *Blindspot: Hidden Biases of Good People* (New York: Random House, 2013), 6.

10 For the most thorough attack on Freud for his failure to be properly scientific, see the work of ex-Freudian Frederick Crews, *Freud: The Making of an Illusion* (New York: Metropolitan Books, 2017).

11 Freud insists that one cannot simply treat unconscious ideas in the same way that one treats conscious ideas. One cannot correct the unconscious by straightforwardly providing someone with the proper idea. This is what Freud objects in his essay on what he calls "wild psychoanalysis." He writes, "If knowledge about the unconscious were as important for the patient as people inexperienced in psychoanalysis imagine, listening to lectures or reading books would be enough to cure him. Such measures, however, have as much influence on the symptoms of nervous illness as a distribution of menu-cards in a time of famine have upon hunger. The analogy goes even further than its immediate application; for informing the patient of his unconscious regularly results in an intensification of the conflict in him and an exacerbation of his troubles."

Sigmund Freud, "Wild Psycho-Analysis" (1910), trans. Joan Riviere, in *The Standard Edition of the Complete Psychological Works of Sigmund Freud*, vol. 11, ed. James Strachey (London: Hogarth Press, 1957), 225. If one tries to correct racist ideas by giving people better information, one inevitably fails because one does not touch the unconscious.

12   Jacques Lacan makes a few prophetic comments about a future increase in racism but provides no sustained analysis of how racism operates psychically. In the interview entitled *Television*, Lacan notes "certain fantasies" are bound to develop that would be "unheard of before the melting pot." Jacques Lacan, *Television*, trans. Denis Hollier, Rosalind Krauss, and Annette Michelson, ed. Joan Copjec (New York: Norton, 1990), 32.

13   David L. Eng and Shinhee Han, *Racial Melancholia, Racial Dissociation: On the Social and Psychic Lives of Asian Americans* (Durham: Duke University Press, 2019), 21.

14   One would expect that a collection entitled *The Psychoanalysis of Race* would provide major insights into the role that the unconscious plays in racism. But that is not what one finds in the book. Despite the many essays dealing with a wide range of topics, no essay included in the collection tries to advance a psychoanalytic theory of racism. Most remain committed to the analysis of particular instances and don't attempt to address how racism as such functions. Perhaps the problem begins with the title that addresses *race* rather than *racism*. See Christopher Lane, ed., *The Psychoanalysis of Race* (New York: Columbia University Press, 1998). The one exception is Slavoj Žižek's essay, which does put forward a theory of racism linked to fantasy, but even here, Žižek devotes only a limited amount of the essay to theorizing racism. See Slavoj Žižek, "Love Thy Neighbor? No, Thanks!" in *The Psychoanalysis of Race*, ed. Christopher Lane (New York: Columbia University Press, 1998), 154–75.

15   See Hortense J. Spillers, "'All the Things You Could Be by Now, If Sigmund Freud's Wife Was Your Mother': Psychoanalysis and Race," *Boundary 2* 23.3 (1996): 75–141.

16   David Marriott, *Haunted Life: Visual Culture and Black Modernity* (New Brunswick, NJ: Rutgers University Press, 2007), 223.

17   See David Marriott, *Lacan Noir: Lacan and Afropessimism* (New York: Palgrave, 2021); Anne Anlin Cheng, *Ornamentalism* (Oxford: Oxford

University Press, 2019); David Eng, *Racial Castration: Managing Masculinity in Asian America* (Durham: Duke University Press, 2001); Kalpana Seshadri-Crooks, *Desiring Whiteness: A Lacanian Analysis of Race* (New York: Routledge, 2000); and Antonio Viego, *Dead Subjects: Toward a Politics of Loss in Latino Studies* (Durham: Duke University Press, 2007).

18   Sheldon George, *Trauma and Race: A Lacanian Study of African American Racial Identity* (Waco, TX: Baylor University Press, 2016), 8. For more psychoanalytic theorization of racism, see also George's coedited collection, Sheldon George and Derek Hook, eds., *Lacan and Race: Racism, Identity, and Psychoanalytic Theory* (New York: Routledge, 2021).

19   Hortense Spillers describes how this excessive sexualization functions during American slavery. In her epochal essay "Mama's Baby, Papa's Maybe: An American Grammar Book," she writes that under slavery "the captive body becomes the source of an irresistible, destructive sensuality" and that "the captured sexualities provide a physical and biological expression of 'otherness.'" Hortense J. Spillers, "Mama's Baby, Papa's Maybe: An American Grammar Book," *Diacritics* 17.2 (1987): 67. The point of departure for Spillers' essay is the Moynihan Report, which laments the dominance of the woman and the failure of the Law of the Father in African American family life. As Spillers shows, this influential document of the 1960s remains ensconced in the racist fantasy structure that prevailed during slavery.

20   Slavoj Žižek delves into the political function of fantasy and often focuses on antisemitism, but he does not go into detail about the structure of the racist fantasy and its ramifications. See Slavoj Žižek, *A Plague of Fantasies* (London: Verso, 1997).

21   Jennifer Friedlander argues that dissipating the power of the racist fantasy requires a radical act. She writes that "the Act performs the ethical task of facilitating an impossible identification with both the Symbolic fiction and intrusions of the meaningless Real. Such a position resists reincorporation into the fantasy of Symbolic closure." Jennifer Friedlander, "In Medium Race: Traversing the Fantasy of Post-Race Discourse," in *Lacan and Race: Racism, Identity, and Psychoanalytic Theory*, ed. Sheldon George and Derek Hook (New York: Routledge,

2021), 117. For Friedlander, one principal danger of the racist fantasy is that it obfuscates the necessary failure of the symbolic structure and causes us to misread the field of possibilities as closed rather than as open.

Chapter 1

1   Jacques Lacan describes fantasy as a relationship between the subject and what he calls the objet a, which is his name for the obstacle that acts as a cause of desire (although he never precisely names it as an obstacle). He states, "The fantasy is the relation between the object *a*—which is what is concentrated through the effect of discourse in order to cause desire—and this something that is condensed around it, as a split, and which is called the subject." Jacques Lacan, *The Seminar of Jacques Lacan, Book XIX:... or Worse*, trans. A. R. Price, ed. Jacques-Alain Miller (Medford, MA: Polity, 2018), 205–6. Lacan contrasts the objet a, which causes desire, with the object of desire, which is what the objet a renders desirable, in order to indicate how we require an obstacle in order to find an object desirable. As Lacan rightly sees it, there is no direct desire for an object. Without the obstacle created by the objet a, the object of desire ceases to be the object of desire.

2   I will use the term *racial other* rather than the more common *racialized other* because there are versions of the racist fantasy in which the racial other is specifically deprived of being a race at all. It is the absence of racialization that defines racial otherness. This is what transpires in the Nazi fantasy of the Jew. In the speech that he made just after *Kristallnacht*, Nazi leader Jules Streciher articulates the party's standard fantasmatic line that Jewishness is not a race, that there is no such thing as Jewish blood. He states, "We know that the Jew received his blood from all the races of the world. Negro blood, Mongolian blood, Nordic blood, Indian blood—the blood of all races flows in this bastard race. As the old German proverb has it: 'He who has mixed blood in his veins follows the worst direction.' That means that he is forced to do wrong. He who has pure blood has a single soul; he who has mixed blood has a divided soul. Sometimes he obeys the good blood, sometimes the

bad. As a bastard, the Jew always follows the dictates of his bad blood." Jules Streicher, "Speech after the Night of Broken Glass," in *Landmark Speeches of National Socialism*, ed. Randall L. Bytwerk (College Station: Texas A&M University Press, 2008), 88. In the Nazi fantasy scenario, Jewishness represents an obstacle to German enjoyment because it is a racial other that is not properly racialized. Jews are what Hitler himself calls a nonrace.

3   The role that scarcity plays in fantasy suggests that scarcity is primarily fantasmatic. Obviously, there are some situations of real scarcity, but often when defenders of capitalism have recourse to natural scarcity, they do so in order to justify capitalist relations of production, not because natural scarcity exists.

4   In the *Wissenschaftslehre*, Fichte lays out why one needs the obstacle. He writes, "The activity of the self consists in unbounded self-assertion: to this there occurs a resistance. If it yielded to this obstacle, then the activity lying beyond the bounds of resistance would be utterly abolished and destroyed; to that extent the self would not posit at all." J. G. Fichte, *The Science of Knowledge*, trans. Peter Heath and John Lachs (Cambridge: Cambridge University Press, 1982), 192. Without the obstacle, as Fichte sees it, no activity of the subject would be possible. The emphasis on the centrality of the *Anstoss* is Fichte's great theoretical contribution and provides, in a sense, the basis for the development of the entire Hegelian dialectical system.

5   The current English translation of the *Wissenschaftslehre* translates *Anstoss*, for better or worse, as "check."

6   It is probably not surprising that the theorist responsible for the discovery of the *Anstoss* was also a German ethnic nationalist who preached anti-Semitism. Although he recognized the centrality of the obstacle, Fichte could not bring himself to see it as structural when thinking about politics. He could not resist the temptation to see the racial other in the position of the obstacle to the constitution of the German nation.

7   This lack of any intrinsic value in the fantasy object becomes apparent when an object drops out of its position within the fantasy. For instance, when we stop fantasizing about a potential love object, all of a sudden it ceases to have any appeal at all.

8   As Juan-David Nasio puts it, "The function of the fantasy is to substitute
     for an impossible real satisfaction a possible fantasized satisfaction."
     Juan-David Nasio, *Le Fantasme: Le plaisir de lire Lacan* (Paris: Petite
     Bibliothèque Payot, 2005), 13.

9   Jacques Lacan, *Le Séminaire XIV: La logique du fantasme, 1966–1967*,
     unpublished manuscript, January 11, 1967.

10   Alfred Hitchcock undoubtedly understood that the obstacle was the
     star of the fantasy. It led him to make his famous remark, "The more
     successful the villain, the more successful the picture." Qtd. in François
     Truffaut, *Hitchcock: The Definitive Study of Alfred Hitchcock by François
     Truffaut*, rev. ed. (New York: Simon and Schuster, 1985), 191.

11   Toni Morrison, *Playing in the Dark: Whiteness and the Literary
     Imagination* (New York: Vintage, 1993), 59.

12   We can recognize the logic of the racist fantasy on ancestry.com. Those
     who are blandly white seek out this website in order to find a hint of
     the racial other in their genetic background. In this way, they hope to
     partake of the enjoyment associated with this figure. Please don't see
     ancestry.com.

13   In *Tarrying with the Negative*, Slavoj Žižek makes his definitive statement
     on the psychic structure of racism. It involves a relationship to the other
     that sees in this figure an obscene enjoyment that cuts off our own. He
     states, "We always impute to the 'other' an excessive enjoyment: he wants
     to steal our enjoyment (by ruining our way of life) and/or he has access
     to some secret, perverse enjoyment. In short, what really bothers us
     about the 'other' is the peculiar way he organizes his enjoyment, precisely
     the surplus, the 'excess' that pertains to this way: the smell of 'their' food,
     'their' noisy songs and dances, 'their' strange manners, 'their' attitude
     toward work." Slavoj Žižek, *Tarrying with the Negative: Kant, Hegel, and
     the Critique of Ideology* (Durham: Duke University Press, 1993), 203.
     What Žižek doesn't add here is that it is through figuring the other's
     enjoyment in this way that we fantasize our own. We have no enjoyment
     of our own outside our relationship to the other's.

14   Adolf Hitler, *Mein Kampf*, trans. Ralph Manheim (Boston: Houghton
     Mifflin, 1971), 325. Hitler is not conscious that this is a fantasy. He
     believes that he is recounting the actual state of things, unaware that
     what he sees has been underwritten by an unconscious racist fantasy.

15 As Derek Hook points out, "There is no such thing as a stand-alone (or purely affective) instance of racist jouissance. There are only distributions, patterns, *arrangements* of racist enjoyment that are structured by fantasy." Derek Hook, "Racism," in *Routledge Handbook of Psychoanalytic Political Theory*, ed. Yannis Stravrakakis (London: Routledge, 2019), 280–1.

16 Karen E. Fields and Barbara J. Fields, *Racecraft: The Soul of Inequality in American Life* (London: Verso, 2012), 96–7. While it might appear at first glance that the Fields advocate a colorblind response to racism because they reject the existence of race, they actually see colorblindness as the refusal to see racism. Their idea is that one must recognize one's own perception of race as the effect of racism and then make that the occasion for the struggle against this social deformation. Colorblindness is an attempt to change the world by closing one's eyes.

17 The insistence on the facticity of racial difference, even if located in culture rather than in biology, has the effect of obscuring the role that capitalism plays in the formation of racial difference. As Touré Reed puts it, "Constructs like underclass ideology, diversity and even intersectionality have helped to displace class-based analyses of race and inequality by reifying culture—uncoupling social relations from their proximate environmental influences." Touré F. Reed, *Toward Freedom: The Case against Race Reductionism* (London: Verso, 2020), 50. The turn from biology to culture as a means of explanation for racial difference can leave the racist fantasy structure fully intact.

18 There is nothing necessary about the role that race plays in the organization of enjoyment. We might just as easily use religion or sexual orientation as the foundational fantasy for contemporary society's distribution of enjoyment. Race plays the leading role for contingent reasons, although there are parts of the world where religion predominates and has the decisive role in the fantasy.

19 Sheldon George, *Trauma and Race: A Lacanian Study of African American Racial Identity*, 4.

20 James Baldwin approaches this phenomenon in *The Fire Next Time*. He claims, "The white man's unadmitted—and apparently, to him, unspeakable—private fears and longings are projected onto the Negro." James Baldwin, *The Fire Next Time* (New York: Vintage, 1962), 96.

Racists see in the racial other precisely what their recoil from in themselves—their own form of enjoyment. But the fantasy isn't so much a projection as a discovery for racists. They discover their own enjoyment through what they fantasize in the racial other.

21 Frantz Fanon, *Black Skin, White Masks*, trans. Richard Philcox (New York: Grove Press, 2008), 154.

22 Achille Mbembe, *Necropolitics*, trans. Steve Corcoran (Durham: Duke University Press, 2019), 62.

23 Saidiya V. Hartman, *Scenes of Subjection: Terror, Slavery, and Self-Making in Nineteenth-Century America* (Oxford: Oxford University Press, 1997), 22–3.

24 One often sees people attack the targets of racism for "playing the victim." But if one takes the racist fantasy into account, it is always the racist that plays the victim. The enjoyment of the racist fantasy depends on the racist subject's self-victimization, a process enacted through the structure of the fantasy.

25 Malcolm X (with Alex Haley), *The Autobiography of Malcolm X* (New York: Ballantine, 1964), 138.

26 Malcolm X, *The Autobiography of Malcolm X*, 139. Malcolm X found himself too light-skinned to work for this pimp. He failed to occupy adequately the correct position within the fantasy.

27 When *Do the Right Thing* came out in 1989, it was a novelty on American screens. Not only were films from Black directors rare, but even rarer was a film that explored the damage that the racist fantasy did to those caught up in it. Although some of the Blaxploitation films of the 1970s did do this, their emphasis on Black sexuality, violence, and drug use often confirmed the racist fantasy as much as challenged it. *Do the Right Thing* marks a turning point, inaugurating the New Black Cinema of the 1990s, a cinema that included a number of films committed to taking on the racist fantasy.

28 Lee's satirical treatment of Buggin' Out's protest rubs Douglas Kellner the wrong way. He proclaims, "Lee presents racism in personal and individualist terms as hostility among members of different groups, thus failing to illuminate the causes and structures of racism. Moreover, the film denigrates political action, caricaturing collective action and the tactic of the economic boycott, which served the Civil Rights movement

so well." Douglas Kellner, "Aesthetics, Ethics and Politics in the Films of Spike Lee," in Mark A. Reid, *Spike Lee's* Do the Right Thing (Cambridge: Cambridge University Press, 1997), 82. What Kellner misses is Lee's critique of the violence that the racist fantasy produces, a critique that is not beset by the middle-class liberalism that Kellner identifies with Lee's politics.

29 For a more extensive analysis of *Do the Right Thing* and the rest of Spike Lee's cinematic output, see Todd McGowan, *Spike Lee* (Urbana: University of Illinois Press, 2014).

30 Edward Said, *Orientalism* (New York: Vintage, 1978), 190.

31 In *Civilizations and Its Discontents*, Freud explores how enjoyment renders life within society inherently contradictory and almost completely unworkable. The discontented are not just those that society leaves behind but everyone, insofar as fitting in is an impossible task. See Sigmund Freud, *Civilization and Its Discontents*, trans. James Strachey, in *The Standard Edition of the Complete Psychological Works of Sigmund Freud*, vol. 21, ed. James Strachey (London: Hogarth, 1961), 57–145.

32 Jacques Lacan, *Le Séminaire XIII: L'objet de la psychanalyse, 1965–1966*, unpublished seminar, session of 27 April 1966.

33 We constantly attempt to avoid confronting our own enjoyment. This is a point that Alenka Zupančič makes in *Ethics of the Real*. She writes, "It is not simply the mode of enjoyment of the neighbour, of the other, that is strange to me. The heart of the problem is that I experience my own enjoyment (which emerges along with the enjoyment of the other, and is even indissociable from it) as strange and hostile." Alenka Zupančič, *Ethics of the Real: Kant, Lacan* (New York: Verso, 2000), 225. The lasting appeal of the racist fantasy is that it helps me to avoid recognizing my own enjoyment as "strange to me" because I attribute my enjoyment to the racial other.

34 Even though the structure of the racist fantasy is masochistic—the subject doesn't enjoy while the racial other does—racist acts are inherently sadistic. This inverse relation between the fantasy and its effects on social reality, while it is commonplace, disguises the psychic structure at work in racism.

35 Although a French court overturned the Burkini ban after the public outcry, many areas in France have left their bans in place or erected them

despite this verdict. Courts are often powerless against the tug of the enjoyment that racism produces.

36 James Wolfreys, *Republic of Islamophobia: The Rise of Respectable Racism in France* (Oxford: Oxford University Press, 2018), 30.

37 Although C. L. R. James draws attention to the solidarity that often formed during the Haitian Revolution in *The Black Jacobins*, he also describes the racism that those with lighter skin experience against those who are darker. He writes, "Even while in words and, by their success in life, in many of their actions, Mulattoes demonstrated the falseness of the white claim to inherent superiority, yet the man of colour who was nearly white despised the man of colour who was only half-white, who in turn despised the man of colour who was only quarter white, and so on through all the shades." C. L. R. James, *The Black Jacobins: Toussaint L'Ouverture and the San Domingo Revolution*, 2nd ed. rev. (New York: Random House, 1963), 43. Those with lighter skin saw their darker compatriots as barriers to their own enjoyment, despite hating this fantasy among whites.

38 The prevalence of the racist fantasy helps to explain why Black civil rights leader Louis Farrakhan went so far as to embrace Donald Trump, despite his unapologetic racism. During the 2016 U. S. Presidential campaign, Farrakhan praised Donald Trump for the position that he took up relative to Jews. He celebrated Trump as "the only member who has stood in front of the Jewish community and said, 'I don't want your money.'" Qtd. in Nolan D. McCaskill, "Louis Farrakhan Praises Donald Trump," *Politico* (1 March 2016): https://www.politico.com/blogs/2016-gop-primary-live-updates-and-results/2016/03/louis-farrakhan-donald-trump–220021. Trump actually ran the most pro-Israel administration since Israel's formation, and yet Farrakhan's investment in the racist fantasy that placed Jews in the position of the racial other permitted him to see a fellow traveler in Trump.

Chapter 2

1 When it comes to racism, Derrida would not just refuse the binary of the racist subject and the racial other, he would also question the idea that

there could be a single racist fantasy. For Derrida, every phenomenon is multiple phenomena. There is no one racist fantasy but multiple racisms. This becomes clear in his brief essay on South African apartheid, in which he insists on the plural to describe racism. See Jacques Derrida, "Racism's Last Word," trans. Peggy Kamuf, *Critical Inquiry* 12.1 (1985): 290–9.

2   Jacques Derrida, *Positions*, trans. Alan Bass (Chicago: University of Chicago Press, 1981), 41.

3   One area where Derrida clearly rejects the binary opposition is the relationship between the human and the animal. In fact, Derrida critiques any discussion of such a relationship because he refuses to group all animals under the category of *animal* in the binary. He states, "one will never have the right to take animals to be the species of a kind that would be named The Animal, or animal in general." Jacques Derrida, *The Animal That Therefore I Am*, trans. David Wills, ed. Marie-Louise Mallet (New York: Fordham University Press, 2008), 31. This is Derrida's approach to what others have called speciesism.

4   One of the leading proponents of cosmopolitanism is Kwame Anthony Appiah. He envisions cosmopolitanism as a philosophy that imagines the possibility of getting along by accommodating radical differences in belief by focusing on how ways of acting actually converge. This leads Appiah to claim, "cosmopolitanism is, in a slogan, universality plus difference." Kwame Anthony Appiah, *Cosmopolitanism: Ethics in a World of Strangers* (New York: Norton, 2006), 151. Appiah's emphasis on a multitude of differences follows from the overcoming of the conception of race in terms of a binary opposition.

5   Gilles Deleuze and Félix Guattari, *A Thousand Plateaus: Capitalism and Schizophrenia*, trans. Brian Massumi (Minneapolis: University of Minnesota Press, 1987), 379. Thinkers indebted to Deleuze and Guattari who discuss race more thoroughly tend to take up the concern for racial multiplicity at the expense of the binary structure of racism. This is evident in the thought of Arun Saldanha. Clarifying the priority that racial multiplicity has in Deleuze and Guattari's thought, Saldanha writes, "The impurities and politics of *race* exceed the purification programmes of *racism*." Arun Saldanha, "Bastard and Mixed-Blood Are the True Names of Race," in *Deleuze and Race*, ed. Arun Saldanha and

Jason Michael Adams (Edinburgh: Edinburgh University Press, 2013),
17. The emphasis on multiplicity is apparent from the title of Saldanha's
essay, with its mention of "bastard" and "mixed-blood."

6   Frank Wilderson laments the turn to more complexity in thinking
about oppressive relations. By moving away from the binary opposition,
he argues, one turns antagonism into conflict and thereby represses
antagonism. He claims, "it is hardly fashionable anymore to think the
vagaries of power through the generic positions within a structure
of power relations—such as man/woman, worker/boss. Instead, the
academy's ensembles of questions are fixated on specific and 'unique'
experiences of the myriad identities that make up those structural
positions." Frank Wilderson, *Red, White, and Black: Cinema and the
Structure of U. S. Antagonisms* (Durham: Duke University Press, 2010),
6. According to Wilderson, the turn away from these binary oppositions
also implies a failure to talk about the structural problem itself.

7   Paul Gilroy, *Against Race: Imagining Political Culture beyond the Color
Line* (Cambridge: Harvard University Press, 2000), 37.

8   Karen E. Fields and Barbara J. Fields, *Racecraft: The Soul of Inequality in
American Life* (London: Verso, 2012), 95.

9   This is the problem with the liberal dream of eliminating racism
through widespread interracial relationships that would produce racially
indistinct offspring. The silent presupposition of this dream is that we
have racism as a result of racial difference, but the causality operates
in the other direction: racism will always find a way to create racial
difference, regardless of how things actually are. To this end, one of the
targets that Karen and Barbara Fields take on in *Racecraft* is that of a
supposed mixed race identity. As they point out, this fiction of interracial
mixing exists only to convince people that race is actual, that there is
such a thing as racial purity.

10   The attack on President Juvénal Habyarimana's plane played the same
role in Rwanda that the Reichstag Fire played in Nazi Germany. We still
do not know with any certainty the culprit for either event, and both
events led directly to draconian racist measures—the Rwandan genocide
and the passing of the Reichstag Fire Decree, which enabled the mass
arrest of communists and the cementing of Nazi political power. Even
though both regimes interpreted these events as attacks, they served

a vital function within the racist fantasy because they showed that the racial other was a threat to the enjoyment of the racist subjects in power.

11 Qtd. in Barrie Collins, *Rwanda 1994: The Myth of the Akuza Genocide Conspiracy and Its Consequences* (New York: Palgrave Macmillan, 2014), 161.

12 As Dale Tatum puts it in his account of the genocide, "The Hutus who believed this fictitious appeal believed that it was simply a matter of 'kill or be killed' by the Tutsis. So, they launched preemptive attacks that they believed were acts of self-defense." Dale C. Tatum, *Genocide at the Dawn of the 21st Century: Rwanda, Bosnia, Kosovo, and Darfur* (New York: Palgrave Macmillan, 2010), 42.

13 Whenever someone invokes ancient ethnic conflicts to make sense of contemporary violence, we can be sure that they are providing ideological cover for the aggressors. Ancient ethnic conflicts only exist insofar as we take them up in the current struggle. We always have the ability to change the political valence of the past, no matter how entrenched it seems to be.

14 Scott Straus, *The Order of Genocide: Race, Power, and War in Rwanda* (Ithaca: Cornell University Press, 2006), 21.

15 Mahmood Mamdani, *When Victims Become Killers: Colonialism, Nativism, and the Genocide in Rwanda* (Princeton: Princeton University Press, 2001), 56.

16 J. Charles Schenking describes the scale of the destruction that the earthquake unleashed: "Within one week, the magnitude 7.9 earthquake, fires, and aftershocks destroyed over 45 percent of the structures in Tokyo and over 90 percent of the structures in Yokohama. Economic costs of the calamity surpassed over 6.5 billion Yen, a figure four times larger than Japan's national budget for 1923." J. Charles Schenking, "The Great Kanto Earthquake and the Culture of Catastrophe and Reconstruction in 1920s Japan," *The Journal of Japanese Studies* 34.2 (2008): 296.

17 This strategy is apparent in the response of Donald Trump to the coronavirus pandemic. In order to both locate blame with the Chinese and to slur them at the same time, Trump often used the racist term *kung flu* to refer to the coronavirus. Despite the critique that the use of this term brought down on Trump, it was nonetheless a revelatory effort to

create an enemy in the face of the possible explosion of universality that the virus portended.

18 J. Michael Allen, "The Price of Identity: The 1923 Kanto Earthquake and Its Aftermath," *Korean Studies* 20 (1996): 66.

19 Byung Wook Jung, "Migrant Labor and Massacres: A Comparison of the 1923 Massacre of Koreans and Chinese during the Great Kanto Earthquake and the 1931 Anti-Chinese Riots and Massacre of Chinese in Colonial Korea," *Cross-Currents: East Asian History and Culture Review* 22 (2017): 45–6.

20 Sonia Ryang, "The Great Kanto Earthquake and the Massacre of Koreans: Notes on Japan's Modern National Sovereignty," *Anthropological Quarterly* 76.4 (2003): 736.

21 One cannot mark a clear and distinct break between blackface and brownface. The term *brownface* is used to refer to actors using dark make-up to impersonate someone who is dark-skinned but not signified as Black. This is much more prevalent in Bollywood than in Hollywood, where blackface was the rule.

22 One of the ironies of the use of blackface and brownface in Bollywood is that many of the stars of this cinema also appear in advertisements for skin-lightening products. For a detailed account of these advertisements and the conflict with the antiracist positions of the stars, see Alia Waheed, "Glamour, Glitz and Artificially Light Skin: Bollywood Stars in Their Own Racism Row," *The Guardian* (28 June 2020): https://www.theguardian.com/film/2020/jun/28/glamour-glitz-and-artificially-light-skin-bollywood-stars-in-their-own-racism-row.

23 Just as Orson Welles employed brownface in *Touch of Evil* (1958), so did Satyajit Ray in *Aranyer Din Ratri* (1970).

24 Rudolf Valentino was, of course, not Arab, and the first film does mention his European ancestry. Nonetheless, the film shows him passing for an Arab. The fact that an Italian could become the iconic representative of the exotic Arab indicates the purely fantasmatic quality of this figure and its distance from any realities of Arab existence.

25 Edward Said, *Orientalism* (New York: Vintage, 1978), 190.

26 The fantasy of the hypersexualized Arab man endures with full force through the 1980s and then abates in the 1990s. As Jack Shaheen notes in his encyclopedia of Hollywood's anti-Arab stereotyping, "The movies

of the 1980s are especially offensive. They display insolent desert sheikhs with thick accents threatening to rape and/or enslave starlets." Jack Shaheen, *Reel Bad Arabs: How Hollywood Villifites a People* (New York: Interlink Books, 2001), 22.

27 Robert A. Pape, *Dying to Win: The Strategic Logic of Suicide Terrorism* (New York: Random House, 2005), 23. Pape's view is not that of a sympathizer with the politics of Arab suicide bombers. He writes in order to help the United States "to win the war on terrorism." Robert A. Pape, *Dying to Win*, 7.

28 Novelle B. De Atkine, Foreword to *The Arab Mind*, rev. ed. (New York: Hatherleigh Press, 2002), x–xviii.

29 Seymour Hersh documents the importance of *The Arab Mind* for the neoconservative movement in general. See Seymour Hersh, "The Gray Zone: How a Secret Pentagon Program Came to Abu Ghraib," *The New Yorker* (24 May 2004): http://www.newyorker.com/ archive/2004/05/24/040524fa_fact.

30 Raphael Patai, *The Arab Mind*, rev. ed. (New York: Hatherleigh Press, 2002), 130.

31 Many journalists and theorists have made the connection between Patai's book and the torture at Abu Ghraib. For instance, Ann Marlowe notes, "There is no straight line from *The Arab Mind* to Abu Ghraib, or to the war in Iraq, but there is a suggestive trail," Ann Marlowe, "Sex, Violence and the Arab Mind," *Salon.com* (8 June 2004): http://dir.salon.com/story/ books/feature/2004/06/08/arab_mind.

32 For an account of the enjoyment at work in torture, see Hilary Neroni, *The Subject of Torture: Psychoanalysis and Biopolitics in Television and Film* (New York: Columbia University Press, 2015).

Chapter 3

1 Benjamin Isaac argues for the existence of racism in classical antiquity, but even he concedes that there is a radical difference between what he finds there and the modern version, which leads him to label what plagues antiquity "proto-racism." He writes, "Obviously, it did not exist in the modern form of a biological determinism which represents a

distortion of Darwin's ideas, nor was there systematic persecution of any ethnic group by another. However, I shall argue that it is justified to speak of 'proto-racism.'" Benjamin Isaac, *The Invention of Racism in Classical Antiquity* (Princeton: Princeton University Press, 2004), 5. Given the distance between how the Greeks and Romans conceived of otherness and modern racism, it seems inexact to employ the term.

2　We owe the term *barbarian* to the Greeks, for whom it denoted one who didn't speak Greek. The foreigner was often deemed to be inferior, but this inferiority was not tied to racial difference.

3　In contrast to racism, sexism seems to exist in both premodern and modern societies. But the nature of this sexism undergoes a change as it becomes modern. Unlike premodern societies, modernity creates the possibility that gender identity will count for nothing, that it will have no bearing on one's subjectivity. In traditional society, one simply is one's gender: gender identity is determinative, which is why there was no Judith Butler among the ancient Chinese or Greeks. After the modern break, it becomes possible to separate subjectivity from gender identity, as the existence of Cartesian philosopher François Poullain de la Barre attests. On the basis of Cartesian doubt, Poullain de la Barre rejects of notion of the biological inferiority of women and theorizes gender equality in 1673. See François Poullain de la Barre, *De l'égalité des deux sexes* (Paris: Folio, 2012).

4　To theorize the fantasmatic role that the idea of salvation plays in the Europe of the Middle Ages is not to take a position on the truth of the Christian doctrine. A doctrine can be absolutely true and nonetheless serve as the ruling fantasy of a social order.

5　In *Mein Kampf*, Hitler goes so far as to attack the anti-Semites that surrounded him as a youth for their lack of human tolerance. As he sees it, Jews are not at all defined by their religion. His hatred for them stems entirely from their status as a racial other. As he puts it, "the Mosaic religion is nothing other than a doctrine for the preservation of the Jewish race." Adolf Hitler, *Mein Kampf*, trans. Ralph Manheim (Boston: Houghton Mifflin, 1971), 150. The religion simply serves the race, not vice versa. Through this reversal, Hitler takes part in the vast modern project of transforming the site of discrimination from religion to racial identity. Even though the target remains the same—it's the Jews as a religious people and then as racial identity—the form of their oppression undergoes a complete shift.

6　Jean-Claude Milner, for one, insists on the radical difference in premodern and modern anti-Semitism. As he puts it, "There is thus no relation between the 'division' that the name Jew entails before Hitler and the division that it entails after Hitler." Jean-Claude Milner, *Clartés de tout: de Lacan à Marx, d'Aristote à Mao*, eds. Fabian Fjanwaks and Juan Pablo Lucchelli (Paris: Verdier, 2011), 175. The religious division associated with this name becomes a racial one.

7　René Descartes, *Discourse on the Method of Rightly Conducting One's Reason and Seeking the Truth in the Sciences*, trans. Robert Stoothoff, in *The Philosophical Writings of Descartes*, vol. 1 (Cambridge: Cambridge University Press, 1985), 119.

8　In his reply to his critics, Descartes claims that the native of Canada or the Hurons, whom his critics name as lacking the idea of God, actually have it in their own way. He writes, "As for those who deny that they have the idea of God, but in its place form some image etc., although they reject the name, they concede the reality." René Descartes, "Second Set of Replies," in *The Philosophical Writings of Descartes*, vol. 2, trans. John Cottingham, Robert Stoothoff, and Dugald Murdoch (Cambridge: Cambridge University Press, 1984), 99. Descartes refuses to give any philosophical significance to the idea of racial difference.

9　According to Henry Louis Gates Jr., Descartes nonetheless paves the way for racism because of the way that he privileges reason. The racist can subsequently deny reason to nonwhites and thereby justify racism. Gates points out that in the aftermath of Descartes, many Enlightenment thinkers "simultaneously used the absence and presence of reason to delimit and circumscribe the very humanity of the cultures and people of color which Europeans had been 'discovering' since the Renaissance." Henry Louis Gates Jr., "Writing 'Race' and the Difference It Makes," in *"Race," Writing, and Difference*, ed. Henry Louis Gates Jr. (Chicago: University of Chicago Press, 1986), 8. Reason becomes the hammer that Europeans employ to justify their racism. It should be said, however, that Descartes explicitly rejects the refusal to see all humans as inherently reasonable beings.

10　See René Descartes, *Meditations on First Philosophy*, trans. John Cottingham (Cambridge: Cambridge University Press, 1986).

11 Even prior to Descartes, Shakespeare inaugurates the modern epoch in 1600 with *Hamlet*. The radicality of this play consists in Hamlet's refusal to obey the dead father and instead to engage in a process of incessant questioning. The supposed problem of the play—Hamlet's inability to act—is actually the form that his action takes. Rather than acting like the son in a typical revenge tragedy and exactly the revenge that the father's death demands, Hamlet decides to find out for himself. This refusal to obey without questioning mirrors the attitude that Descartes takes up in philosophy. It reflects the absence of anyone to rely on, an absence that characterizes modernity.

12 Paul Gilroy, *Against Race: Imagining Political Culture beyond the Color Line* (Cambridge: Harvard University Press, 2000), 65.

13 For an examination of the role of racism in Western philosophy, see Robert Bernasconi with Sybol Cook, eds., *Race and Racism in Continental Philosophy* (Bloomington: Indiana University Press, 2003); Andrew Valls, ed. *Race and Racism in Modern Philosophy* (Ithaca: Cornell University Press, 2005); and Peter K. J. Park, *Africa, Asia, and the History of Philosophy: Racism in the Formation of the Philosophical Canon, 1780–1830* (Albany: SUNY Press, 2013).

14 Heidegger's infamous support for Nazism stems directly from his fear of the spirit of the Jewish world taking over the world. In his private writing, he uses the same word for world Jewry—*Weltjudentum*—that the Nazis constantly employ.

15 Charles W. Mills, *The Racial Contract* (Ithaca: Cornell University Press, 1997), 16.

16 Immanuel Kant, "Of the Different Races of Human Beings," trans. Holly Wilson and Günther Zöller, in *Anthropology, History, and Education*, ed. Günther Zöller and Robert B. Louden (New York: Cambridge University Press, 2007), 93. Just after this remark, Kant adds, "humid warmth is beneficial to the growth of animals in general and, in short, this results in the Negro, who is well suited to his climate, namely strong, fleshy, supple, but who, given the abundant provision of his mother land, is lazy, soft and trifling." Immanuel Kant, "Of the Different Races of Human Beings," 93. This essay contains Kant's most egregious racist speculation, although it is not the only place where this tendency crops up.

17 The comments from his essay on race are not the end of Kant's racist speculations. They also appear in his treatise *Observations on the Feeling*

of the Beautiful and Sublime. Here, Kant brings up the opinion of a "Negro carpenter," an opinion he begins to credit just before saying, "There might be something here worth considering, except for the fact that this scoundrel was completely black from head to foot, a distinct proof that what he said was stupid." Immanuel Kant, "*Observations on the Feeling of the Beautiful and Sublime*," trans. Paul Guyer, in *Anthropology, History and Education*, ed. Günter Zöller and Robert B. Louden (Cambridge: Cambridge University Press, 2007), 61. Kant makes a direct appeal of racism and calls it an argument, despite the fact that it isn't one at all. Although both of these examples of Kant's racism come prior to the critical turn in 1781 when Kant becomes Kant, there is no evidence to suggest that his critique of the over-extension of reason or his discovery of the categorical imperative ameliorates the racism that he expresses in these earlier works. As a matter of fact, the evidence points in the opposite direction, especially when one considers that Kant includes a racist joke at the expense of an Indian in the 1790 *Critique of the Power of Judgment*. The joke goes as follows: "If someone tells this story: An Indian, at the table of an Englishman in Surat, seeing a bottle of ale being opened and all the beer, transformed into foam, spill out, displayed his great amazement with many exclamations, and in reply to the Englishman's question 'What is so amazing here?' answered, 'I'm not amazed that it's coming out, but by how you got it all in,' we laugh, and it gives us a hearty pleasure: not because we find ourselves cleverer than this ignorant person, or because of any other pleasing thing that the understanding allows us to note here, but because our expectation was heightened and suddenly disappeared into nothing." Immanuel Kant, *Critique of the Power of Judgment*, trans. Paul Guyer and Eric Matthews (Cambridge: Cambridge University Press, 2000), 209. Even though Kant claims here that the ignorance of the Indian is not the source of the humor in the joke, it is nonetheless part of the enjoyment that the joke delivers for Kant, which is the index of its racism.

18   In his magisterial interpretation of Kant's morality, Henry Allison recognizes the great breakthrough of the *Critique of Practical Reason*. In this work, Kant discovers a proof for our freedom, which he had not yet formulated in the earlier *Groundwork of the Metaphysics of Morals*. But nowhere in his discussion does Allison addresses Kant's racism.

See Henry E. Allison, *Kant's Theory of Freedom* (Cambridge: Cambridge University Press, 1990).

19 In *Culture and Imperialism*, Edward Said laments the inability of ideals of equality to impact the project of British imperialism. He writes, "it is genuinely troubling to see how little Britain's great humanistic ideas, institutions, and monuments, which we still celebrate as having the power ahistorically to command our approval, how little they stand in the way of the accelerating imperial process." Edward Said, *Culture and Imperialism* (New York: Vintage, 1993), 82. While Said's analysis is undoubtedly correct, what he doesn't discuss here is the role that fantasy plays in the imperial process that he diagnoses.

20 Achille Mbembe, *Critique of Black Reason*, trans. Laurent Dubois (Durham: Duke University Press, 2017), 54. Along the same lines, Paul Gilroy points out how the idea of race enables us to believe in a hierarchy that would totter without this ideological support. He states, "the 'race' idea is powerful precisely because it supplies a foundational understanding of natural hierarchy on which a host of other supplementary social and political conflicts have come to rely. Race remains the self-evident force of nature in society." Paul Gilroy, *Postcolonial Melancholia* (New York: Columbia University Press, 2005), 8. Race works to provide this sense of hierarchy because it appears empirically self-evident. One simply looks and sees race everywhere as a plain fact. Efforts to say that there is no such thing meet up with the barrier of the fact that I trust my eyes. But this trust has its psychic basis not in empiricist philosophy but in the racist fantasy. This is the ubiquitous invisible support that props up the apparent visibility of race.

21 Thomas Jefferson, *Autobiography, 1743–1790*, in *Thomas Jefferson Writings* (New York: Library of America, 1984), 22.

22 Thomas Jefferson, *Notes on the State of Virginia*, in *Thomas Jefferson Writings* (New York: Library of America, 1984), 265.

23 Thomas Jefferson, *Notes on the State of Virginia*, 265.

24 In *After Finitude*, Quentin Meillassoux describes the process of God losing his authoritative status as the emergence of a general fideism. As he puts it, "The destruction of the metaphysical rationalization of Christian theology has resulted in a generalized becoming-religious of thought, viz., in *a fideism of any belief whatsoever*." Quentin Meillassoux,

After Finitude: An Essay on the Necessity of Contingency, trans. Ray
Brassier (New York: Continuum, 2008), 46. What Meillassoux doesn't
see—perhaps because of his own investment in it—is that the one point
at which this fideism stops is at the authority of biology. Biology now
functions in the way that God once did.

25   Karen E. Fields and Barbara J. Fields, *Racecraft: The Soul of Inequality in
American Life* (London: Verso, 2012), 40.

26   See Angela Saini, *Superior: The Return of Race Science* (Boston: Beacon
Press, 2019).

27   It is not just racism that biology supports. As Mari Ruti shows in *The Age
of Scientific Sexism*, thinkers today marshal biology in the service of their
sexism. She claims, "the more modern men and women deviate from the
evolutionary mantra, the more desperately (some) evolutionary thinkers
seem to want to assert it as the 'truth' about human nature." Mari Ruti,
The Age of Scientific Sexism (New York: Bloomsbury, 2015), 11. Ruti notes
that while today most biologists go out of their way to deny the reality
of race, they fervently maintain the biological reality of sexual difference
and insist on its ramifications for modern life.

28   Adrian Desmond and James Moore make Darwin's opposition to slavery
into a motivating force for writing *The Origin of the Species* in 1859.
They go so far as to say that he rushed it into publication in order to
help turn the United States against its slaveholders. The problem is that
the evidence for this claim is quite thin, despite the fact that Desmond
and Moore have written a hefty book devoted to supporting it. They do
at least show that Darwin conceived of himself as an antiracist and that
he did not see his work as a possible support for racist ideas. For their
account, see Adrian Desmond and James Moore, *Darwin's Sacred Cause:
How a Hatred of Slavery Shaped Darwin's Views on Human Evolution*
(New York: Houghton Mifflin Harcourt, 2009).

29   Charles Darwin, *The Descent of Man, and Selection in Relation to Sex,
Part I, Volume 21*, eds. Paul H. Barrett and R. B. Freeman (New York:
New York University Press, 1989), 133.

30   Further along in *The Descent of Man*, Darwin begins to speculate about
the impact of the theory of natural selection on eugenics. He writes, "we
build asylums for the imbecile, the maimed, and the sick; we institute
poor-laws; and our medical men exert their utmost skill to save the

life of every one to the last moment. There is reason to believe that vaccination has preserved thousands, who from a weak constitution would formerly have succumbed to small-pox. Thus the weak members of civilized society propagate their kind. No one who has attended to the breeding of domestic animals will doubt that this must be highly injurious to the race of man. It is surprising how soon a want of care, or care wrongly directed, leads to the degeneration of a domestic race; but excepting in the case of man himself, hardly anyone is so ignorant as to allow his worst animals to breed." Charles Darwin, *The Descent of Man*, 139. Darwin's belief in degeneration leads to this statement that sounds almost exactly like the lament of a Social Darwinist.

31 André Pichot, *The Pure Society: From Darwin to Hitler*, trans. David Fernbach (New York: Verso, 2009), 256.

32 Pichot explores the link between Darwin and capitalism, but this link has not received near the attention that it deserves. The fact that reading Thomas Robert Malthus's *An Essay on Population* played a crucial role in helping him to conceive of natural selection should be proclaimed loudly when one talks about the theory. Natural selection has its basis in the idea of an existential scarcity of resources and an inevitable struggle between beings to gather as much of those resources as possible. The parallel between this image of natural life and the image of life theorized by the exponents of capitalism is not simply an accident. The theory of natural selection is the theory of a capitalist thinker. This doesn't mean that it doesn't have any validity but just that we should measure its validity in this context.

33 Dorothy Roberts, *Fatal Invention: How Science, Politics, and Big Business Re-Create Race in the 21st Century* (New York: New Press, 2011), 52.

34 In *Race Decoded*, Catherine Bliss names this position *antiracist racialism*. She chronicles how widespread it has become among genetic researchers. Bliss writes, "What I call antiracist racialism, or the idea that there is no rank to races but that there are nevertheless discrete populations worth studying, now prevails across science and society." Catherine Bliss, *Race Decoded: The Genomic Fight for Social Justice* (Stanford: Stanford University Press, 2012), 15–16. The popular idea that there are distinct races existing in a nonhierarchical relation with each other prevails in a significant number of geneticists.

35 Octave Manoni, "'I Know Well, But All the Same …'" trans. G. M. Goshgarian, in *Perversion and the Social Relation*, eds. Molly Anne Rothenberg, Dennis Foster, and Slavoj Žižek (Durham: Duke University Press, 2003), 70.

36 In *Seminar XI*, Lacan provides a justification for the psychoanalytic intervention in these terms. He says, "It is clear that those with whom we deal, the patients, are not satisfied, as one says, with what they are. And yet, we know that everything they are, everything they experience, even their symptoms, involves satisfaction. … Let us say that, for this sort of satisfaction, they give themselves too much trouble. Up to a point, it is this *too much trouble* that is the sole justification of our intervention." Jacques Lacan, *The Seminar of Jacques Lacan, Book XI: The Four Fundamental Concepts of Psychoanalysis*, trans. Alan Sheridan, ed. Jacques-Alain Miller (New York: Norton, 1978) 166. We could think about antiracist politics in just this way.

37 Milton Friedman, *Capitalism and Freedom* (Chicago: University of Chicago Press, 2002), 21.

38 The problem with Friedman's thesis is not confined to its failure to consider the racist fantasy. It also doesn't take into account the effect of prejudices that are so widespread that playing into them helps one's profitability rather than harming it. In the Jim Crow American South, for instance, the decision to serve Black customers at one's restaurant might have the effect of alienating all potential white customers, thereby leading to the restaurant's failure. Friedman doesn't include this possibility because he thinks of prejudice as only an individual phenomenon. Or, he thinks in terms of prejudice instead of racism and sexism, which are inherently structural.

39 Touré F. Reed, *Toward Freedom: The Case against Race Reductionism* (London: Verso, 2020), 12.

40 Please don't see Stephen R. Soukup, *The Dictatorship of Woke Capitalism: How Political Correctness Captured Big Business* (New York: Encounter Books, 2021). Soukup's work is one of several conservative broadsides against the supposed leftist turn taken by the corporate world. This turn is just as false as the claim that Dwight D. Eisenhower was a communist.

41 Colin Kaepernick is a significant exception: his critique of racism includes a critique of capitalism. The radicality of his protest certainly

played a part in his ostracism from the National Football League during the prime of his career.

42 Adam Smith, *The Theory of Moral Sentiments* (New York: Penguin, 2009), 214.

Chapter 4

1 At times, Sigmund Freud argues for the priority of fantasy to any experience of reality, but on other occasions, he resorts to a more traditional opposition between reality and fantasy. This move appears, for instance, in his important essay on aesthetics, "Creative Writers and Day-Dreaming." Freud writes, "We may lay it down that a happy person never phantasizes, only an unsatisfied one. The motive force of phantasies are unsatisfied wishes, and every single phantasy is the fulfilment of a wish, a correction of unsatisfying reality." Sigmund Freud, "Creative Writers and Day-Dreaming" (1908), trans. I. F. Grant Duff, in *The Standard Edition of the Complete Psychological Works of Sigmund Freud*, vol. 9, ed. James Strachey (London: Hogarth Press, 1959), 146. This reduction of fantasy to a secondary status marks a moment where Freud steps back from his most radical insights. Such moments are, fortunately, very rare.

2 Jacques Lacan, *The Seminar of Jacques Lacan, Book XX: Encore 1972–1973*, trans. Bruce Fink (New York: Norton, 1998), 95.

3 When people are in the position of the racial other, they often don't share the same reality because they don't share the same fantasy. In this situation, one receives questions that make sense only from the perspective of the fantasy but that make no sense to the one to whom the question is directed. Daniel Cho relates a common experience along these lines. He states, "I cannot tell you how many times I'm asked where I'm 'from.' The racist white person sees in me the secrets of the orient, and therefore they see me as coming from some far away land. But I see myself as a Californian. So, I usually reply 'Oh, I'm from California. How did you know I'm not from Ohio?' To which they reply, 'No, where are you REALLY from?' We don't share the same fantasy space, and so our everyday social interaction completely breaks down and often becomes antagonistic. One time I was asked 'If I go to Korea, what should I get as

a souvenir?' This is after I had already explained to the person that I was born in the US and have never been to Korea. But because they fantasize that I have a secret, they can't help but ask." Daniel Cho, Otterbein University, private message, October 16, 2020.

4   In his *Seminar XIX*, Jacques Lacan states, "You derive jouissance only from your fantasies. This is what gives birth to idealism, which no one, by the way, despite the fact that it is incontestable, takes seriously. What is important is that your fantasies enjoy you." Jacques Lacan, *The Seminar of Jacques Lacan, Book XIX:… or Worse*, trans. A. R. Price, ed. Jacques-Alain Miller (Medford, MA: Polity, 2018), 97 (translation modified). Fantasy is the site of an enjoyment that both captures the subject and enjoys at the expense of the subject, which is what Lacan stresses in the final line.

5   Molly Anne Rothenberg, *The Excessive Subject: A New Theory of Social Change* (Malden, MA: Polity, 2010), 206.

6   This is why membership in a community depends not on an official process of initiation but on adopting the fundamental fantasy frame. As Slavoj Žižek states, "One becomes a full member of a community not simply by identifying with its explicit symbolic tradition, but when one also assumes the spectral dimension that sustains this tradition: the undead ghosts that haunt the living, the secret history of traumatic fantasies transmitted 'between the lines,' through its lacks and distortions." Slavoj Žižek, *The Fragile Absolute, or, Why Is the Christian Legacy Worth Fighting For?* (New York: Verso, 2000), 64.

7   Freud envisions the act that forms society as a shared transgression—the murder of the primal father. Even if this figure has only a mythic status, the crime that eliminates him is real because, as Freud sees it, there is no way to imagine the social bond without a shared crime at the origin.

8   Fraternities almost always include illegal acts in their initiation rites so that those who enter into the fraternity share the bond of guilt. It is this bond, not the deep friendships that form over the years of living together, that constitutes the fraternity as such. Without the transgressive initiation, the fraternal bond would not exist.

9   William Faulkner, *Absalom, Absalom!* (New York: Vintage, 1990), 168.

10   William Faulkner, *Light in August* (New York: Vintage, 1990), 464.

11   For the most insightful account of the investigation into Hollywood and the subsequent blacklist, see Larry Ceplair and Steven Englund,

The Inquisition in Hollywood: Politics in the Film Community, 1930–60 (Urbana: University of Illinois Press, 2003).

12   For many, like Lee Edelman, enjoyment marks the point at which the subject closes in on itself, a point at which the subject turns away from others and does its own thing. As Edelman puts it, "jouissance can only fuck up the very logic of reproduction." Lee Edelman, *No Future: Queer Theory and the Death Drive* (Durham: Duke University Press, 2004), 60. Enjoyment cannot be marshaled to the benefit of the society because it is fundamentally anti-social. For others, like Slavoj Žižek and Joan Copjec, enjoyment is always the enjoyment of the other. Rather than idiosyncratically finding our own form of enjoyment, we discover it through experiencing how the other enjoys. The very existence of racism enables us to resolve this dilemma in favor of the latter position (which sheds light on the affective structure of racism).

13   As Jacques Lacan never tires of repeating, our desire is the desire of the Other. See, for instance, Jacques Lacan, *The Seminar of Jacques Lacan, Book XI: The Four Fundamental Concepts of Psychoanalysis*, trans. Alan Sheridan, ed. Jacques-Alain Miller (New York: Norton, 1978), 38.

14   While Martin Heidegger correctly apprehends that the social authority functions through the anonymous figure of the They (*das Man*), he assumes that the desire of the They is straightforward. Hewing to the desire of the They enables one, as Heidegger sees it, to avoid confronting the abyss of one's own existence. What he misses is that the attempt to follow the dictates of the They always runs into the problem of desire and its interpretation. One cannot just follow the They without interpreting what this figure desires.

15   Mari Ruti points out that the act of interpreting the desire of the social authority is the way in which the subject constitutes itself as singular. She writes, "we individuate ourselves through the specificity of our desire." Mari Ruti, *Distillations: Theory, Ethics, Affect* (New York: Bloomsbury, 2018), 188. The specificity of desire is the individual interpretation that one makes of the social authority's desire.

16   This mistake about the knowledge of the social authority is what psychoanalytic thought calls the transference. In the terms of Jacques Lacan, one takes the social authority as a subject supposed to know and thus seeks out the desire of this subject. This supposition of knowledge

is not just a mistake, however. Without it, the subject would not begin to desire. It is a necessary error.

17 Jacques Lacan points out that "desire … cannot be indicated anywhere in a signifier of any demand whatsoever, for it cannot be articulated in the signifier even though it is articulated there." Jacques Lacan, "Kant with Sade," in *Écrits: The First Complete Edition in English*, trans. Bruce Fink (New York: Norton, 2006), 652–3. That is, we cannot speak desire directly but must announce it through a demand or through the interpretation of a demand coming from the social authority. Because desire is unconscious, it cannot be straightforwardly announced.

18 The fact that the desire of the social authority is never a desire for pure obedience leads Jacques Lacan to claim that "the truth of desire is in and of itself an offense against the authority of the law." Jacques Lacan, *The Seminar of Jacques Lacan, Book VI: Desire and Its Interpretation*, trans. Bruce Fink, ed. Jacques-Alain Miller (Cambridge: Polity, 2019), 74. In order to comply, one must disobey. This is the contradiction at the heart of all desire.

19 Sheldon George, *Trauma and Race: A Lacanian Study of African American Racial Identity* (Waco, TX: Baylor University Press, 2016), 25.

20 It is the role that the slave woman plays in the master's sexual enjoyment that leads Jacobs to proclaim, "Slavery is terrible for men; but it is far more terrible for women. Superadded to the burden common to all, *they* have wrongs, and sufferings, and mortifications peculiarly their own." Harriet Jacobs, *Incidents in the Life of a Slave Girl* (New York: Penguin, 2000), 85. This is the point at which the patriarchal structure of the American South comes together with the institution of slavery to place female slaves in a position of constant danger of sexual violence.

21 Frantz Fanon, *Black Skin, White Masks*, trans. Richard Philcox (New York: Grove Press, 2008), 154.

22 The racist fantasy doesn't necessarily link the racial other with carnality. In her penetrating study of anti-Asian racism in the United States, Anne Anlin Cheng points out that "Asiatic femininity has always been prosthetic. The dream of the yellow woman subsumes a dream about the inorganic. She is an, if not the, original cyborg." Anne Anlin Cheng, *Ornamentalism* (Oxford: Oxford University Press, 2019), 131. The racist fantasy that engulfs Asian women involves ornamental rather than

carnality. But what stays consistent is the relationship to enjoyment. Even though she is specifically not carnal, the Asian woman caught up in the racist fantasy is a site of enjoyment.

23 Dr. Flint is actually the father of her master, his daughter. Jacobs is able to resist Dr. Flint solely because of the fact that it is his daughter rather than he who is her master.

24 Harriet Jacobs, *Incidents in the Life of a Slave Girl*, 30.

25 Thavolia Glymph points out that white women were simply part of the oppressive structure in the slave system. She writes, "In the antebellum period, white women were clearly subordinate in fundamental ways to white men, but far from being victims of the slave system, they dominated slaves." Thavolia Glymph, *Out of the House of Bondage: The Transformation of the Plantation Household* (Durham: Duke University Press, 2008), 4. Despite attempts by certain white feminist scholars to celebrate instances of solidarity between white women and slaves, Glymph shows that these cases are exceptions, not the rule.

26 Stephanie Jones-Rogers, "Rethinking Sexual Violence and the Market-Place of Slavery: White Women, the Slave Market, and Enslaved People's Sexualized Bodies in the Nineteenth-Century South," in *Sexuality and Slavery: Reclaiming Intimate Histories in the Americas*, eds. Daina Ramey Berry and Leslie M. Harris (Athens: University of Georgia Press, 2018), 116.

27 The fundamental claim of Afropessimism is that blackness becomes identified with nothingness throughout the history of modernity. This explains the nonstop racist violence that occurs against blackness. If blackness is nothingness, destroying blackness provides a way of gaining some purchase on nothingness, which represents an insoluble ontological problem. As Calvin Warren puts it, "Antiblack violence is violence against nothing, the nothing that unsettles the human because it can never be captured and dominated. Blacks, then, allow the human to engage in a fantasy—the domination of nothing." Calvin L. Warren, *Ontological Terror: Blackness, Nihilism, and Emancipation* (Durham: Duke University Press, 2018), 21. For Warren, the confrontation with the nothing becomes endurable thanks to the violence against its Black representative. All I would add to this claim is that this figure of nothingness is necessarily sexualized.

28 Ibram X. Kendi, *Stamped from the Beginning: The Definitive History of Racist Ideas in America* (New York: Nation Books, 2016), 505.

29 David Marriott, *Whither Fanon? Studies in the Blackness of Being* (Stanford: Stanford University Press, 2018), 125.

30 When Freud theorizes a fundamental antagonism between the individual and the social order, he focuses on the incompatibility between the individual's form of enjoyment and the functioning of the social order. He sees the path of sublimation as the only hope for the individual's enjoyment to serve the ends of society, but even here, civilization ultimately cuts into the individual's capacity for enjoyment. In *The Future of an Illusion*, Freud states, "every individual is virtually an enemy of civilization, though civilization is supposed to be an object of universal human interest." Sigmund Freud, *The Future of an Illusion*, trans. James Strachey, in *The Complete Psychological Works of Sigmund Freud*, vol. 21, ed. James Strachey (London: Hogarth, 1961), 6. The common result of this struggle between the individual and the social order is repression, which channels individual enjoyment through fantasy.

31 One of the most compelling depictions of the desire of social authority for what defies all authority—the enjoyment of nonbelonging—comes from David Lynch's *Twin Peaks: Fire Walk with Me* (1992). The figure of phallic social authority in the film, BOB (Frank Silva), is consumed by a desire for the enjoyment of nonbelonging that he attributes to Laura Palmer (Sheryl Lee). This desire leads him to proclaim to her, "I want to taste through your mouth." It is precisely Laura's defiance of him and his regime that renders her desirable.

32 Joan Copjec, *Imagine There's No Woman* (Cambridge: MIT Press, 2002), 167.

Chapter 5

1 Frank B. Wilderson III, *Afropessimism* (New York: Liveright, 2020), 90.

2 Violence comes in many forms, one of them verbal. Perhaps the most common form of racist violence is the racist epithet. The enjoyment that the racist epithet provides has its origins in the racist fantasy. When one uses it, one shows that one shares the fantasy with others. One exposes

oneself enjoying alongside others who partake in this same enjoyment. This is why people often avoid using such epithets among those being targeted by them. In *Black Is the Body*, Emily Bernard recounts pointing out to her (all white) students that they shouldn't believe that the n-word has a special status for her because she is Black. She states, "I don't think I feel more offended by it than you do. What I mean is, I don't think I have a special place of pain inside of me that the word touches because I am black." Emily Bernard, *Black Is the Body: Stories from My Grandmother's Time, My Mother's Time, and Mine* (New York: Vintage, 2019), 24. By stripping away the notion that the word wounds her more than them, Bernard forces her students to confront their recoil from saying it in front of her, to recognize the factor of enjoyment present in the n-word. The recoil is their own enjoyment that they don't want to display to someone not sharing in it.

3   The racist fantasy of the Black criminal leads directly to the actual criminalization of Black subjects. This is the process that Michelle Alexander documents in *The New Jim Crow*. As criminals, they become the targets of racist invective that the purveyors do not recognize as racist. She writes, "Criminals, it turns out, are the one social group in America we have permission to hate. In 'colorblind' America, criminals are the new whipping boys." Michelle Alexander, *The New Jim Crow: Mass Incarceration in the Age of Colorblindness* (New York: The New Press, 2010), 138. This criminalization indicates the power that the racist fantasy has to destroy people's lives. The fantasy has real effects.

4   The mass incarceration of Black men in the United States has its legal origins in inegalitarian laws and racist policing practices. But its psychic origin lies in the racist fantasy and the image of Black male criminality that this fantasy requires.

5   In the colonial situation, the colonial powers typically interpret the resistance of the colonized as an indication of an inherent criminality. That is, they interpret it through the racist fantasy. In *The Wretched of the Earth*, Frantz Fanon describes how this happens in Algeria during the time of French colonization. He states, "One of the characteristics of the Algerian people established by colonialism is their appalling criminality. Prior to 1954 magistrates, police, lawyers, journalists, and medical examiners were unanimous that the Algerian's criminality posed

a problem. The Algerian, it was claimed, was a born criminal. A theory was elaborated and scientific proof was furnished." Frantz Fanon, *The Wretched of the Earth*, trans. Richard Philcox (New York: Grove Press, 2004), 221. The scientific proof of criminality that Fanon ironically alludes to here has its basis on empirical analysis, but this empirical analysis is itself rooted in the racist fantasy. The fantasy shapes how the French social scientists work when they approach Algerians.

6   The trickster figure has a radical ideological ambiguity in American history because of its complex relationship to the racist fantasy. Joel Chandler Harris presents the trickster figure through the plantation tales of Uncle Remus. In these tales, the trickster often has the ability to manipulate for the sake of illicit enjoyment. In the plantation tales of Charles Chesnutt, in contrast, the trickster figure uses rhetorical manipulation specifically to combat racism or to highlight its injustice.

7   This is what Amy Louise Wood emphasizes in *Lynching as Spectacle*. She states that "countless southern defenders of lynching saw the violence as an inevitable and justifiable substitution for capital punishment, in particular because the legal system bestowed too many rights on black criminals and offered too little respect for white victims. Certainly the state provided little recourse for black criminals in the South—they were often inadequately defended, convicted, and sentenced by all-white juries in exceptionally hasty trials, and they were more likely to be sentenced to death than were white criminals. Nevertheless, white southerners who justified lynching regularly expressed frustration with the slow, bureaucratic wheels of justice." Amy Louise Wood, *Lynching as Spectacle: Witnessing Racial Violence in America, 1870–1940* (Chapel Hill: University of North Carolina Press, 2009), 25. Even though we recognize that the authorities in the American South were utterly enmeshed in the society's racism, from the perspective of the lynch mob, they were never racist enough because they played the part of the dupe in the racist fantasy.

8   For a thorough account of the significant role that lynching played in disciplining blackness, see Philip Dray, *At the Hands of Persons Unknown: The Lynching of Black America* (New York: Random House, 2002).

9   Many of the rape accusations that occasioned lynchings were false, although their truth or falsity is entirely beside the point. The point is the

position that the victim to be lynched occupies in the fantasy structure of the lynching party. For the lynching party, innocence serves just as well as guilt in the fantasized target. For a thorough account of the relationship the complicated role that Southern women played in the practice of lynching, see Crystal M. Feinster, *Southern Horrors: Women and the Politics of Rape and Lynching* (Cambridge: Harvard University Press, 2011).

10   Isabel Wilkerson, *Caste: The Origins of Our Discontents* (New York: Random House, 2020), 149.

11   See Isabel Wilkerson, *Caste: The Origins of Our Discontents*, 149–50.

12   The enjoyment perpetuated by the lynching party has to be extralegal. This is what accounts for the intensity of the revelry: the group of white murderers have the thrill of breaking the law while secure in the knowledge that they are obeying the social demand and thus securing their belonging in white Southern society.

13   Historians have reached no definitive conclusions about the guilt or innocence of Washington, although his guilt has nothing at all to do with the act of lynching. Given the position of Black enjoyment in the racist fantasy, every Black man was already guilty of the same crime, no matter what he actually did.

14   Jean Laplanche and Jean-Betrand Pontalis, *Fantasme originaire, fantasme des origines, origines du fantasme* (Paris: Pluriel, 1985), 96.

15   This is Freud's theory of the relationship between the psyche of the artists and the artwork. In "Creative Writers and Day-Dreaming," Freud notes, "The creative writer does the same as the child at play. He creates a world of phantasy which he takes very seriously—that is, which he invests with large amounts of emotion—while separating it sharply from reality." Sigmund Freud, "Creative Writers and Day-Dreaming" (1908), trans. I. F. Grant Duff, in *The Standard Edition of the Complete Psychological Works of Sigmund Freud*, vol. 9, ed. James Strachey (London: Hogarth Press, 1959), 144. Through this process, Freud contends, the artist is able to allow others to enjoy what would otherwise be a private fantasy. The magic of art consists in this translation of the private fantasy to the public work of art.

16   For instance, Jean Mitry exclaims, "It is an undeniable fact that the cinema *as an art* was born in 1915, i.e., with *Birth of a Nation*, Griffith's

first successful film, the cinema's first masterpiece." Jean Mitry, *The Aesthetics and Psychology of the Cinema*, trans. Christopher King (Bloomington: Indiana University Press, 1997), 67. Mitry does not temper this praise with an acknowledgment of the fundamental racism of *Birth of a Nation*.

17   While the extreme racism of *Birth of a Nation* has marred Griffith's reputation as a filmmaker and made it almost impossible to see anything positive about him, for most of the twentieth century film theorists and historians held him up as perhaps the greatest innovator in the history of cinema. Through his development of continuity editing and his working out of epic cinematic storytelling, Griffith established a model for cinema history that remains in force to this day. It was very common for even left-leaning film theorists to simply look over his ugly racism. For instance, even Gilles Deleuze manages to praise Griffith in the first of his books on cinema without mentioning his blatant racism. Deleuze points out that "the American cinema constantly shoots and reshoots a single fundamental film, which is the birth of the nation-civilisation, whose first version was provided by Griffith." Gilles Deleuze, *Cinema 1: The Movement-Image*, trans. Hugh Tomlinson and Barbara Habberjam (London: Athlone Press, 1992), 148. While Deleuze is certainly correct to credit Griffith for his role in creating the pattern for American filmmaking (especially in its epic version), the omission of any discussion of racism in *Birth of a Nation* is nonetheless striking. Deleuze's point unfortunately resonates not just on the level of form but also in filmic content. One could certainly say that American cinema constantly shoots and reshoots the stereotypes that Griffith proffers.

18   Jacques Lacan, *Le Séminaire, livre XVI: D'un Autre à l'autre, 1968–1969*, ed. Jacques-Alain Miller (Paris: Seuil, 2006), 115.

19   Walter Long, the actor playing Gus, was a white actor using blackface. Griffith resorted to the use of blackface in *Birth of a Nation* because he feared Black enjoyment to such an extent that he did not want Black male actors in proximity to the white female leads. The idea of Gus pursuing Flora and proposing to her so repulsed him that he could not even witness the threat of this enjoyment being acted out with an actual Black man.

20   *Birth of a Nation* was not the first feature film. (It is difficult to say what film holds this honor because of the inaccuracy of the historical record.)

But it was definitely the first feature film event. Tickets for the film were $2.00 in 1915, which translates to over $50 today. This was a lot of money to pay to see a film, completely unheard of at the time. Even at this price and despite the fact that several states banned its release because of its racist content, *Birth of a Nation* was the most commercially successful ever after its release. Everyone saw it and had an opinion. Even those who hated it and protested it, such as writer Charles Chesnutt, often recognized its formal significance.

21   Michelle Alexander, *The New Jim Crow: Mass Incarceration in the Age of Colorblindness*, 13.

22   In *Are Prisons Obsolete?*, Angela Davis stresses the role that the prison plays as a space of nonbelonging, a space to deposit the racial others whose fantasized enjoyment functions as a threat to the social order. She writes, "Because of the persistent power of racism, 'criminals' and 'evildoers' are, in the collective imagination, fantasized as people of color. The prison therefore functions ideologically as an abstract site into which undesirables are deposited, relieving us of the responsibility of thinking about the real issues afflicting those communities from which prisoners are drawn in such disproportionate numbers. This is the ideological work that the prison performs—it relieves us of the responsibility of seriously engaging with the problems of our society, especially those produced by racism and, increasingly, global capitalism." Angela Davis, *Are Prisons Obsolete?* (New York: Seven Stories Press, 2003), 16.

23   This is a point that Emily Bernard (University of Vermont, private conversation, June 6, 2020) insists on. She notes that it is only because Black existence is so devalued that a mass audience can repeatedly watch the murder of a Black man, which is what happened in the aftermath of George Floyd's death. Anyone with an investment in universal equality would simply find the footage unwatchable. Despite the important political reaction that the widespread visibility of Floyd's death provoked, I find Bernard's argument here convincing.

24   The transition from a critique of capitalism to a critique of power has had disastrous consequences for the Left. Power is an amorphous entity that often functions beneficently. What's more, when one thinks in terms of the evil of power, one misses the primacy of capital in determining all social relations today. At the exact moment one needs a little power to

confront the ubiquitous workings of capital, power becomes anathema. Far from abdicating power, we should marshal it in the effort to fight capitalism and racism. But this is what biopolitical critique doesn't allow because it sees such efforts as guilty for their complicity with structures of power. The dominance of the critique of power distorts not only the contemporary critique of racism but also the entire political field.

25   In *History at the Limit of World-History*, Ranajit Guha interprets world history as a narrative that Western philosophy has imposed on the other. This imposition is an act of power associated primarily with the state. As Guha puts it, "The noise of World-history and its statist concerns has made historiography insensitive to the sighs and whispers of everyday life." Ranajit Guha, *History at the Limit of World-History* (New York: Columbia University, 2002), 73. For Guha, the state's dominance is what we must constantly contest. He fails to see that the state might be the only structure powerful enough to counteract the dominance of capital.

26   Foucault theorizes the move from the regime of punishment to that of biopower as a transition away from sovereignty. This is a point of contention with later biopolitical theorists. Giorgio Agamben, for one, sees biopower working through the figure of the sovereign exception. For him, sovereignty in some form or another is integral to the working of power, which is why he does not believe that the biopolitical regime no longer makes use of the sovereign, as Foucault does.

27   Michel Foucault, *"Society Must Be Defended": Lectures at the Collège de France, 1975–1976*, trans. David Macey (New York: Picador, 2003), 256.

28   Roberto Esposito, *Bíos: Biopolitics and Philosophy*, trans. Timothy Campbell (Minneapolis: University of Minnesota Press, 2008), 128.

29   When Freud conceives of the unconscious, he does not use the most common German word for it, a word in currency during Freud's life. Rather than the more common *bewusstlos*, Freud uses the term *unbewusst*. Although he does not invent this latter term, he popularizes its use. Through this decision, Freud indicates that his notion of the unconscious is not reducible to what is not conscious (*bewusstlos*) but is rather operating in a different—and even opposed—way than consciousness, indicated by the prefix *un-*.

30   Arno J. Mayer, *Why Did the Heavens Not Darken?: The "Final Solution" in History* (London: Verso, 2012), 15.

31 Friedrich Nietzsche, *Writings from the Late Notebooks*, ed. Rüdiger Bittner, trans. Kate Sturge (Cambridge: Cambridge University Press, 2003), 46.

32 Nietzsche's insistence on power as a universal explanation is miles away from Freud's theorization of unconscious desire as what drives us. The fact that Freud claimed to have avoided reading Nietzsche because he recognized that their thinking was too similar has led some critics to accuse Freud of attempting to obfuscate his debt to Nietzsche. While it is true that Freud's paradoxical denial suggests an influence—even an unconscious one—the distance that separates the two thinkers is immense. Nietzsche's celebration of the explanatory power of power has absolutely no correlate in Freud's thought.

33 This understanding of the unconscious as satisfying itself through undermining our power becomes apparent only after Freud's discovery of the death drive in 1920. From that point on, Freud turns to a new chapter in his theorization of the unconscious, even though he himself never comments on this shift.

34 Giorgio Agamben, *Homo Sacer: Sovereign Power and Bare Life*, trans. Daniel Heller-Roazen (Stanford: Stanford University Press, 1998), 114.

35 Frank Wilderson points out that Agamben radically misunderstands the figure of the Muselmann because he fails to see it in terms of the history of racism. He writes, "The Muselmann, then, can be seen as a provisional moment within existential Whiteness, when Jews were subjected to Blackness and Redness—and the explanatory power of the Muselmann can find its way back to sociology, history, or political science, where it more rightfully belongs." Frank Wilderson, *Red, White, and Black: Cinema and the Structure of U. S. Antagonisms* (Durham: Duke University Press, 2010), 36. One could put it this way: Agamben fails to see that the Muselmann is a political category.

36 Adolf Hitler, *Mein Kampf*, trans. Ralph Manheim (Boston: Houghton Mifflin, 1971), 623. Hitler's fellow high-ranking Nazis all talk of Jews in similar terms. For instance, in his "Total War" speech, Joseph Goebbels warns of "the acute and life-threatening danger from Jewry." Joseph Goebbels, "Total War," in *Landmark Speeches of National Socialism*, ed. Randall L. Bytwerk (College Station: Texas A&M University Press, 2008), 120.

37 Zahi Zalloua points out the problem with privilege theory's insistence
that white privilege is real. He states, "The assumption of privilege theory
is that if the unprivileged only had the same privileges, they would be
happy too." Zahi Zalloua, *Žižek on Race: Toward an Anti-Racist Future*
(New York: Bloomsbury, 2020), 29. If one understands the belonging
attached to whiteness as a false solution to the problem of subjectivity,
then it becomes clear that any talk of a privilege attached to this position
misses what's at stake.

Chapter 6

1 In *Caste*, Isabel Wilkerson notes, "Even now, in a 2020 ranking of the
richest African-Americans, seventeen of the top twenty—from Oprah
Winfrey to Jay-Z to Michael Jordan—made their wealth as innovators,
and then moguls, in the entertainment industry or in sports." Isabel
Wilkerson, *Caste: The Origins of Our Discontents* (Durham: Duke
University Press, 2020), 137.

2 When the Black athlete or entertainer takes up a political position
against racist society, the widespread acceptance of this figure quickly
disappears. This is what happened in the case of Paul Robeson, one of the
great renaissance figures of the twentieth century. Robeson was a stellar
athlete, a breathtaking singer, and a powerful actor. But because he added
political activism to this combination, white American society rejected
him, and the United States government persecuted him, going so far
as to restrict his ability to travel. Robeson's trajectory reveals that the
Black athlete or entertainer remains acceptable only as long as this figure
remains within the confines of the racist fantasy. Becoming political
disturbs the fantasy structure.

3 Frantz Fanon, *Black Skin, White Masks*, trans. Richard Philcox (New
York: Grove Press, 2008), 136.

4 Michelle Alexander, *The New Jim Crow: Mass Incarceration in the Age of
Colorblindness* (New York: The New Press, 2010), 169.

5 I heard this song being played loudly by a group of young suburban
white guys playing basketball at a local gym. Despite the lyrics, none of

the gym officials asked the group to change its music selection. It passed
the social censor because it fit the racist fantasy.

6   Cornell West, *Race Matters* (New York: Vintage, 1993), 128.

7   I owe this point and this example to my son, Dashiell Neroni, who
insisted that there was an antiracist way for a white teen to listen to hip
hop, and I owe the identification of the song "Da Real Hoodbabies" (after
we heard it together) to his twin brother Theo, who, as always, insisted
the converse.

8   Perhaps the most notorious film depiction of imaginary interracial
healing occurs in the risible *Crash* (Paul Haggis, 2004). The film shows
a multitude of interracial encounters in contemporary Los Angeles but
highlights the transformation of racist police officer John Ryan (Matt
Dillon) who saves the life of Christine Thayer (Thandiwe Newton).
Despite earlier molesting Christine during a traffic stop, he pulls her
from a burning car just before it explodes.

9   White savior films have had a lasting popularity, a popularity that,
despite abundant critiques levelled against them, shows little sign of
waning, given that *Green Book* (Peter Farrelly, 2018) won the Academy
Award for Best Picture. While *Green Book* seems to improve on the locus
classicus for the formula, *Dangerous Minds* (John N. Smith, 1995), by
giving much of the agency in the film to the Black character, it is finally
the white character who has the most to teach, even though he is much
less educated. Throughout the film, Italian Tony Lip (Viggo Mortensen)
instructs jazz pianist Don Shirley (Mahershala Ali) how to enjoy himself.
This includes a revelatory scene in which Lip shows Shirley how to eat
fried chicken properly—how to really enjoy it. Here, the white savior
doesn't rescue the Black man so much as rescue the racist fantasy. In this
sense, its variance from the formula confirms the racist structure rather
than challenging it.

10   Michael Oher himself points out that the film *The Blind Side* takes
liberties with its depiction of his ignorance. By showing Michael to be
ignorant, the film simultaneously highlights the role of the white savior
in coming to his rescue and emphasizes Michael's lack of enjoyment.
As the film constructs it, his ignorance produces innocence—and thus
separates him from the threat of Black enjoyment. See Michael Oher,
I Beat the Odds: From Homelessness, to the Blind Side, and beyond
(New York: Avery, 2012).

11 C. L. R. James claims that the moment of class solidarity between the working class in France and the slaves in what would become Haiti actually saved the French Revolution. In *The Black Jacobins*, he writes, "The great gesture of the French working people towards the black slaves, against their own white ruling class, had helped to save their revolution from reactionary Europe." C. L. R. James, *The Black Jacobins: Toussaint L'Ouverture and the San Domingo Revolution*, 2nd ed. rev. (New York: Random House, 1963), 214. Despite this great gesture, the class solidarity did not survive the defeat of the Jacobins and the rise of Napoleon, who reinstituted slavery in Haiti in the years prior to independence.

12 Kubrick himself was so convinced about the reality of this fantasy that he feared the forces of extreme wealth in America would come after him for depicting this scene of their unrestrained enjoyment. The fact that he died of a mysterious heart attack soon after finishing the editing of *Eyes Wide Shut* suggests that perhaps he was right.

13 Instead of associating wealth with enjoyment and working-class existence with misery, most Hollywood films reverse these associations. For instance, in a crucial moment in *Titanic* (James Cameron, 1998), we see a clear contrast in enjoyment between the staid dinner in the upper decks and the wild festivities in steerage. When Jack (Leonardo DiCaprio) goes to dinner with Rose (Kate Winslet) among the ship's wealthy voyagers, the constraint of manners and decorum stifle any moment of amusement. But after dinner, he takes her to a dance in the lower decks, where both of them experience enjoyment untrammeled by this constraint.

14 For a more hopeful take on the politics of *The Wolf of Wall Street*, see Clint Burnham, *Fredric Jameson and the Wolf of Wall Street* (New York: Bloomsbury, 2016).

15 This is a point that Freud obliquely makes when discussing comedy. He points out that among the lower classes, one can tell jokes in a much more ribald fashion than when one rises in class status. Once one is in the upper class, the joke requires a circuitous path to deliver its enjoyment because higher class status entails more repression. Freud goes so far as to suggest that for those in the lower class, a direct expression of smut can replace the joke altogether.

16   The great lie of Robert Heinlein's science fiction classic *Stranger in a Strange Land* is that the wealthy millionaire Jubal Harshaw lives a life replete with enjoyment. The problem is that no matter how many millions millionaires have, they can never buy freedom from repression since repression inheres within the very class status that the wealth purchases.

17   The power of this identification with the billionaire leads majorities in the United States to oppose taxes levied against wealthy estates, even when they learn that such a tax would never apply to them, no matter how successful they became.

18   Carl Schmitt, *The Concept of the Political*, trans. George Schwab (Chicago: University of Chicago Press, 1996), 67.

19   According to Chantal Mouffe, the disappearance of political antagonism creates a breeding ground for rightist extremism, which sells its program as the rebirth of genuine antagonism. She writes, "as a consequence of the blurring of the frontiers between left and right and the absence of an agonistic debate among democratic parties, a confrontation between different political projects, voters did not have the possibility of identifying with a differentiated range of democratic political identities. This created a void that was likely to be occupied by other forms of identifications which could become problematic for the working of the democratic system." Chantal Mouffe, *On the Political* (New York: Routledge, 2005), 69. By erasing political antagonism, modern democracy threatens its own foundation and paves the way for antidemocratic forces to arise as its champions.

20   Toni Morrison, *Sula* (New York: Plume, 1973), 136.

21   In the final line of the novel, Morrison recounts Nel weeping. She writes, "It was a fine cry—loud and long—but it had no bottom and it had no top, just circles and circles of sorrow." Toni Morrison, *Sula*, 174. This line captures how Nel's suffering is intrinsically linked to her enjoyment. Morrison paints the sorrow as a form of enjoyment.

22   In *The Philosophical Discourse of Modernity*, Habermas describes the moral power of the ideal speech situation. He claims, "Once participants enter into argumentation, they cannot avoid supposing, in a reciprocal way, that the conditions for an ideal speech situation have been sufficiently met." Jürgen Habermas, *The Philosophical Discourse of*

Modernity: Twelve Lectures, trans. Frederick G. Lawrence (Cambridge: MIT Press, 1987), 323. Reciprocity is inherent in speaking, and this reciprocity is already the germ of full-fledged mutual recognition.

23 Jürgen Habermas, *Moral Consciousness and Communicative Action*, trans. Christian Lenhardt and Shierry Weber Nicholsen (Cambridge: MIT Press, 1990), 200.

24 Most theorists of mutual recognition base their approach in a liberal interpretation of Hegel's philosophy, one that typically focuses on the dialectic of the master and the slave in the *Phenomenology of Spirit*.

25 Judith Butler, *Undoing Gender* (New York: Routledge, 2004), 144.

26 Robert Pippin justifies mutual recognition as a political position on Hegelian grounds. He writes, "It is in *being successfully recognized as such a free subject*, where 'successfully' has to do with the achievement of a successful form of mutual justification, that one can then *be* such a free subject, can thereby come to regard one's own life as self-determined and so one's own." Robert Pippin, *Hegel's Practical Philosophy: Rational Agency as Ethical Life* (Cambridge: Cambridge University Press, 2008), 209. The problem with Pippin's attribution of this position to Hegel is that he fails to see how Hegel always shows the failure of mutual recognition, not its success. If my freedom depends solely on a world of mutual recognition, I'm in trouble.

27 Christina Sharpe, *In the Wake: On Blackness and Being* (Durham: Duke University Press, 2016), 83.

Index

www.ingramcontent.com/pod-product-compliance
Ingram Content Group UK Ltd.
Pitfield, Milton Keynes, MK11 3LW, UK
UKHW031249020325
455689UK00008B/152